Nuala O'Faolain

A Radiant Life

ABRAMS IMAGE

NEW YORK

Library of Congress Cataloging-in-Publication Data

O'Faolain, Nuala.
  A radiant life / Nuala O'Faolain ; [introduction by Fintan O'Toole].
     p. cm.
  Selected columns previously published in the The Irish times, and other
writings, from the 1980's through 2008.
  ISBN 978-0-8109-9806-3 (alk. paper)
  I. O'Toole, Fintan, 1958- II. Irish times (Dublin, Ireland : 1874) III.
Title.
  PN5146.O39A25 2011
  824'.92--dc22
                              2010037687

Originally published as *A More Complex Truth* © New Island, Dublin, 2010

Printed in the U.S.A.
10 9 8 7 6 5 4 3 2 1

Abrams Image books are available at special discounts when purchased in
quantity for premiums and promotions as well as fundraising or educational
use. Special editions can also be created to specification. For details, contact
specialmarkets@abramsbooks.com or the address below.

THE ART OF BOOKS SINCE 1949
115 West 18th Street
New York, NY 10011
www.abramsbooks.com

Contents

2000–2008

Note on the American Edition

Nuala O'Faolain changed lives – knowing her changed mine. After her memoir, *Are You Somebody?*, became an international bestseller, hundreds of people wrote to Nuala – some to thank her, many to confess their own secrets. For these readers Nuala spoke with a frankness that, despite differences of circumstance, named a common anguish. But Nuala was an influential journalist before she was a memoirist. For the first time, American admirers can read for themselves a selection of Nuala's eloquent columns, spanning nearly twenty years, from *The Irish Times* and the *Sunday Tribune*.

Nuala O'Faolain was part of a noble tradition of female dissent in a country that had little value for its women (or its children) and even less for the childless, aging woman who had no "tribal function, and must invent her own self-importance." Her feminism was an outgrowth of a sense of social justice, the moral response to the conditions in which she lived and those she witnessed. But Nuala was nonetheless a feminist who acknowledged that her convictions were compromised in her dealings with men, once claiming she "would still walk across 59 women to get to one man if I was attracted to him." The experience of being a middle-aged woman was never more candidly conveyed: "There's nothing genteel about the life inside me," she wrote. "In there it is as if I live in a condition of turbulence, always moving between opposites – wellbeing and sadness, delight and dullness, acceptance and restless regret." The capacity to make use of the restiveness of such a nature to purposeful effect is in part what made

Nuala a great columnist and journalist, not to mention an extraordinary person.

We were friends for the last ten years of her life, years she divided between Ireland and New York, after the success of *Are You Somebody?* changed her own life. Nuala had a gift for friendship, and it was a deep privilege to know and love her. Which is not to say that intimacy was easy for her; the contradictions in her nature were often present in her dealings with those she loved. Sudden reversals and shifts of mood could be frightening, just as her equally unexpected generosity could astonish.

Nuala discovered she was ill with advanced cancer in New York, late in February 2008. She returned home to Ireland. After she underwent radiation treatment, I visited her cottage in Clare in March to help out. I found a book of Rilke's poems on her shelf; I had the same collection at home. Radiation had left her weak and exhausted and she hated almost every minute of my time with her. She longed to be alone but could not manage most things. I sat, reading in the next room, trying to leave her be. I remember calling out a line of Rilke's to her through the doorway: "I hold this to be the highest task of a bond between two people that each should stand guard over the solitude of the other."

"Well," she answered crisply from the next room. "Then perhaps you should shut the fuck up?"

After I returned to New York, Nuala sent me an e-mail: "This place has never been the same since you left. Mabel [her dog] hasn't been the same. I haven't been the same. But not worse, more somber, more solitary – even though there are far too many people around. I am moving, in other words, into the dark – but at the enemy's pace."

None of Nuala's family and friends thought she had so little time, but I see now that she sensed it. She knew she could not tolerate hospitals or invalidism and declined chemotherapy. Instead, in a wheelchair, she went with friends to Paris, Madrid, back to New York to say goodbye, to Berlin for the opera, and to Sicily for a long-planned holiday with her sisters and brother, and her boyfriend, John. She died in Dublin, on May 9, a few days after that final trip. It was almost exactly three months to the day that John and I had sat with her in the emergency room at New York Hospital as the doctors discovered she had cancer.

But for the moment, Nuala's voice is here again. Here she is, addressing the reader in her intimate way, passing on trenchant observations about the country she loved and sometimes witheringly criticized. If Nuala's eye was unremitting, her vulnerability left her open to the sufferings of others, to the inequities of culture, and to the play of power in the dealings between women and men. These columns are free of polemic, but score direct hits on the complex subjects under consideration. "I was blinded by the habit of translating everything into personal terms," she writes apologetically, but it is her source of power. Through the prism of casual, everyday encounters, Nuala presses her subject, reaching beyond the prompting of the moment to transcend topicality. The result is a cumulative historical narrative, an inadvertent chronicle of a transformed Ireland by one of its sharpest critics.

The voice in these columns is vintage Nuala in its directness, its plain-spokeness, but it is also a voice made subtle by erudition and intellectual reach. The paradoxical combination of frankness and an academically trained mind (Nuala had an undergraduate degree in medieval English from Hull and a postgraduate degree in nineteenth-century literature from Oxford) results in a lightness of touch, of great facility. Unpretentious for all her scholarship, Nuala did not think herself wise. And yet what else is there to call it when she reminds us that "the powerful have a duty to be self-conscious"?

Once Nuala spent more time in Manhattan, American concerns began appearing in her writing. She wrote, "I wanted to borrow the immigrant energy of the great city. I wanted to escape the despair and lethargy that still clings to the Irish countryside." But it was to Ireland that Nuala returned when she knew she was dying. She wrote to me after recording her last, painful radio interview with her dear friend Marian Finucane – "I am just so grateful and privileged to be allowed to speak my truth out. After all, I have this community, Ireland, instead of a family of my own."

The title of this collection is not something Nuala would have chosen. She would not have described her life with such a word as "radiant." Anguish was, for her, all too present and traceable, as readers of her memoirs know. That she set aside personal turbulence when contemplating the world she describes in these columns is a measure of both method and necessity. But for those who knew and loved Nuala – as well as for her devoted readers – "radiant" aptly describes the intelligence at work in these pages. I, for one, can vouch for her radiance, even as these columns demonstrate the brilliant illumination we have lost with her passing.

Sheridan Hay
New York, 2010

Editor's Note

In December 1995, Nuala O'Faolain and I met up in Dublin to discuss the possibility of a book of her selected columns from *The Irish Times*. "I'm never late," Nuala announced, when she turned up late, "but I had to wait for the bin-men to give them their Christmas tip." Bewley's coffee house was packed, so we went into a nearby, since-vanished café, where Nuala, over a plate of beans on toast, agreed to do the book if she could write an introductory 5,000-word autobiographical essay to provide a context for her public voice. An essay that famously evolved into *Are You Somebody?,* which appeared in October 1996, and stayed in the Irish bestsellers for five months. Published in the United States with the subtitle *The Accidental Memoir of a Dublin Woman,* it reached No. 1 on the *New York Times* bestseller list, and went on to sell over a million copies worldwide.

The initial Irish edition of the memoir included thirty-one of her newspaper columns – essays, in fact – under four thematic headings: People, The Times, Issues, and Belief. Twelve of those number among the seventy-one columns feature pieces and reviews which make up the current selection, and which appear here in chronological order, dating from 1985 to 2007, a year before Nuala's untimely death in May 2008.

I would like to record my sincere thanks to the following individuals for their help in compiling the selection: Gerry Smyth, Managing Editor, *The Irish Times*; Noirín Hegarty, Editor, the *Sunday Tribune*; Máiréad Brady, Librarian, South

Dublin County Library; Irene Stevenson, Librarian, *The Irish Times*; Caroline Walsh, Literary Editor, *The Irish Times*; Patsey Murphy, Editor, *The Irish Times Magazine*; Fintan O'Toole, Assistant Editor, *The Irish Times*; Deirdre Brady, author, Dublin; Dr. James Skelly, Magee College, University of Ulster, Derry, Northern Ireland; and Dublin City University Library.

In an iconic radio interview four weeks before her death, Nuala told RTÉ broadcaster Marian Finucane: "What matters now in life is health and reflectiveness. I just shot around. I would like it if I had been a better thinker." With all due respect to dearest Nuala, the evidence herein suggests a more reflective thinker would be difficult to find.

Anthony Glavin
December 2009

The 1980s

Liberty and Showbiz

I was watching the other night the show that American television put on to celebrate the refurbished Statue of Liberty. The occasion was attended by Presidents Reagan and Mitterand and by loads of other people, all obviously freezing half-to-death on a windy platform in New York harbor.

It was fascinating, as always, to see what a nation chooses to display as expressing itself. You will recall that when the eyes of millions of viewers were upon us, at Ballyporeen, we – or somebody – settled on Derek Davis and some small Irish dancers to encapsulate the mystery of Irishness. The Americans have a great deal more confidence than we have when it comes to patriotic showbiz, as well they might. All the same, Liberty weekend was, from a European point of view, a very, very odd occasion.

For one thing, America's royalty, the stars, were playing amazing roles. President Mitterand was introduced by that well-known statesman, Gregory Peck; Robert De Niro, with a microphone that didn't work, introduced the Chief Justice, who in turn administered the oath of allegiance to thousands of new citizens in a simultaneous nationwide telecast.

This ceremony could have been the emotional highlight of the night. The Statue of Liberty stands for the millions of immigrants who founded modern America, and citizenship of the States is still the goal, the almost religious aspiration, of millions of people all over the globe. As the cameras panned over the new citizens you could see one reason at least

1

why American-ness means liberty. There they were; people of all shapes, sizes, and colors, not knowing the words of the oath, yawning, shuffling, casually dressed. Nobody had drilled them into deference. They are, like the earlier immigrants, free now from lords and bishops and the oppression of class. They are equal; the old countries of Europe, even the socialist ones, have never achieved such an ideal. This is to put to one side, of course, the questions raised by the show's opening with a little African American boy singing the National Anthem.

Andy Williams and Mireille Mathieu demonstrated détente. The camera never got to the Secretary of Transportation – whose reason for giving a speech I didn't catch – so we never saw her. "I Want to Be in America" was danced with the marvellous Busby Berkeley–type precision that is one of America's real arts. Bob Hope was given a medal in the company of Elie Wiesel, chronicler of the Holocaust, Mr. Wang of computers, Kissinger, a token woman, and Irving Berlin, who not only typifies immigrant success but also wrote "White Christmas," America's folk anthem.

The video from Lawrence, Kansas, didn't show up. Coretta Scott King shivered in the audience along with Senator Robert Dole, Steven Spielberg, and a glowing George Shultz. Mrs. Mitterand looked as if she would never smile again. When President Reagan turned on the lights of the Statue of Liberty and no flames came out of her torch, I thought it was another technical hitch. In fact, they turned on the torch in a later part of the ceremony. And the flames didn't work.

But by then the viewer was reeling. The Fonz, a chillingly popular television star with close-set eyes, questioned a resettled Vietnamese teenager about Communism. The Communists, she said, were "cruel, stern, and ill-tempered" and she is very glad to be in the Land of the Free. Well, I don't know about ill-tempered. I'm not sure that the manners of the millions of people on this planet who live by Communism are even relevant. But the Fonz was overcome with emotion. So were the Reagans. Nancy had been in her misty-eyed mode from the very start and couldn't do much more. But the President got even more broken-voiced sincerity into saying "God Bless America" at the end than he had in the beginning.

The sanitization of good and evil continued. A crowd of extras, tastefully dressed as huddled masses, formed tableaux as Neil Diamond in two different shirts sang "Yes, to America." This dissolved into a barn-dance sequence about freedom, with girls in gingham dresses and boys in denim. Tactically, that was a mistake. The whole night was asserting that there was no one else in America before the ships arrived at Ellis Island, that the state was born of innocence and hard work, that America has no colonizing past. But you can't conjure up the settlement of the interior without reminding people of the aboriginals, the Native American, who were completely ignored on Liberty weekend and whose hearts are buried at Wounded Knee. I bet they thought the new Americans were cruel, stern, and ill-tempered.

It was a splendidly elitist night. Nobody was there because they matter in their own small community, or because they had spent a lifetime in the service of others. You had to be either a Republican politician or a top star to be allowed to talk. And when it comes to choosing between politicians and stars, the producers spoke for all of us, and brought on the real King and Queen, Sinatra and Elizabeth Taylor.

The latter, and not the Statue of Liberty, was the evening's memorable woman; $265 million it cost to refurbish Liberty:

3

Miss Taylor did it by willpower. When last seen, she was fat, she was sad, and she was visibly getting old. But in a scene of rebirth as stunning as the chrysanthemums coming back to life in *E.T.*, she is now slim and beautiful and younger than ever. It was a joy to behold.

And it was joyous, too, to listen to Sinatra singing. Cracked and scratchy as his voice is now, it is still the voice of America. Millions of people courted to his music, danced, played his records to suit their moods, had babies to it, and will go on loving it as long as ballads survive. The producers of the show dissolved to a shot of the Reagans as he sang. But popular as they are, they are not as potent as Ol' Blue Eyes, and the camera returned to him. And so to the fireworks and the end of the show.

It was a new way of displaying power. What the English say with the Royal Family, what the Russians say with tank parades, what the Vatican says with St. Peter's, the Americans said with entertainment. The images were so familiar and benevolent, the verbal content was so irrelevant, that the state behind the glitter was forgotten, the state that bombed Libya and terrorizes Nicaragua and ignores the anti-nuclear movement.

State occasions – and Liberty weekend was a state occasion – usually say something. But Reagan's America baffled these expectations. It covers its idea of itself in sentimentality and gloss. And since most of us have reason to be grateful to America and do love it, we are inclined to take it at its own valuation. It seems bad-mannered to insist that what matters to us now is not the America that once gave shelter to our emigrants, but the modern America that exercises foreign policies to which we are vulnerable.

The Americans have every right to celebrate themselves. But do they extend the same rights to everyone else? Would they lend Sinatra to the Sandinistas to celebrate their revolution? That sense of the world outside its shores which America once had, the generosity toward ethnic identity which it exemplified, was altogether missing from Liberty weekend. Between the song and dance, the speeches betrayed an isolation, a wilfully simple self-approval, which no non-American can be happy with. Liberty is not their property, even if the Statue is.

The Irish Times, July 8, 1986

U2: The Myth & The Mystery

U2 are genuinely so marvelous that a certain amount of music penetrated through the sound at Croke Park last weekend. But, basically, there were slow numbers, fast numbers, and very fast numbers. You couldn't hear the words – not that it mattered, since everyone knew the words.

What survived the massive amplification and the concrete reverberations of the stands were tempo and beat. You lost the intros because the crowd had started cheering in recognition. You lost the closing chords, because they'd started cheering again. You lost the middles, because the songs were so well-known to the audience that they were singing along, so that your experience of "With or Without You" was far more of the two girls beside you bellowing it out in a Westmeath accent, slightly behind Bono's beat, than of Bono singing it.

Rock critics wrote about the concerts as if they were LPs, as if nuance was detectable. But whatever Croke Park was about, it was not about listening to music. What, indeed, was it about? For all the thousands and thousands of words I've read about last weekend's concerts, nobody seems able to explain just why U2 is the voice of the *zeitgeist*. This is not to question the individual brilliance of the band's members. They are, each, wonderfully talented. But what are these orchestrations, these tempi, these developments of an opening theme, this level of difficulty or easiness, these sentiments – all that comes out of Bono and the others as they invent and shape a song – why is this meaningful all over the world? By what process does significance leave one kind of music or one performer or one band, so that it suddenly seems old-fashioned and irrelevant, and what happens to make the new band seem significant? On what level does rock music work? The audiences in Milan and Cork and Boston are quite different from each other: what is it in U2 that is meaningful to all of them? The words? The level of performance? Something no one can explain?

What journalism does, vaguely aware that there's a mystery here, is to divide the answer between descriptions of the music, "the Edge's driving guitar soars past the most committed drum solo that even Larry has ever attempted" kind of thing, and the biographical "Bono stared out into the hot New Mexico night" kind of thing. But these don't add up to any kind of intelligible discussion. Given the overwhelming importance of rock music in popular culture, it is a great pity that the newspapers, in particular, don't give more space to thoughtful writing about rock.

The "color-piece" writers, too, seemed to be in the grip of a benign myth, so much so that they referred to Sunday's rain, which made you wet, the same as any other rain, as "a light drizzle." The crowds were celebratory, welcoming their own back, cheerful, joyful, etc. Well, as a matter of fact, the concert I was at was a distinctly poignant occasion, precisely because U2 are from Dublin, and were the only four millionaires there. The kids in the audience looked so poor. They *are* poor. They were by far the least privileged crowd U2 have so far played to (Belfast at least is in a welfare state). In comparison to playing in Basel, it must have been like playing in Soweto. They were awfully young and thin and plain, as far as the eye could see, ungainly when they danced, keeping to their own groups, generally humble. The one thing they had was energy. It is a stirring sight to see 40,000 people jumping up and down in unison, but the unison would be just as complete for Ronnie Drew and "Alive, Alive O-O" as it was for "Where the Streets Have No Name." Unison isn't of itself *about* anything: you get it in Croke Park at a great goal the same as you get it at U2.

So what was distinctively "U2-ish" about the occasion? In what ways was it different from any other very popular, very well-hyped rock concert? The answer surely is only in a sad way, really. The members of the band are even more not one of us than, say, the Rolling Stones, because they were, once, one of us. The gap between them and their audience is felt, no doubt on both sides. The bouncers, terrifying as Alsatians, mark the boundary of worlds. Bono can bend toward us from the ramp, but never come among us. People talk of "national pride" being evoked by U2, but it is difficult to see just how any nation can take any credit for their talent or their luck. Rock concerts are a conspiracy to make musicians – the build-up, the lights, the shrieks – seem like superior beings, but how do you believe in superior beings from Artane? The relationship between Ireland and U2 is far more complex than journalism admits.

The Irish Times, July 4, 1987

Irish Atheism

I was talking to a woman the other day, a single parent, who supports herself and her daughter by long, night hours of cleaning. She had just got a note from her daughter's school, telling her that she'll be making her First Holy Communion in June. This woman dreads the expense; it is not just the outfit for the little girl, but something presentable for herself that she has to get. Why, she wanted to know, can they not wear their school uniforms? Why indeed. As it is, I've met mothers who shoplift to clothe their children for these occasions.

However, the grumble about the clothes turned into a larger complaint. Had I seen, she wanted to know, the amount of money that children collect on their Communion visits these days? Fivers and tenners, single pounds are too small to offer. "Surely it's meant to be religious," she said, "not all about what you're wearing and how much money did you get?"

Well, yes. It is. But what interested me about her disgust at the secularization of this sacrament was that, as far as I know, she doesn't believe in God herself. She certainly doesn't practice the Catholicism she grew up in. So what's it to her, if the material is wiping out the spiritual?

She belongs to what I think might be quite a sizable number of people, former Catholics, who go along with the externals of belief, so that their children won't feel like outsiders. The implications of this position don't really worry her at all, and she wouldn't call herself a hypocrite. Neither would I use the word hypocrisy in this context. Whatever it is these people are doing, it is much more vague and instinctive and pragmatic than hypocrisy is.

It starts with marriage. Imagine a man and a woman, neither of whom would dream of accepting Catholic teaching on celibacy before marriage, or the procreative purpose of marriage, or anything else the Church might preach. They haven't been to Mass in years or to confession for decades. But they want to get married in a Catholic ceremony in a church, and they'll readily lie about their beliefs, even all the way through a premarriage course, to get that kind of wedding. They say that they don't want to upset the mammies and the grandas and so on, and, of course, that's true. But it is also true that their nonbelief doesn't seem to them an important thing, worth arguing about in the open. It is not a positive unbelief; it is not convinced atheism. It really just boils down to not liking and not practicing the religion they were brought up in.

And anyway, people usually get married so as to celebrate each other, and to say to the world, in the most solemn terms they know, that they commit themselves to each other. In this culture the vast majority of people don't know any terms more solemn than those arrived at during the history of Christianity. It takes real independence to turn one's back on this huge reservoir of meaningfulness, and to settle for the literalness of the registry office.

Next, there's the question of baptism. Again, the emotions cry out for the big gesture, and endorsement by tradition. A christening is a welcoming of the baby to this earth, and an induction of the new human being into the community, leaving aside its denominational aspect. And, in any case, I suppose that atheist parents think that it doesn't matter very much, because the baby doesn't know what's happening. Their own example of unbelief, they assume, will set the child right.

And so it all begins. But is it a good way to live – to see to it that the children appear to be Catholics, while steering clear of the whole thing yourself? To exploit their powerlessness? To send them out to Mass, while you stay in bed? To give them money for missions in which you don't believe? To accompany them proudly to First Communions and Confirmations, even though they have never seen you pray?

I see why people do this, of course. They want to give their children protective color. It is extremely hard on a child to bear the burden of dissenting from the majority. Only a few children in the country can get through the educational system without encountering teachers and schoolmates and schoolmates' parents who would make no bones about their hostility to unbelief. How could any loving parent ask a child to pay for his or her parent's views? Outside Dublin it is very difficult even for an adult to retain standing while eschewing communal practices.

The children know. They know that some of the people around them really believe, and they know that no one at home does. But they have to live as best they can by the double standard. It is only about religion that this arises. Whatever other convictions the parents may have, even minority convictions, like vegetarianism, or using Irish as the language of the home, the children will be reared by them, quite straightforwardly. After all, what else can you rear children by, except your own convictions? But few people will take the risk of not hedging their bets on this profound subject.

But if this leads to anything it must be to the creation of

adults who take neither belief nor unbelief seriously. Perhaps that is why there are so many socialists in this country, and even communists, who are perfectly at ease with religion. It used to be part of the work of the Left to attempt to disenchant people with heaven, so that they would cry for justice here on earth. But Irish socialists are as keen on heaven as anyone else: they have to be. To stand on atheist principle, to refuse to join in prayers, say, at funerals, to say that religious funerals are so much mumbo-jumbo, would be to proclaim yourself utterly marginal. A nutter. Offensive. Nobody would dream of doing it.

Nobody is supposed to take any ideology seriously enough to make a display of it. Any nonreligious ideology, that is. So people stay quiet, and somehow believe that by not going to Mass they are taking a stand against religion or the Church or clerical power or something – that like Stephen Dedalus they are flying by the net of religion. But are they?

All religions must have members who fall away. It must always be a personal difficulty for anyone, of any religion. But Catholicism is so vast here, so saturates all aspects of life and death, that to leave it means leaving the protection of the pack, being alone.

It is a process or a decision with myriad social consequences. Perhaps in this sense it is right for parents to keep their children enrolled in Catholicism as a way of life, even though they do not accept it as a revelation of the truth. Perhaps, too, Irish atheism is rarely more than tentative, as if God might come along at any minute and prove it wrong. The woman who faces her daughter's Communion wouldn't be complaining about the cost of it if she had money. But she would still disapprove of commercializing the sacraments she doesn't believe in. Nostalgia and wistful hope are far, far more powerful over the human heart than the dry pleasure of having a perfectly logical position.

The Irish Times, February 1, 1988

An Ugly Little War

I know a woman who is getting on in years but still, until recently, she held down a part-time job, played bridge, and took an active interest in life. Then, at a traffic light one day, a boy threw a rock through her passenger window and snatched her handbag. And it's no exaggeration to say that she has become old since then. She's shaky and she falls silent all the time. And it wasn't the shock of the incident that did that to her. It was losing her belongings. She just can't get over that.

Handbags are actually part of people. When my grandmother was dying, she was calm and happy, but her hand used to stray across the bedclothes to check that her handbag was still there. It had everything in it – her pension book, photos, memoriam cards, old letters, her purse, her glasses, her receipts from the landlord. The bag was by far her most intimate possession. No one else would dream of opening it. She would never say to us children: "Take a shilling from my bag." She'd say: "Hand me over my bag," and extract the money from its depths herself.

Old ladies, particularly old ladies of no property, like her, keep everything they've got in their bags. All their money, all their valuables. Words can't easily describe what it means to them to have their bag stolen. And even modern women, whose money is in the bank, always have other things in there that are special and worth carrying around. A love letter or a Mass card or a diary or a child's birth-tag. These things are of no value to the robbers. But then, you realize, neither are you yourself. They don't care about you. You are shaken in your own humanity, you feel cold and lonely when you have to stand there and realize that you are nothing to someone else, that they will throw your precious bits and pieces into a ditch.

Old ladies are not being used for their sentiment here. They are, in fact, the people whose bags mean most to them and who are simultaneously most vulnerable to being robbed. Still, worse could happen to them: they could be raped. The existence of rape changes the structure of the world for women – it literally shrinks the world, since women cannot, for instance, walk on their own after dark. Property crime does not have such far-reaching effects. But it does change and color the quality of life. People in cities are warier now than they used to be. Hatred is nearer the surface. And a lot of people are walking around with wounds inside them that no one knows about. Because society doesn't allow you to mourn for possessions.

A friend of mine has an elderly mother who prided herself on living alone. But she was followed home, twice, on pension day, and was mugged as she went to put her key in the lock. She is afraid to live in her house now. The loss of her own place is the second worst thing that has ever happened to her – after being widowed – but nobody would tolerate her talking about it and crying about it for more than a few days. She just had to bear it in silence.

Everybody I know has been robbed, whether it was a car vandalized, or a burgled house come home to, or a purse snatched in a shop. Everybody. I also know a few who do these things. The ones I know are very stupid and limited. I remember a friend being absolutely devastated by the theft of her bag because her address book was in it, twenty years of addresses, the central tool of her trade.

You can take it for granted that whoever stole her bag

15

doesn't have an address book. Doesn't keep a diary. Doesn't have a checkbook. Owning these things, like owning a house, makes us seem to the young criminals a different species. To them, they and their peers, who own nothing but clothes and videos, are the real people. We are the aliens.

They can be sorry for themselves, and for their own kind, but not for us. Some girls took my neighbor's bag, and she is so small and old that they looked through it in front of her. She had no money at all – there was nothing there except her medical card and her free-travel pass and that sort of thing. They took the bag anyway. She had to spend weeks queuing up to replace all that, anxiously explaining herself to the ESB, to the Social Welfare, to CIÉ, to the Eastern Health Board.

This would be classified as a petty crime. What's petty about it? In her way, this lady is a representative twentieth-century figure. She did nothing to deserve what happened to her. The crime against her was arbitrary, motiveless. And the girls humiliated her for their own amusement. The best that can be said about what happened to her is that she's much more willing to die than she was before.

But we fail the humanity of the thieves, just as they fail ours, when we write them off as animals. It is open to anyone to spend a day in the courts. If you do, and you look and listen to the people up on robbery charges, you have to recognize that they have been stunted by unvalued lives. You have to recognize that they were made, not born. This has nothing to do with bleeding-heart liberalism: I don't feel one bit liberal about the strutting boys in their trainers who terrorize their fellow-poor and anyone less strong than they are. I feel the rush of hatred, too, and the lust for revenge. But the courts strip the inequities of our society bare. These callous kids were babies once, and babies are pure potential. You know that you could have stood in the maternity ward all those years ago and, on the basis of home address alone, said: "This one will be the judge. This one will be the man in the anorak standing in front of the judge."

What can we expect, in a society so dreadfully divided between the haves and the have-nots, but that some of the latter will prey on the former? We accept that a third of the population live on the poverty line. We accept that only a handful of the most exceptional of the children of the poor will make it through to third-level education. We accept massive examples of greed and dishonesty in public life. We accept the values of materialism. What do we expect then – to be left unharassed, we who have all the privileges?

People do grow out of crime. It comes about when the girlfriend gets pregnant, or they start making good money at the job, or they get a house, or they win a cup at weightlifting. As soon as they have something – as the rest of us have – to protect. Jail doesn't decriminalize people; a stake in society may. But we've got thousands and thousands of young people who cannot expect a stake in society. Is it reasonable to expect them to oblige us and respect us? To be nice? To accept their lot?

There is a low-level war on the streets of Dublin. But it is an ugly little war. It is not against the rich: the rich don't allow themselves to be vulnerable. It is essentially a war between the poor and the not-much-better-off. The little old ladies, for example, are frontline troops. More and more of them are finding that their declining years have been poisoned by the spread of street crime. And, for all we know what to do about it, so will ours be.

The Irish Times, August 8, 1988

Power and Obedience

In Galway the other night the company I was in started talking about a local controversy. Some Leaving Cert girls, it seems, as an end-of-school prank, had invited a male stripper to lay on a surprise performance for the teachers, religious and lay, and for the girls. This was very much unappreciated by their elders. The head nun canceled revision classes, canceled the debs' ball, and in general demonstrated to the girls where, as a matter of fact, power lies.

The people I was with never got round to discussing the rights and wrongs of this event. We were all so astonished at the girls having even thought of such a thing that we got no further. Even the youngest among us, not long out of school, could hardly believe the change there has been since her day. It would never have crossed our minds – any of the men and women there – to try even the mildest joke on the authorities in our schools. And as for a male stripper! The world would have come to an end. God knows what would have happened. We'd have been murdered, for sure.

"But then it's all different now," someone said. "Kids *like* going to school these days. They don't dread it the way we used to." And then, the horrible, unforgotten stories began to be told. One woman, when she was five or six – before her First Communion, anyway – had been slapped by a nun. When she told her mother, her mother took her back to the school to demand an explanation. The nun looked the mother right in the eye and denied ever touching the child. Next day, the nun assembled the school, and made the child kneel in front of it and repeat after her, "I am a liar. I am a liar." In this woman's voice, you could hear the bewilderment of the child she once was, as well as an enduring bitterness.

A man said that it hadn't been too bad for him. There were only two masters in his school who beat pupils and one of them only punished you "when it was reasonable. If you were messing, or that." But the other was a sadist, who used to lift the boys up by the short hairs beside their ears. He taught math. Once a boy explained a math problem he'd written out on the board to others, when the master was out of the room. For that, he was beaten so savagely that he was left unconscious. "What was his crime?" the man who was telling us this is still asking, thirty years later. "What was his crime?"

All of us could remember the special pain when the cane missed your palm, and caught your fingertips instead. We all, the men and women there, know what it's like to have your ears twisted. Chair-legs, pointers, fists – anything and everything was used against children in those days.

And it was no use appealing to home. Most parents thought that if you were chastised you deserved it, and probably deserved more of the same. Or that it was the school's business, and that parents couldn't interfere with a school. Or, that they'd been beaten themselves and that it hadn't done them a pick of harm.

That's the question, isn't it? Was it harmful? Because if it was, then most people over the age of about twenty-five years are likely to have been harmed. Not that they'd admit it. Men, especially, sturdily insist that if anything, being hit did them good. Made men of them. Should be brought back for joyriders, vandals, hooligans – other people's children, in short.

19

I think it is true, myself, that just being hit, as such, doesn't harm you, or at least that it didn't in that culture, where it was altogether accepted. But the context did matter. Where it was unfair, or out of control, or part of personal vendetta, then it terribly disturbed the child's task of making sense of the world. And I think that it was, generally, harmful. That it inculcated a sense of powerlessness on the one hand, while teaching authoritarianism on the other. The individual was a nobody, in a world of more powerful beings. Power was always out there, in the hands of the wielder of punishment. The notion of personal authority, of rightly having your own place in power relations, simply couldn't develop in the climate of fear.

I think of a quiet man I knew, who once told me about his school. Everyone bullied him, because he was so meek. But one Brother hated him. One icy winter's day, for example, the Brother soaked his scarf in water, and sent him out to stand in the yard until the scarf should freeze. It took five hours. This man never asserted himself in life. He married a forceful woman, who walked all over him. He did his little job, quiet as a mouse. It is hard for me to see no connection between what he suffered as a child and his subsequent timidity. It is hard not to believe that if he'd gone to a child-loving school, his natural sweetness might have led to his being valued, and thus to valuing himself.

In fact, I find it difficult to believe that there is no relationship between our society at large and what we witnessed as children. And it was as small children we witnessed it, at least for me. Secondary girls' schools didn't use corporal punishment, the ones I went to anyway. Yet we might have been better able to take it when we were older, instead of at seven or eight or nine.

What threat, I ask myself, did people so small appear to pose, that they could be treated like that? What was going on? However bold we were, how could they have done it to people so much smaller than themselves? Make them flinch and howl and be humiliated? "Ah, sure, we got over it," people say. But if they did, how is it that those episodes are always remembered, when so much else of childhood is forgotten?

How did all this affect the relationship of ordinary people to the other people, the ones who have power over them? You notice that we have no Tiananmen Squares here, that we don't assemble to demand accountability, no matter how bad things are. We don't go after the people in power, we don't follow them around saying, "What happened to the promises you made?" Or, "You lied to us." Or, "You let us down." Grievances we have in plenty, but what about outrage? What about confronting them – making them pay? No, that's not something we do, and I don't think it is altogether fanciful to see a link between that passivity and the prudent passivity we learnt at school.

The kind of country we have is commonly called "conservative." Well, if conservatism includes an unwillingness to rock the boat, a fear of change, a dull acceptance of the status quo, those are all attitudes that were inculcated in us, from our earliest years. It isn't as if we chose them, from a wide menu of things we might have been. To be like that was the wisest course. And not just in the schools, of course. From de Valera down to the parish priest, from the home to the guards' barracks to the doctor's surgery, the two poles of that world were authority and obedience.

Now, we have a more diverse kind of world struggling to come about, and young people to cope with it who never knew what it was like to be afraid to go to school. Here's hoping that that will make a difference, and that enough of them will stay here long enough for us to see the difference. The male stripper, it seems to me, was an awfully bad idea, on several grounds. But the road that led to him has been climbing all the way.

The Irish Times, June 5, 1989

Knowing Travellers

Someone I know bought a derelict cottage recently. He was working on it at weekends, and one weekend the copper-piping for the plumbing was delivered to the site. A local came up to see him and said that Travellers had been noticed looking at the copper. So he slept in the shell of the building for a few nights until all the copper had been installed and the place was secure.

When he told me this little story he said to me: "I'm only telling you this in private. I'd never say it in public." In other words, he's a decent man who wouldn't dream of contributing to the anti-Traveller feeling around. On the other hand, he un-hesitatingly believed that the Travellers were going to steal the copper.

There are not many subjects on which such doublethink is commonplace. Abortion is similar, in the passions it arouses and the absence of a middle ground. But liberals here are actually more free to express their views on abortion than on the Travelling people. They may have worries about the whole Travelling way of life, and fear an element within the Travelling people. But they will not give voice to any of this, for fear of being seen to line up with the vociferous minority which would be glad to see the Travellers in punishment camps, and their women sterilized.

Thus, the argument about Travellers polarizes people into those who hate them, and those who are driven by that hate into a blanket defense of the Travelling people which ordinary people cannot quite accept. Claims are made for the Travelling way of life which settled people, by definition, cannot understand. And the Travellers are charged with so many and such horrible crimes by their detractors that their defenders have to deny any criminality at all.

Dublin County Council recently had a special meeting about their plan for halting sites. During the meeting, one councillor said that there was a fear among settled communities that the presence of Travellers would lead to an increase of rape and in attacks on old people. He was shouted down, and withdrew the remark.

I'm glad that he did so. But it is more of the doublespeak. He was only reporting, accurately, what some people do fear. If those fears didn't exist there would be no problem. But the fact is that there is a problem. I don't see what is gained by acknowledging the problem, but refusing to acknowledge the reasons for it.

I have never had the opportunity of knowing a Traveller on equal terms. The closest I've come was a settled Traveller I met in Cork. She always kept her hand over her mouth, because her lips were split and her teeth missing, thanks to her late husband. But she was the gentlest, most good-humored of women. When I met her, her children were teaching her to read and write and she was learning at a great rate, because she wanted to be able to help them at their homework.

Just one meeting like that can dissolve the stereotypes. But anyone with eyes in their head can see the healthy children and the spotless caravans that some Travellers can manage to present in seas of mud and in rain and frost. And anyone can listen. More and more, Travellers' own voices are being heard. There was a young woman on the *Gay Byrne Show* not long ago,

24

talking to him about the way Travellers handle courtship and marriage. She was wonderful. If anything, she was patronizing the rest of us.

If this smacks of a naive plea to recognize the humanity of the Travellers, that is because their enemies deny their humanity, so you have to start the discussion at zero. "Animals," people say. "Savages." "They've all got AIDS." Journalists get long, usually anonymous, letters about the filth of the Travellers, their neglect of their children, their thieving ways, the viciousness of their assaults, the way they terrorize old people all over the country. Usually, one thing has been done to the writer by a Traveller, or someone thought to be a Traveller. And in their distress and fear they see Travellers everywhere and crime everywhere and the whole of living ruined for everyone by all Travellers.

You can assert to such people that Travellers *are* humans, that they are our fellow Irish people, and are, on the whole, as law-abiding as the settled people, on the whole, are. But this cuts no ice. The one thing that stops the tirade is to point out that which is self-evidently true: the babies of Travellers come into the world as innocent as you or I, and whatever it is that goes wrong happens in and through society.

Almost the whole of Travellers' lives is on view. A man beats his wife in the street and a hundred people see. Settled wife-beating happens behind closed doors. The Travellers line up outside the employment exchange with bottles of wine in their hands, or sit in their vans swigging from the bottles. Meanwhile thousands and thousands of settled people are drinking in pubs or in front of the telly or handing around the sherries. Many people neglect their children, but hardly anyone knows. Yet everyone sees the Travelling children sniffing glue. Everyone sees the women with sunburnt babies sitting all day in front of a cardboard box.

Everyone can identify a Traveller at once, the weather-beaten faces and the motley clothes. Their beautiful women and children, such as Nan Joyce and her children, have a special sort of beauty. So the Travellers have no privacy from us. They are "other." Their otherness is more than disquieting: between us and them there is an abyss of understanding, and in that abyss the nightmares about their nature swirl. What you have no understanding of you can endow with any feature.

It is this mythic element that makes reasonable planning for the Travellers so difficult. Because, on the face of it, the problem they present is soluble, and it should be possible to bring about an Ireland where everyone has access to water and sanitation, and where we, the comfortable ones, don't have to put the others out of our minds on cold winter nights. There are about 12,000 persons – persons, not families – on the road or staying at halting sites. Even if that figure is a great under-estimate, that's still a very small number of people. There are millions of us – surely it is possible to set up a network of sites and schemes where Travellers can escape from the de-graded living conditions which we impose on them, and then calmly blame them for?

Or, do we want to go on like this forever? The argument for compassion has never worked: we've accepted for decades that Travelling children suffer and die in far greater numbers than our children, and not many people care.

But what about the argument from self-interest? The very people who most loathe and fear the Travellers must see that the cycle has to be broken sometime. They must see that while attitudes to the Travellers remain so hostile, Traveller children are born to alienation, born to be increasingly hardened by their experience of life, born to grow up unable to like or pity or make common cause with their oppressors. "Why don't *they* do something? Why don't they understand us?" some settled people cry. But truly, what society has done to them is so much worse than what they do back, and all of us are so multiply advantaged compared to them, that it will take a long process of reparation before we can talk of mutuality.

The Irish Times, July 10, 1989

The Mystery of the General Good

On my way in to work I pass beggars with their babies, and women in furs going into boutiques to collect dresses that have been flown in from England. I could buy a mackerel on the way for 25p, or I could buy handmade chocolates. I pass chip shops and dining clubs, brasseries and hermetic pubs, vegetable stalls and gourmet delicatessens.

In the bank this morning, the man in front of me in the queue was the cart-pusher, who comes along the gutter in the morning vaguely trailing his sweeping-brush. The woman behind is famous for her dinner parties. Each thing is part of the whole: privilege and poverty all in an intimate, intricate mix together.

Even the people most trapped in ghettos – the very rich, the too-famous-to-go-out, the very poor – know what the others do, and a little bit about what it's like. There's bound to be a relative somewhere whose condition is quite different from the rest of the family's. Even politicians, who never travel on a bus, meet an awful lot of people who never travel in a car. You can't really seal yourself into just one way of life here. Other people keep breaking in.

RTÉ television shows ads for expensive toys, and at the same time shows scenes of deprivation from home and from abroad. *The Irish Times* talks about champagne and golden baubles, and also talks about the homeless and malnourished and hopeless. The mix reflects the way things are. It wouldn't make sense, to most people, to censor affluence because of guilt about misery. Not only are a lot of people in actual fact comfortable enough: in actual fact, that is what everybody aspires to be. Having money is cheerful and exciting. Who ever wanted as badly to be poor?

But it jars, the mix. It jars, the silk lingerie alongside the itinerants. It is just not okay to come out of a shop with your parcels and stumble across a glue-sniffing child. Whatever there is left in us of a desire for social justice, even if it is no more than a persistent unease, comes alive at Christmastime. You make yourself conscious of your own good fortune by conjuring up what the opposite would be – what it would be like if you had no home or if you lost the children or if nobody wanted you.

Ordinary people don't know why things are as they are. They don't know how it comes about that some are fortunate and some are not. They feel themselves to be individually compassionate – they would make things better for other people if they could. But they see no route from themselves to the general good. They don't know what to do, except be charitable.

In theory, that is what politics are for. We are an electoral democracy and we can use the ballot to express, through legislation, the will of the people. In practice, this is not how politics in this country is perceived. People grasp that they can elect politicians, and choose between the persons offered to them. They can even elect parties. But the connection between party and policy has long since been lost, at least in the Center and on the Right. Nobody even listens to what politicians say before an election. And after an election, what power have the people then? If we were asked, for instance, by referendum, whether we want the recommendations of the Commission on Social Welfare implemented, I have no doubt that we would say that we most certainly do. But no government implements them. Something stops them: the size of the task, or the Department of Finance or, for all I know, the International Monetary Fund. We really have no way of making the government's priorities the same as our own.

And leaving politics aside, most people don't know anything about economics. They see no connection between their own good fortune and the bad fortune of others. Nobody ever points out any connection, except in the line of making them feel guilty. But they don't want to feel guilty, and they don't believe they are guilty. They're glad that they're safe and warm and have money to spend, and they really, really don't understand why someone mightn't have worked for five years, or why a single mother would trap herself with more than one baby, or why a poor man would spend his whole dole money on drink.

If it were clear to people that mortgage tax relief, for instance, or private schools, are in fact connected with the despair of the underprivileged, they might allow their moral sensibility to open up to those things. But they're trapped in little pieces of information, and anecdotal knowledge, and a view of the poor based on the cleaning woman.

Yet, if asked, of course everybody would say that they want things to be better, that they don't want anybody to suffer; that of course they don't want itinerant children to burn to death in a field of mud; of course they don't want teenagers exploited in low-paid jobs; of course they don't want there to be women who can only get through Christmas on Valium.

And it's not just because it's more comfortable for yourself if everybody around you is comfortable. It is because – in my opinion, anyway – people would much rather be good than bad. And they have an idea of the good, which derives from Christianity, and it has to do with other people. The thing that baffles them is, how do you get from here to there? How can one person, in one life, move a whole society toward social justice?

Can there be any kind of plan? But then do people at heart believe in planning? At Christmas you notice more than any other time how great the role the accidental and the random play in the individual life. There are going to be people who are dreadfully unhappy this week and all by accident, through no fault of their own or ours, nothing to do with money, even. That your lover left, or the daughter moved to Australia, or all the old neighbors are gone. It is known by everybody that even leaving aside the big things, like whether we have good health, or when we die, the way our lives work out is essentially un- governable. This is never mentioned as a factor in political cul- ture. Some politics depend on the notion of steady progress toward an achievable goal. But, deep down, people don't be- lieve that events can be made as orderly as that. So those pol- itics appear unreal, and that in turn affects their chance of success.

It goes against the grain of experience to believe that general reform is possible all at once, or that it can be brought about increment by increment, with everybody knowing where they're going. But piecemeal, minor reforms are within our grasp. One family can look after one other, less fortunate, family. One pressure group can establish a need, and struggle to meet it: think back ten years ago, there was no one to help the victims of rape. Twenty years ago there was no single parent's allowance. A hundred years ago there was no alternative to the workhouse. Obviously things do get better, even if it is obscure to most of us how it is that they get better, or when the exact moment of change is, or what are the ideas that eventually move in from the edges and become the center.

It seems reasonable, if not to believe, then to hope that things will continue, bit by bit, to improve. That there might be a Christmas when there will be less to hurt the conscience.

We're hardly going to go on, are we, letting the number of our homeless grow and grow? Or are we? Is it endemic to our economic system that an underclass must develop, and that we must harden our hearts?

The Irish Times, December 18, 1989

The 1990s

On Human Dignity

I was walking past O'Connell Bridge House the other day when this man stopped me. He showed me a piece of paper with "Driver Testing Centre, O'Connell Bridge House" written on it. "Could you tell me where that is?" he said. "You're standing in front of it," I said. "Look, it's written on the door." "Oh, is it?" he said. "The thing is, I can't read."

I went on my way, idly wondering whether people who can't read should be allowed to drive cars. How many road signs are symbols, and how many depend on words? And also wondering, as always, how *anybody* learns to read. How does the miracle work? What happens? I remember the exact moment myself, and it was the only transcendent thing that ever happened to me. There were still words in the sentence that I was looking at that I couldn't understand, and they were like black holes. But light seemed to jump from each word I could understand to the next word I could understand, so that I could grasp the general meaning of the whole shape. I ran all the way to the shop, to tell them all there. There was no one much to show off to at home.

The miracle doesn't happen to everyone. Last week, I went to a little event in a room in Mountjoy Square in Dublin. Men and women who have been learning how to read and write, through the Dublin Literacy Scheme, were reading their first pieces of work in public. Need I say that the atmosphere of first-night nerves was intense, that people were standing outside on the steps, dragging desperately on cigarettes, that in the room, practically every pair of hands you could see were shaking. Yet, they did it. Haltingly, or helter-skelter. "I have a dog called Max." "Being un-em-ployed is very bor-ing." "Christmas is a happy occ-asion for all fam-il-ies." All ages and accents. All kinds of faces. As each person read aloud, the others followed the words in a booklet. Some of them followed the lines with their fingers: adults, using the gestures of children.

Nobody went out and found these people. They came to look for literacy themselves, most of them in fear and trembling. When you can't read or write, they were telling me afterwards, you think you're nobody. You have no confidence. You lie and deceive to cover up. So you have to face your whole self when you go to inquire about classes. It is much more than just seeking a skill.

And it isn't easy to acquire the skill at the wrong time of your life. These were adults, who talk and think with all the sophistication of adults, yet they had to go back to being like children. They could only express themselves in writing like six-year-olds, yet what they wanted to express had to do with jobs, journeys, Nelson Mandela, bringing up children, Shamrock Rovers, money. This must be the hardest thing – to be able to run like a hare in your mind, but be hobbled by words.

As they read, you could hear that their mouths were dry with nervousness. When they'd come to a shaky stop, the others would applaud and applaud. There were three women who were more or less holding each other's hands to keep each other going. That's how they must have learnt, too: together. These particular women were from a notoriously deprived area of the north inner-city. Usually, they would be described as under-privileged. So they are, on many levels. But not that night. When you saw their courage and determination, and the

36

resource they have in each other, and the amount of laughs they were getting out of the situation, you couldn't but see them as privileged. Other people leave school and never face another challenge in their lives.

Not that literacy is just a problem of the poor, or of women. Most students are men, as a matter of fact, probably because the scheme – relying as it does on voluntary labor – can offer one-to-one tuition, so you don't have to face a group to start with. A learner gets two hours tuition a week for thirty weeks and that, even though it is only the equivalent of two weeks at school, is enough to get them started. But three-quarters of all the people who turn up at Mountjoy Square are unemployed. They could easily do a full-time course, and that's what they want to do. The Dublin Literacy Scheme, however, doesn't have the funds or staff to run full-time courses. Even though it has almost as much funding as the rest of the country's literacy schemes put together.

One woman read out a piece about being able to under-stand her Christmas cards for the first time. She had kept all her cards over the years, but only now can she read them. This is the least of the pains of illiteracy. You can't read instruc-tions so you're afraid, say, giving medicine to a child, that you're making a mistake. You can't read the signs in railway stations, so you're not sure of your stop. You can't hope for promotion in your work. You can't write letters home. You can't help your children with their schoolwork. You can't buy own-brand goods, because there are no pictures on the labels. The Na-tional Adult Literacy Agency has an information pack about its work, and it quotes a few sentences that sum up a social tragedy. "Any time the AGM came up I was put forward as secretary and I could never take it. Then they'd say, 'There are people in the club for many years and they get a lot of pleas-

ure out of it, but they're not willing to put anything into it."
Now I was willing and I'd love to but I couldn't, and I
couldn't turn around and say: 'I can't spell, I can't read.' "

Chance, or ill-luck, kept these people back. They were put
down the back of the class and forgotten, or they were out of
school a lot with sickness, or they'd had to help at home, or
they had worked from childhood and been too tired to learn.
One beautiful girl had been to a very fashionable school. Her
English teacher, infuriated by her slowness, had slapped her
head, and this girl wouldn't even try after that. As it turns out,
she's dyslexic. But nobody understood that, or cared. She left
school unable to read. But she can read now. I heard her. Her
tutor sat beside her, beaming and nodding, like a hen with a
chick.

There is no fee for being taught to read or write.
The scheme takes the view that literacy is a right, and you
shouldn't have to pay for your rights. But this means that it
just barely survives. It has one full-time paid organizer, and
one assistant. Between them, they have to test and train the
voluntary tutors, compile teaching materials, administer all the
meetings of the students and the teachers, do what research
they can, and try to develop outlets for the students who master literacy and are now longing to go on to more learning. If
one of those two people gets sick, I don't know what happens.
Even so, the Dublin scheme is much the most fortunate in the
country. You can get some help in most places through the
VECs, but there is no real state scheme.

More and more people are looking for help with reading
and writing. The Altrusa/VEC scheme in Cork, for example,
has 150 working couples "and more coming all the time."
Presumably, life has become impossible to manage without

literacy. Presumably, too, this is one problem which a single big push would almost solve. It is a legacy of the past: of school classes of fifty or sixty children; of unkindness towards children; of a time when if the family failed the child, there were no other sources of help. The Department of Education could increase its small grant towards literacy provision for, say, five years: perhaps the teachers' unions – some of whose predecessors short-changed these people – would care to lobby?

There was nothing at all dramatic about the reading in Mountjoy Square. We were all squashed in on plastic chairs, and someone had to run out for milk for the paper cups of tea. It wasn't even funny. There was too much tension in the room for that. But look at all that was happening in that room. Here were human beings who had been denied their birthright of literacy, and who had sturdily set out to retrieve it. They were the last people you'd be sorry for. So, if the reading threatened to move the spectator to tears, it wasn't from pity. It was because you don't often see, overcoming all the awkwardness, such a display of human dignity.

The Irish Times, May 14, 1990

Innocence Ruined

One morning last week I was walking down the Rathmines Road at about eight o'clock. I was going for a swim. Going past McDonald's I saw a woman, surrounded by children. She was calling in to someone inside the restaurant, asking what time it would be open. She was a small woman, and the children were very small. I counted them – six little girls, and the baby she was carrying looked like a boy. The older children were laden down with bags and bundles. McDonald's wouldn't be open for another hour, so they walked on. A duck and her ducklings.

I said to the woman that there was another café around the corner, and because she was so burdened I ran round to it to see when it would be open. It would be open at half past eight. I could guess what this little troupe were doing on the street, but the woman told me anyway. They'd run away from the caravan they live in at first light. Her husband had been beating her. You could see the bruises.

There's a refuge for battered women in Rathmines. She'd been there already, but she'd been told to come back at half past ten when the health people would be there. So she and the seven children were looking for somewhere to shelter for the next few hours. They stood there, all with the same blue eyes. Matter-of-fact, they were, as if it's just another thing you do in life, to pack up all your worldly goods and set out. The mother had organized the evacuation with such precision: the baby's food had been prepared, the bundles were distributed according to what each child could carry. And they were all spotlessly clean, hair and clothes. How she had managed this, in a caravan, I just don't know. I thought maybe I should go with them to the café in case they were refused service. The woman had a Traveller's voice. But they were such an orderly group that I expected they would be all right.

So I went for the swim. There was me, paying money to get exercise. There was she, getting miles of exercise, whether she liked it or not. I went home via the café. They were sitting at some tables outside its door. They had no cups or anything in front of them, so I don't know whether they'd eaten. The baby was chuckling away, but the little girls were bored. "What time is it?" one of them asked me. She had her schoolbag with her. Maybe she would have preferred being at school to trailing around with her mother, though you could see the confidence they had in her. I said to the woman: "There are eight of you, there's only one of him. Could you not have thrown him out?" "That's easier said than done," she said.

I rang the refuge later. They have twelve families there at the moment instead of ten which is their maximum, and the place is so crowded that they're sleeping on floors. But they had made room for her. She's there now.

I could go and see her. She's used to people with accents like mine asking her intimate questions. I could give her advice about housing and contraception and barring orders. But who am I to exploit her powerlessness further? The rich and powerful never tell you anything – you wouldn't dream of asking. People like her tell you everything, because you might be able to help them. But I can't help her.

Except by asking the broad question – what put her on the street? And you may say that whatever it was, it has nothing to do with us. We can't help it if he beats her. It's between themselves. We have nothing to do with it. As a community, we designate people to protect the weak. We designate the Garda. Of course, it's hard to get to the phone when you're being beaten up, and of course this woman had no phone. Still, in theory, you can always send for the guards. And we do provide refuges for battered women. Not nearly enough of them, but some. Not many women have to walk the streets with their children all night. Only a few. You could say that there is no more the community can do about what is essentially a private matter.

But there is more the community could do. It could begin to become conscious of the extent to which some men think they own their women and children, and the extent to which they feel entitled to wreak their power over them. Everyone assents to this. Beating your own wife is far more acceptable than beating someone else's wife. Why?

Why is it that no one interferes? Why is it that wife-beating is considered distasteful and upsetting, but isn't considered a grave offense? It is accepted as a part of life, something that always happened and always will happen, as if it were part of "nature." But there is no one nature. We construct nature. What we think is natural, and therefore outside human manipulation, changes all the time. For example, it once seemed natural to be amused by the mad, and people went to Bedlam to laugh at the inmates. For example, it once seemed natural to do anything you liked to animals. You could prod a poor bear to dance in the street. That's over now: what is "natural" has been reconstructed. To the point where I can say that if a man cruelly beat a harmless and devoted pet animal there would be public outrage. Whereas there is no outrage at a man beating the woman who "belongs" to him.

"Why doesn't she leave him?" is what people say. Why is it assumed that she is free to change things, but he isn't? Why is he assumed to be changeless? Why are there refuges for women, instead of refuges for men, where they could go or be sent to sort themselves out, and try to find some insight into their behavior? There is one self-help group, in north Dublin, where men who habitually assault their partners have come together to confront what they do. Why is there only one such group in the country? Look at what women have done, for themselves and for other women, over the past twenty years. First they started all the services that men's abuse of women make necessary – services for single mothers, rape counseling, refuges. Then they moved on and today, literally all over Ireland, women are involved in self-development through schemes and groups and personal initiatives, and through the arts. Thousands of them are hoping to change themselves to understand things better, with the hope of living more fully.

Where is the corresponding vitality in the world of men? You'd think that they were perfect the way they are. You'd think patriarchy was perfect, even though patriarchy underpins beatings and abuse and rape and walking away from the responsibility of your own child. "Feminist" men claim to be such because they are personally blameless and because they support women. But why don't they support men? Why aren't they out there working with rapists, the same as women work with rape victims? Why does no man take responsibility for his brothers? Even about themselves too many men are lazy, and get by on the minimum of insight. In practice, the only men you meet who know anything much about themselves are men who have struggled to give up drink, because they have had to reflect.

Of course, someone is going to say that I'm generalizing about men. Yes, that's exactly what I'm doing. Individual men are as likely as anyone else to give their time to the Vincent de

Paul Society, or to be dedicated probation workers, or to lend their energies to social change, including all the changes that have come for women. But it is on the general level, it is as a mass, as a gender, that men are to date much less conscious than women.

Yet it is on the level of consciousness that change must come. Just as it did about Bedlam. Barring orders and more refuge places aren't the answer to wife-beating. The answer is self-education, especially the self-education of men. The ideal people to get a process of self-education going are not officials, not social workers, not doctors, but other men. Ordinary men. But that kind of thing is not the kind of thing men do for each other.

I don't know why that man beat up the woman I met. I don't suppose he knows either. I don't suppose she knows. And above all, I don't suppose that the children know. But they were there when it happened. They were learning. So that's seven more small human beings who have seen with their own eyes that brute violence makes things happen. The implications of such a lesson are social as well as personal. We will be dealing with them. But even if it meant nothing in social terms – even if the only victims of that night's violence were the women and the seven children – look at the extent of what those children have lost. Theirs is innocence ruined, even though their mother is so brave.

The Irish Times, June 10, 1991

The Other World

There are some apparitions happening again in County Cork and I see the Bishop of Cork and Ross quoted as saying about them that "it's a silly season for silly people." Oddly enough, the last time I heard the word "silly" used like this was in Mostar, a town near Medjugorje. The local doctor, a committed socialist, was talking with contempt about the pilgrims who flock to Medjugorje. "They're children," he said. "When you think of all that the world needs – they're so *silly*."

I said that I didn't think they were silly: I thought they were needy. What's more, I thought that on a human level, Medjugorje was a wonderful place. People seemed to expand there – to be more whole. Even I felt it. Irrespective of visions and visionaries and dancing suns and rosary beads changing color. The doctor, however, continued to be as scathing as the Bishop of Cork and Ross.

The doctor wanted to build a just and reasonable society. He found mystery distasteful. But the mysterious exists, and some people have an appetite for it. A few years ago, thousands were traveling to Ballinspittle. Why that year, and not the years in between? Some commentators said it was the abortion referendum, and the psychic upheavals it led to. I don't know that the *zeitgeist* is so easily explained. Why Cork? A Mayoman said to me that it's because Cork isn't in an all-Ireland final this year. Not that Mayo is an entirely rational place. I was there on Midsummer Eve and there were bonfires all over the place.

Did committed socialists – like the doctor – see fairies (as I did) when they were children? I'm not suggesting that fairies and religious apparitions have anything in common. Fairies have no doctrinal or ethical implications. Mine didn't have, anyway. It is just that in both cases, other people don't believe you. Most people probably do not believe that there are manifestations of the Virgin Mary in County Cork at the moment. Yet they must know that the people concerned are not telling lies. There are, of course, impostors and hysterics and the like in the apparition business. But that is as nothing compared to the thousands, if not millions, of people whose lives have been transformed by the inexplicable.

People who were quite indifferent – who couldn't care less – did see the sun dance at Fátima, and did leave their crutches at Lourdes and did see the statue move at Ballinspittle and do fast and pray with a special intensity because of the message promulgated at Medjugorje. And those are just examples from within one Church in one place – Europe. If you were to contemplate all the magical and miraculous elements in all the religions of all the world – the chicken-bones on altar-steps, the white rags tied to desert tombs – then you'd begin to wonder whether "silliness" is the right word for what is going on.

In Ireland, things are always turning out to be multidimensional. At the well of St. Gobnait in Ballyvourney recently, some woman had left her rings. There were bright toggles – that teenagers tie their hair up with – twisted around the little rail of offerings, under ancient trees. At a remote well in the Burren – a toothache-cure well – someone had left a coat-hanger. What were they doing with a coat-hanger, miles from the road? In Leitrim, the lady went to get me a piece of string. If I rubbed this piece of string on a certain tomb, and then wore it, I'd never have back trouble. All perfectly normal. Perfectly normal to go seven times around a bed of stones on your knees. To find a rock in a field with a cross scratched into it. For fifteen-year-old Ann Lovett to have gone to a grotto to have company in her terror of secretly giving birth.

There are invisible presences everywhere. My five-year-old friend, Jack, has an invisible friend called Billy. We – the adults – have to hang around, waiting for Billy to find his coat. A teacher – a practical woman – called to see her mother. She met a tiny little old lady coming out of her mother's house. This was, of course, the banshee, and sure enough, she found her mother dying. A colleague at *The Irish Times* was shown his way home one night on the Aran Islands by people who had drowned seventy years before. In these circumstances, why wouldn't statues move? Given that religion is the great repository of images, given that it engages the deepest emotions, given the daring acts of the imagination that it exacts on a daily basis.

The stir of cities hides the numinous. But think what space there is for visions in other lives. How desolate Knock must have been, thirty years after the Famine. How remote Garabandal and Medjugorje are. How lonely the life of a little girl like Bernadette, gathering firewood, or the children at Fátima, minding the sheep. I can't pronounce on the authenticity of Marian apparitions, but I can say that it is evident that we need to believe that we have a mother, who loves us.

Parish priests get caught in the middle. So one was saying to me, recently. On the one hand, he has his congregation, proud and excited if there are manifestations in their midst. On the other, he has the higher authorities, who very understandably want this kind of thing kept in check. Quite apart from the problem of meaning – and some visions seem, like my fairies, to be meaningless – there is a materialization of faith implicit in the miraculous. "Give us a sign!" people shout at the Creator. As if there were nothing there without a sign.

I can quite see why a teaching Church cannot allow the folk to run hither and thither. But for myself, I like it that people persist in mingling the everyday and the otherworldly. It is an ancient and a universal practice. And although, on a public level, one would like Ireland to be run in a reasonable, pluralist, modern way, there is more to living here than being a citizen. There is a capaciousness not so much of belief as of endlessly suspended judgment, which to my mind is precious.

This is not to say that everything is the same as everything else. I met a woman once who was bottling plums in brandy, at enormous expense, as part of some obscure act of worship picked up by her from a visionary in northern Italy called Mamma Rosa. I wouldn't put that kind of thing even on the same spectrum, however far away, as belief in, say, the Resurrection. But people will do anything to try to make sense of the uncertainties of life and the certainty of death. They use the senseless to make sense. They make a construct out of what they have to hand, often with enormous ingenuity. I never saw a statue move, and don't expect to, and don't want to, but I've met people who have seen such things. It's the people who leave you awestruck – not the statues.

The Irish Times, September 2, 1991

Birth

The streets are so empty in the first wash of light that seagulls inhabit them, tearing at food, high-stepping down the middle of Fitzwilliam Street. In the whole long Georgian vista down to Holles Street Hospital, nothing moves in the dawn. But see that sash window high up at the back of the hospital, pushed up to let in the summer morning?

Inside that room, the radio plays cha-cha-cha music, and on the bed a young woman with sweat in her hair is trying to push her first baby into the world. Her man has red hair and an earring, and he is bent in to her shoulder. He's holding her lovely, strong hand. "Oh Jesus," she says. "Oh fuck." The midwife is listening to the heartbeat through a little rubber thing that she moves around the big belly. The midwife feels another pain coming. "Ah, it's only a little one," Patricia says, laughing a bit. But sometimes she swears again, not even knowing she's doing it, utterly absorbed in her huge effort, as the lounge-bar music plays imperturbably, on and on.

Just after 5:00 AM it was when Patricia went into labor. Now it is 6:00 AM, a most beautiful morning of rose and pearl. Sometimes they whisper a little joke to each other, the young woman and man. The nurse is swabbing between Patricia's legs. I can see the top of the baby's head. But it goes back in again, then peeks again, then disappears again.

Patricia's face goes purple with the effort of pushing. She braces her feet against the bodies of the nurse and the midwife. "Ten more minutes," the midwife says to her, working with her, urging her, praising her. Time is not like time anywhere else – there is only the pace of the event, nothing can make it go faster, or slower, once the birth begins. There is nothing in the world but this.

The midwife picks up a scissors. Patricia starts to pant and grabs the gas mask. You could faint with the intensity of the scene.

Then, most amazingly, the baby slides out to be one of the human beings in the room. All purple and covered in slime, but perfect, perfect. Little Tony, from Wicklow. The nurse puts him on his mother's stomach and big Tony, overcome, runs out of the room.

"Oh, I don't believe it," Patricia says. Her face is completely simplified. Everything here is more real and true than anything else imaginable. She takes the tiny naked being and bends and kisses his silky head with ecstatic tenderness. "I don't believe it," she says, over and over again. And she says to the nurse and midwife who have been with her all night, "Oh, thank you, thank you!"

"Sure you did all the work," the midwife says.

They're like goddesses, those midwives and nurses. In simple pastel shifts, white shoes on their tanned legs, supple and fit and bright-eyed – they could do anything. Four babies they've delivered since midnight, each delivery an absolute event. They don't get tired because they don't get bored. And because the delivery ward is such a place of joy. Outside, in rows of beds, the new mothers sleep like felled oxen, exhausted. Babies wail in their cots. But that is for the future. When a healthy baby is born, the most fundamental event there is has happened.

Night or day, it makes no difference to the delivery ward.

Elsewhere, the business of a big hospital is beginning. At 5:00 AM, the newspapers arrive. The cook comes in. Sliced pans are delivered, great stacks of them. Night sister prepares her morning report for matron. Matron – on that day – was gathering her papers for a trip to Brussels, as an adviser to an EC committee on biomedical and health research. The Master was in his office. It was almost a shock to see him, so overwhelmingly a world of women is a maternity hospital at night.

Up on the top floor is the other place where there is no night or day. In the intensive-care ward, you hear the silence of the babies. You long for them to cry but they can't cry, because they are sedated. Tiny little starfish things, literal scraps of life. The nurses watch the respirators, adjust the dials, move the tubes. Somewhere the radio news was talking about Bosnia. Here, the parents of the sickest baby had just left after a night beside its cot. Sister did not think that that baby would live.

Still, when you looked out the window, and tried to believe in the outside world, there was hardly any traffic. The ordinary day had not begun. The quietness – the sense of beginning – made the scene back in the delivery ward even more precious.

Patricia had been tidied up and washed, and she had a mug of tea. Tony was sitting beside the bed in the calm sunshine that flooded the room. Little Tony – pink and beautiful now – was between them in his cot. They gazed at him. He slept. Sparrows skittered across the roofs outside. A new family; a new day.

The Irish Times, July 21, 1992

Housework

I was on a package holiday, cycling in Austria, and the group included two very pleasant English couples. We came to Mauthausen. The Nazi concentration camp there, and its terrible adjoining quarry, where thousands and thousands of people died horribly, can be visited, if you can bear it. There was a quick discussion between the two husbands and two wives. The wives made little *moues* of distress and became all helplessly feminine at the thought of going near such a place. The husbands began to puff up, manly and protective. The decision was reached that the big strong men would brave the visit to the camp, and the little wifeys would go shopping. And so they both did, each sex well content with the other.

Those couples were thriving, as far as I could see, on the traditional distinction between the public and the private spheres. He'll mind the world out there: she'll mind the home. I can see that it is in the interest of the human race as a species that this should sometimes be the case. Sometimes. When women are very pregnant, or when there are small children to be reared, the woman needs protection and support – not that many women don't manage without it. But that fleeting time in the individual woman's life has been extended to define womanhood altogether. Minding children for five or ten or fifteen years incorporates, in our system, the task of minding their fathers for fifty.

Which – if it suits both parties – is one way of spending your life. But there's no particular reason why the idea of women in the home should be favored over other ideas about women. There is nothing more normal about being a housewife than not being. If you ask yourself in whose interest it is to promote the notion that women are homebodies and men are out in the world, you may reply that it is in men's interests. They are made relatively free by this arrangement. And so it is a notion most powerfully propagated, and represented as "natural." The Englishwomen at Mauthausen were formed and shaped by century upon century of propaganda about how they should behave so as to be what the world calls womanly. The conditioning is so strong that I felt for a moment "unnatural" myself, for feeling that I had to go to the quarry.

Inherited stereotypes make it hard to discuss the perceived conflict between women who do paid work outside the home and women who work unpaid within the home. I say perceived conflict, because, mostly, more has been made of it by people hostile to women than by women themselves. The overwhelming majority of women are in perfect agreement on the matter. They would like both. All things being equal, they would like, at different times in their lives, and in different proportions at different times, to bear and raise children *and* to do interesting and useful work outside the home and earn money.

Almost anyone who impedes women from one or another of these fulfilments is an ideologue. There are mothers, and promoters of motherhood, who make a huge fetish of that particular role, and denigrate the many other marvelous things a woman might do with her life. And there are some women – usually sickened by the world they see around them – who want nothing to do with any of it. If they could, they'd destroy the present world, motherhood and all. A detail of the

Kilkenny incest case – that neighboring men, when they got out of the pub, rang the poor abused daughter and her mother with obscene proposals – is the kind of thing, repeated, that can make you a separatist.

Ireland has more mothers working full-time in the home than any other EC country. This is simply because there are fewer opportunities to work outside the home here than anywhere else. There are very many women who would work outside the home if they possibly could. They are full-time mothers, certainly, but how often is that their choice? And if one of the young women in Ireland who has no hope of a job, much less a career, chooses to have a baby, the choice is not the same as it would be if she'd thrown up a highly paid job as a hairdresser on a cruise ship, say, going around the world. Numbers, in other words, mean nothing. That a lot of women are full-time mothers but no woman has ever been, say, chief executive of a major bank, doesn't make motherhood more "natural" to women than running a bank. But, of course, motherhood may be more desirable than anything else around.

Lots of women in societies like ours do decide, usually along with their partners, to get pregnant such-and-such a number of times, and have such-and-such a number of children, and to work full-time in the home for such-and-such an amount of time. They make a general plan about reproduction based on their resources and values. Having children is by far the most interesting thing they can do.

They choose. They make a choice. A choice that has the whole dignity of the human being behind it. The dignity of the choice should be kept separate from the issue of how undervalued the work of mothering is. For the world as it has been run so far does indeed undervalue work in the home. But the woman who freely chooses to do it has given it her value – has honored the work with her self. She should fight for improvements in pay and conditions, the same as in any job. But let it be clear that that is not the same as resenting the job in itself.

The note of resentment that often characterizes housewives' descriptions of themselves comes from interiorizing the values of the world. They sense that work with children in the home is looked on with contempt. They feel that women who work outside the home are treated with more respect. They try to win respect for what they do, partly by stressing the alleged element of sacrifice in their work and partly by denigrating non-mothering women.

But it wasn't women who designed a world where paid work is admired but unpaid work is not. It wasn't women who designed a world in which childcare is unpaid. It isn't women who ask the mothers of toddlers, "But what do you do all day?" The value system we have inherited is challenged by feminism. It is that value system that says that women and housework are relatively unimportant. Not feminism.

When it is firmly established that to choose to work fulltime in the home *is* an important choice, and is a *choice*, then rearing your own children in your own home can be looked at for what it is. It is an extremely demanding job, but it is also an exceptionally varied, interesting, contenting, and comprehensive job. I have never seen a woman, no matter how successful, move around the workplace with the same fluent ownership of the space as women display in their homes.

I have never seen a woman in the workplace who is not sometimes or always alienated by the work she does. Minding the children of your own body is not alienating. When the situation is not distorted by something else – by poverty, by having no loving support, by having had no choice, by having nothing else to look forward to – then surely there is no better job.

All my sisters have had children. I haven't. But as far as I know, there is no fight between us because we've had different lives. So easy is it, in fact, not just for us but for women in general to appreciate that circumstances and choices have led one to this destiny, another to that, that I mistrust most discussions about women's roles. The problem is not between real women. It is between external views of what women are or should be.

And it is not being born female that is problematical. The problem is absence of opportunity and absence of financial independence. And absence of intellectual confidence. That last one is the one that can be tackled now, today. Fight: don't whine.

Don't fall into a role. When a woman says that she's "only a housewife," or when she complains that she hasn't had a holiday for ten years because she has so many children – as if her fecundity had nothing to do with her – or when she decides that remembering the Holocaust in a concentration camp would injure her delicacy, she's propping up the old roles.

But they're not worth it. Men are not the strong ones, women are not the weak ones, and motherhood is not what makes women valuable. We need truthful, particular ways to describe human diversity.

The Irish Times, March 8, 1993

Designer Poverty

I came out of *Les Misérables* superficially elated. But irritated, underneath – knowing I'd been got at, in some way I didn't like, but not knowing exactly how. It wasn't that the cast had cheated me: they did their best. It wasn't the staging: it was terrific. It wasn't the music. It is a one-song musical, but then "Bring Him Home" is a wonderful song (and one, incidentally, which bears out my theory that the best love stories of our time are buddy-buddy stories – between men – and the most convinced love songs are evoked by male relationships. "Rhinestone Cowboy" is just one of the many examples that spring to mind).

It wasn't the place: for once, The Point was the right venue. It wasn't the money. Tickets for *Les Misérables* are horribly expensive, but at least you can see what the profits are being spent on. There's so much advertising, for instance, that the image of the waif in the beret is practically unavoidable.

But that's just it. That intensely sentimental image is part of it. What it is, I think, that is ripped off by this show, is the human capacity to feel real pity, and to be dynamically outraged on behalf of the oppressed. You come out of *Les Misérables* high on barricades and red flags and justified revolution and the unstoppable power of the people and the injustice of the coexistence of riches and poverty. You come out excited by the Géricaultian tableaux of the wretched of the earth striking out for liberty, the masses marching forward together toward the light, the hopeless but beautiful protests of people with nothing to lose. Then you get into your car, and pausing only to avoid running over the odd tramp or beggar, you go to your comfortable home.

It's only a *musical* for God's sake, you may say. It's only *entertainment*. You're not *supposed* to take it seriously. But what the thing is exploiting and trivializing – what it's using to make big bucks out of – is serious. There is a basic generosity towards each other that we need so as to be able to live in societies. It is what prevents the human world, at least potentially, from being as red in tooth and claw as the natural world. This is the theme of Hugo's book, and he didn't mean it as showbiz – he was serious.

And the ideal of social justice that lies behind *Les Misérables* is taken seriously. The desire for justice is not just another plot-line, another random narrative. Indeed, the authors turned to Hugo's book not just because it was out of copyright but because we can still respond emotionally to it. We can be relied upon to be thrilled by the idea of the poor finding peace and love and hope. We come out of the theater under the impression that it was the articulation of that idea that was thrilling. But it's all a slick illusion: the poor are where they always were, outside the door of the theater, and the authors of *Les Misérables* are multimillionaires, thanks to the power of the rhetoric the show deploys.

The world has watched with delight the failure of state socialism. The whole of Eastern Europe opened up to the operations of the market! Cuba to become an economic appendage of the U.S.A. any day now! Maybe China, even, when Chinese socialism is redefined as Chinese capitalism! North Korea a world laughing stock! Communist and socialist parties everywhere converging on the center! The rout is almost complete.

But what socialism stood for is not dead in ordinary life.

There, it is quite clear that the belief persists that humans deserve shelter and food and work. And justice. *All* humans. That even if a political form has not yet been found for the ideals of socialism – even if socialism itself is not necessary to their achievement – those ideals are valuable and necessary. People, generally, are on the side of the underdog, and whatever about opera, very rich people aren't usually the heroes of musicals. Heroines aren't noted for greed and ruthlessness. The audience at The Point are not themselves the underprivileged, but they know well that privilege and the lack of it exists, and that a society like ours punishes some people unduly, and rewards others, equally unduly. This doesn't seem right in the post-revolutionary First World. Most people now alive surely believe that every human born has a right to liberty, equality, and fraternity.

Hence the popularity of the concept of revolution. All that stuff in *Les Misérables* about when tomorrow comes and hearing the distant drum of freedom and the future belonging to the people – all that refers to a living ideal. It is an uneasy experience, to see it trotted out as light entertainment to a comfortable, bourgeois audience. Yet it is remarkable that even a bourgeois audience recognizes that there is a possible social goodness greater than anything they know. They might not move a finger to bring justice about, themselves. But if justice somehow happened, without disturbing anybody – if overnight, a world was made in which Jean Valjeans are not falsely imprisoned, in which Fantines do not have to whore to buy medicine for their daughters, in which Cosettes are not cruelly used – if such a world were made, it is agreed that it would be superior to the world we've got.

But where, exactly, is this ideal placed? Does it refer to the future? Or is it comfortably placed in the past? The text of the *Les Misérables* program emphasizes the historic. "Living conditions for the French poor in the early nineteenth century were almost unimaginably bad," it says. "Even compared to Britain." They were pretty bad in Ireland too, you think, but then you remember that you're not talking about reality here. The status of reality is confused. On the one hand, the show doesn't work unless you believe that this suffering really happened. On the other, the authors want you to have a good time. On the one hand, the suffering happened in France. On the other, "France" is just a theatrical mirage, and *Les Misérables* is about as convincingly French as *Carousel* is convincingly set in heaven. The only certain, undeniable reality is that the *Les Misérables* event trundles massively and expensively around the world, taking in and paying out money. Going to a performance is closer to worshipping the Golden Calf than any other kind of experience.

It is not clear or convinced about what it is doing, I thought, and therefore bitty, and uneven, and third-rate in parts. It's a Euroshow. And all the worse for that. Genteel English voices twitter their way through the rhymes of the libretto, and you long for an American musical, full of drive and self-belief. If Lerner and Loewe, or Leonard Bernstein, or Rogers and Hammerstein, or Gershwin, or Adolph Comdon and Betty Green had turned their attention to *Misérables* past or present we'd know all about it, I can tell you. We'd be swept into a clear emotional position.

But the contemporary British musical is a pallid little thing, and as for the French — I don't know that they go in for the form at all. The musicals the common person thinks are French or English, *Gigi*, or *My Fair Lady*, for example, are by Americans. Andrew Lloyd Webber changed this for a while.

But I notice a critic saying, about the new show, *Sunset Boulevard*, that "it is extraordinary, considering the investment riding on this production, that, far more than in the film, poverty should be presented as the touchstone of integrity." Evidently there is the same shameless disjunction as in *Les Misérables* between what the show seems to endorse and what it really endorses. Poverty and suffering are touchstones of integrity, but they are designer poverty, designer suffering. Just vehicles, really, for stage effects.

The gasps and applause at The Point had nothing to do with man's inhumanity to man. They were for inventions of lighting and set-design and movement. Clapping for them was infantile; we were like children rapt by conjuror's tricks. But at least it is an honest and joyful thing to do – to rise in your seat and show your delight at displays of technical skill. It beats the hell out of being manipulated into a facile response to what, in its day, was a pioneering piece of polemical journalism. Hugo's *Les Misérables* had an effect something like Pilger on Cambodia in our time, or *Cathy Come Home*, or the "In the Eyes of the Law" series about the Dublin District Courts.

Nothing I say is meant to put anyone off going to *Les Misérables*. But if there are others who came out of it feeling – arid, I think would be the best word – then perhaps they'll consider what I suggest here. Let great showbiz juggernauts like this be what they want. Let them offer themselves in the marketplace. But let us, at least, be alert to what they do. We don't have to say they're wonderful just because they're big.

The Irish Times, July 26, 1993

Let Us Now Praise Famous Women

The Penguin Book of Women's Lives, Phyllis Rose (ed.), Viking

Written by Herself: Autobiographies of American Women, Jill Ker Conway (ed.), Vintage

Y ou have only to murmur the titles of these two anthologies to hear the ghostly chorus squeaking and muttering: "Why not men's lives?" "What about us?" But we're adding to, at this stage in history, not substituting for, or taking from. The exemplary lives of men – St. Augustine, Rousseau, Samuel Butler, *A Portrait of the Artist*, whatever you're having yourself – stare at us from the shelf, as always. Only now, we see the development of women, too, as filled with drama and challenge, and as potentially instructive. That's the tactful thing to say to pretend it's all equal. It is not. I can't be the only woman who has come to find most accounts of women's lives a good deal more suggestive than most men's, and to find myself falling on them with ravenous appetite.

The need to read them went into the writing of them. There is no thought of the public world here, applauding a dutiful life, dutifully recounted. "The buried model of the autobiographer can change from the boastful man to the confiding woman," the Penguin editor, Phyllis Rose remarks. "Sharing her experience with friends, she may be gossipy, artful, tutorial, cool, forthcoming, evasive, maternal, childish, stoic, narcissistic, boastful or modest, depending on her nature, but at some level she always feels the autobiographer's characteristic urge: the urge to preserve herself by giving herself away."

These tales had to be told. What happened has to be told. The telling of it is indistinguishably a raid on expressiveness or truthfulness. The critic Cynthia Ozick, who grew up in a pharmacy in the Bronx, talks about being "buffeted into being" as a writer. "But after a while other ambushes begin: sorrows, deaths, disappointments, subtle diseases, delays, guilts, the spite of the private haters of the poetry side of life, the snubs of the glamorous, the bitterness of those for whom resentment is a daily gruel, and so on and so on and then one day you find yourself leaning here, writing at that self-same round glass table salvaged from the Park View Pharmacy, writing this, an impossibility, a summary of how you came to be where you are now, and where God knows, is that? Your hair is whitening, you are a well of tears, what you meant to do (beauty and justice) you have not done, Papa and Mama are under the earth, you live in panic and dread, the future shrinks and darkens, stories are your only vapour, your inmost craving is for nothing but an old scarred pen, and what, God knows, is that?"

There are maybe 60 extracts from memoirs or autobiographies in the Penguin book; 832 pages. No themes. "The units I wanted above all to avoid," the editor says, "would have been on the order of 'Work,' 'Family,' 'Love,' 'Power.' I think we need to rid our minds of these false divisions in women's experience, and this seemed to me as good a place to start as any. My Borgesian decision was to take refuge in a bibliographic reality, to organise the selections alphabetically."

So we begin with Maya Angelou's brave grandmother in Arkansas, facing the taunting white kids singing a hymn. Next is de Beauvoir, and the lifelong deal she came to with Sartre. Through to the Leo-centered suffering of Sophia Tolstoy ("Maybe if I am gentle with him, he will grow more fond of me too, and will not want to leave me."). To Virginia Woolf's diary at the end: she met Mrs. T. S. Eliot. "… this last making me almost vomit, so scented, so powdered, so egotistic, so weakly."

Between, there are confidences from all over the world, and from many cultures. Nisa is a Khung hunter-gatherer from a remote part of the Kalahari. Her long rage and mourning at being put away from her mother's breasts is the kind of thing Western consciousness will not allow. In an alphabetical run, Janet Frame, Anne Frank, and Natalia Ginzburg each people the prisons they find themselves in. Being trapped, and escaping, is the basic narrative of many of these women's lives, whether the escape is from literal imprisonment, or from analogues, like Colette's marriage to Wily or Jessica Mitford's class background, or Mary McCarthy's Catholicism, or Emily Hahn's addiction to opium.

Ireland is strangely represented by an extract from Bernadette Devlin's *The Price of My Soul* about teaching the Mother Superior of her grammar school the difference between bigotry and patriotism. But then, nothing here represents. Editor Phyllis Rose's deceptively relaxed introduction could not put it more humbly: "The book is a product of a lifelong and personal interest in women's autobiographical writing, an interest which had little material to feed on in my childhood but now is treated to a rich harvest." She herself had been an ambitious child. She had wanted to be a cowgirl. But "what did it mean to live life to the full? How fully could a woman live? These were the questions that I wanted biography and autobiography to answer …"

You read their lives to see how it might otherwise have been, your life. As if women's writing was a shared, not an individual act, and each writer stood for the whole class of women. Even though some are stunning and some plain. And even though this incoherent possessiveness is not a publicly acknowledged motive. "The selections," the editor of the Vintage American anthology, Jill Ker Conway, says sniffily, "are chosen to exemplify the range of activities, occupations, and social situations which have prompted the autobiographical muse for American women … The aim of the whole is to give the reader a feel for the texture and imagery of women's writing and a sense of the kinds of narrative problems which a woman autobiographer must resolve." That sounds academic enough. But you take away from the book 25 long pieces, 672 pages, not the apologia for it, but the blistering personal moments it contains.

The poet Louise Bogan, for instance, writing in the 1930s about revisiting the mean Boston streets of her childhood. She goes to the local library.

No book of mine was listed in the catalogue. (A slight paranoid shudder passed over me.) I felt the consuming, destroying, deforming passage of time; and the spectacle of my family's complete helplessness in the face of their difficulties, swept over me. With no weapons against what was already becoming an overwhelming series of disasters, no insight, no self-knowledge, no inherited wisdom, I saw my father and mother (and my brother) as helpless victims of ignorance, wilfulness, and temperamental disabilities of a near-psychotic order facing a period (after 1918) where even this small store of pathetic acquisitions would be swept away. The anguish which filled my spirit and mind may, perhaps, be said to have engendered (and reawakened) poisons long since dissipated, so that they gathered, like some noxious gas, at the centre of my being. The modern horrors of the district also became part of this miasma; certainly the people in these newly over-crowded streets were as lost as those members of generations preceding them ... But those were my first years of adolescence and of the creative impulse and of hard and definitive schooling. And, as I remember, in spite of the growing sense of crisis by which I was continually surrounded, they were years of a beginning variety of interests of growth and of hope ...

This kind of speaking may stop you in your tracks. In which case, these books are waiting for you.

The Irish Times, April 30, 1994

Being Free

A few weeks ago, I went around the travel agencies in Dublin looking for a cheap ticket to anywhere where the skies would be blue. I arrived at one agency at the start of the lunch hour. Most of the staff seemed to have gone to lunch, even though the place was packed with customers, themselves free for just that hour. Service was so slow that person after person gave up after waiting 30 minutes or so, and went away. Those in the queue stood, because there were only a few seats. It was almost unbelievable that paying customers were being treated that way.

But nobody complained. Far from it: when they did at last get to one of the assistants, each person put on an ingratiating little smile, and began by apologizing, as if being there at all was their own fault. When they were shown, say, a brochure – a brochure soliciting, after all, their money – they'd say humbly "Is it all right if I keep this?" It couldn't have been more clear that a holiday is a thing so special and desired, and everything to do with planning a holiday casts such a radiance, that even propping up the wall of a Dublin travel agency is all right. Magic phrases rose above the confessional murmurs … "Two adults, two children, Orlando"; "Alcudia, half-board"; "on the beach, about a mile from Rhodes town …"

As far as I know, in some hundreds of years of social theorizing, it never occurred to any prophet to mention holidays. Not even the most prescient political scientist guessed what leisure was going to mean to the masses by the end of the twentieth century. The thought quite gives one pause. How likely are contemporary Marxes and Proudhons and Pol Pots and Socialist Workers to be right in their forecasts, if the forecasters of the nineteenth century got it so wrong? Or got part of it so wrong? Only futurists of a Jules Verne–like brilliance could have foreseen cheap air travel and all that flows from it. But an exceptionally gifted student of the human soul might have intuited that workers – white collar as much as blue – would themselves take in hand their sense of their own condition, and manage to infuse it with elements of anticipation and reward.

Not that sunshine holidays bought off the revolution, exactly, but that they make people happy, and are an area in which people feel autonomous. Having something wonderful to look forward to in the future alleviates even a near-intolerable present, and holidays are easier to access than heaven. You can see that sunshine holidays have become the heart of the heartless world by the way people carry themselves on holiday.

People of different backgrounds may find different forms of play to pass the day in, and may pass it in different company; the working class mostly with their families; the middle classes, it seems, more often with friends than relations; the wealthy always with their peer group. But there is one central sensation which is the quintessence of the sunshine holiday, and it is the same whether you spent the day with a puzzle book on your beach lounger, or studying Piero della Francesca's narrative technique, or water-skiing behind one of your yacht's motorboats. That is the evening sensation. The sensation of being showered and fresh after a hot day. Of having a drink and a meal ahead of you. Of looking as nice as you're ever going to look, in your tan and your light clothes. "This is the life," they say as they step out arm-in-arm into the warm foreign dusk. And it is, oh it is, the life.

This is the sensation which best sums up, at least in these times and in the so-called First World, the feeling of being free. (And who would have thought, 100 years ago, that freedom would be a sensation, not a condition!) And the privileged can't buy a keener sense of it than the under-privileged: it is the same for everybody. Everybody who can get to it, that is.

For the great Mediterranean tourism industry is under-pinned by people who have never felt this ease. Through windows, down the back alleys of fashionable Greek islands you glimpse sweat-stained kitchen-hands. Kurds. Egyptians. Grim men far from their homes in Africa stalk beach restaurants with their trays of woodcarvings. Tired Moroccans slowly pull sweeping brushes across the floors of airports.

But their day may come. Nobody ever thought, after all, that in Europe unemployed youths and obscure clerks and laundry women and widows with nothing but their pensions would pause at the top of airplane steps to put on their sunglasses before going down on to the sizzling tarmac.

And at the same time, millions of peasants are being freed from terrible lives by the spread of tourism. Yet "blight" is what the privileged feel free to call the tourist urbanizations that now command the east coast of Italy and the east and south of Spain and parts of Turkey and the Algarve and Majorca and so on. The place where I went on my cheap ticket last week, halfway between Almeria and Málaga, was exactly what is meant by "blighted." The bare, beautiful mountains once swept down in folds to the sea, and in the valleys between ridges there were orchards and olive groves, and there were little white-walled villages above shingle beaches where the men brought up their fishing boats.

Now, the headlands have been sliced away and gouged by earthmoving machines and skyscraper-blocks of cement apartments stand side by side for miles on end, so close to each other that they cut out the other's light, above the gray rubble beaches. Anywhere a few almond trees are left, the bulldozers are moving in. The villages have been swallowed by hypermarkets and concrete esplanades and highways. There is no nature for miles.

But who would choose the peasant life, now? Those orchards weeded by hand, irrigated by hand? Those white-walled villages with one communal pump for water? Those baking hillsides, and the labor of harvesting olives for pence, for half-pence? Those who would prefer their landscapes unspoiled – as I do – should consider whether they want other people's human potential to be trapped forever within the simple life, for the sake of the tourist's patronage.

The huge hotels and shopping malls and bingo halls and fish restaurants that cover what once were dry clay fields around the Mediterranean are industries, exactly as if factories belching smoke and clanging with the noise of forklift trucks had been built on the fields. The innocence of swimming and the brilliant blue of each day and the physical release of shorts and flip-flops transform these places in the tourist's perception. But they are industries, heavy industries, even, in the environmental destruction they wreak, and their profligate use of water.

Some day these places will be archaeology. In the meantime, they offer what most people both want and can have.

They are hallowed, however ugly they may be, by the happy ease they offer to burdened humans. They are huge sites of transformation.

The Irish Times, June 12, 1995

Horse-drawn Holidays

Laois had always seemed to me to be one of the flatter counties. But that was before going around it with a horse and a caravan. In fact, the roads of Laois go up gently and down gently all the time. It would be unfair to sit up on the caravan when the horse is going uphill; and it doesn't feel right when he's going downhill, either. And it's as well to get down and lead the horse in traffic, or going around corners. Thus, the general upshot was that my friend Aideen and myself went for a rather long walk around southeast Laois. In the company of a horse. A very horsey horse. As holidays go, it was the exact opposite of lying beside a swimming pool.

There's no getting away from it: there's a lot of work in minding a horse and keeping a caravan shipshape. But it's pretend work. The inside of the caravan is miniaturized, and you play at "house," just as you're playing at traveling. That's exactly what stressed executives from the Ruhr Valley and Lombardy love about it: the holiday is full of innocent activity. You should see their ecstatic accounts in the visitors' book at the headquarters of Kilvahan Horse-Drawn Caravans. They send parcels of chocolates and carrots back to the horses. They send them Christmas cards. But I, for one, prefer my horses in the parade ring. Horses smell. Horses come up behind you and snuffle. When Henry at Kilvahan instructed me to prop the horse's huge foot on my knee and gouge the gunk out of it with a pick, I nearly went home.

Yet the very first thing that happened was that we began to admire the horse. Henry waved us off on our journey at the top of a hill in a little country lane. Birds sang. Honeysuckle swayed in the summer breeze. We were only three miles from our night's stopping place. Nothing could go wrong. But what Henry didn't know was that we more or less drove into the ditch any time a motor vehicle passed. Because we didn't realize that Zulu, quite the wrong name for so peaceable a horse, could cope with absolutely anything. He took advantage, of course, of our many visits to the ditch, and we approached Timahoe with him chewing on a great wodge of weeds and branches, including, we feared, bits of trees that looked as if they'd been planted for the Tidy Towns. But if a horse can be bovine, Zulu was bovine.

He didn't even panic when we somehow wedged the caravan between a pole and a wall coming into the village. We were trying to reverse out, in a cloud of flies with dogs yapping around us, and helpless with laughter anyway, when a strap in a bit of the harness snapped. We were as nearly in real trouble as horse-drawn caravanners ever get. But men and women appeared as if from nowhere, and within a twinkling we were mended, and parked in a lovely field, and the horse was led away for the night, and we'd showered in a bathroom attached to the pub, and we were getting a lift into Stradbally to get something to eat.

And that was the beginning of the revelation. Horse-drawn caravanning, in Laois anyway, is not about horses. Or caravans. It is about people. It only works because people react to you at every turn, whether to help you or just to talk to you or – in our case – to have a gentle little laugh at you. There is very little tourism around these parts, and the locals seem delighted to encounter people doing something as fundamentally absurd as clopping along at two miles an hour.

We got stuck up a cul-de-sac: a man came out and turned

us and told us about his two new hips. We stopped to look at a strange round church: a man appeared as if from nowhere and told us it was a church of the Serbian Orthodox Rite, just being erected, in darkest Laois, by the local landowner. When we couldn't get an *Irish Times* in one shop, the people came out with us to be sure we could get it in the next shop. We were pressed to sit in people's porches, and offered water, and pointed in the right directions. When we couldn't find a place to eat in Stradbally, and bought a loaf and cheese, the woman who gave us a lift back to our caravan in the field sent a child up with lettuce and scallions.

Henry Fingleton at Kilvahan Horse-Drawn Caravans is one of the first people to exploit what Laois has to offer. And it has skills and talents as well as landscape. The caravans, for instance, are made locally – the chassis by one craftsman, the joinery by another, the upholstery by another. Even the way they're painted is local and distinctive. He meets the guests at the Kilvahan center and introduces them to one of the dozen or so horses who used to draw coal carts in Dublin, and who have been chosen for their quiet temperaments. Then they set off on circuits of stopping places which have been set up in Laois and Kilkenny. Just outside Abbeyleix they stay in the yard of a handsome eighteenth-century manor house, and there's a sitting room to use as well as a bathroom. At Ballyroan you're welcome to relax in the house's old conservatory. At Vicarstown – where Aideen and I swam in the soft, reedy Grand Canal – there's traditional music in the pub. Under the Rock of Dunamase, Julia does a four-course meal for £10 and English visitors told us it was just gorgeous. Every stop has some little attraction and exceptionally welcoming people.

There are drawbacks. The English visitors, for instance, remarked somewhat huffily that in England, unlike certain places they could mention, there are always signposts at crossroads. And some of the pubs should do sandwiches. But apart from that, south Laois has everything. There was one morning when I went across the dewy grass in the early sunlight with my towel and soap, to walk down the road to a bathroom. The kettle was getting ready to sing on the stove in the caravan. Zulu was munching away on the other side of the hedge. The day's labors and the day's laughs were still hours away. I can see clearly why the internal-combustion engine took over from the horse, but all the same, at that precise moment – well, a motoring holiday just doesn't have moments like that.

The Irish Times, July 17, 1995

A Radiant Life

U sually, columns like this are part of a commentary on the news. But I've just read an account of a life lived very far away from the news. It came my way when the Fianna Fáil TD, Eoin Ryan, rang me to tell me about a book by an Irishwoman: she had been a friend who died young, is hardly known in Ireland, but is increasingly renowned elsewhere.

In fact, there is a statue to her in Japan. She is venerated there as being "of the same heart and mind as the Great Teacher Buddha." When I heard the word "Buddhist" I got a bit wary. I said to Eoin Ryan that I'm not very religious. "Oh, that's OK," he said. "Neither was she."

Maura "Soshin" O'Halloran is so vivid a presence to me now, from her book, that I'm impatient to get the formal details over with. She was the daughter of an American mother and Irish father, and grew up in both countries. Maura went to the Loreto nuns here and to Trinity. The book itself is made up of journal entries Maura made in her Japanese monastery, and letters home. She was killed in a bus crash in Thailand in 1982, when she was 27.

"Although her passport and journal were stolen with her luggage, the police were able to identify her by means of a ticket stub they found in the pocket-like sleeve of her monk's robe ... " There is a photo of her on the book cover, and wonderful little drawings inside. The monk's robe looks exactly right on her, as does the shaved head.

People who knew her must have loved her. She was very

clever, and she was good. She lived frugally, she did the most demanding kind of voluntary work, and though she could lose herself in meditation, she was a serious fighter against social injustice as well.

It seems to have been almost an accident that, when she was visiting a temple soon after she arrived in Tokyo, its master, Go Roshi, asked her whether she was willing to shave her head and go begging. Go Roshi was clearly a man of the most exceptional perspicacity. It was extremely unusual to allow a Westerner, especially a Western woman, to study in a temple. How, indeed, would she study, knowing no Japanese? Yet he told Maura at the beginning, "without fail, you will attain enlightenment."

She plunged into a life of cleaning and cooking and begging and meditation and the learning of Zen paradoxes and chopping wood and chanting and dealing with the complexities of living with the personalities of other monks. She never exactly explains what kind of Zen training she was following, or what the name is for what she was doing. Her journal entries are simply personal notes jotted down during the doing of it.

To me, it is almost irrelevant that she was a Zen monk. The joy she took in existence, and the simplicity and truth of her responses, and the extreme beauty of her descriptions of the world might have been available to her wherever she was and whatever she was doing. But perhaps there are not many places where there is as much laughter as there seems to be in Zen temples. For Maura and Go Roshi are always breaking into laughter at the most solemn moments. The reader gets to know Maura as what is called a perfectly normal young woman: she had hopes and regrets, she loved parties, she missed her family, she wasn't sure what to do, she had moods, she didn't get on with some people and she went so far as to have a crush on others. Yet everything she writes seems suffused with a sweetness that is not, unfortunately, normal. I don't know when I've read an autobiography that so often and so completely convincingly mentions being happy.

I cannot hope to give more than a hint of the flavor of this young woman. Almost at random I pick a diary entry:

> … two years ago I felt very old, very afraid of growing old. Now I feel 18; I don't look it, and no one else thinks of me that way, but the world and my relationship to it feels like when I was that tender age.
>
> I'm relishing growing old; as my body decays, my spirit is only going to soar all the more. The morning was rain. Not like yesterday's heavy, pounding rain, but a soft, gray vaporous rain. Went to Sasaki san for daffodil bulbs. It was cold, we agreed, not like May. Ojiichan loosened them with a big fork. I cleaned them off with a trowel. It took all his strength to lift and aim his blows but each one was perfect.
>
> He gave me purple rubber gloves for my bluish hands. He smiled and continued down the row. We filled two boxes with daffodils and narcissi. They were heavy. I washed the rubber gloves in a puddle and gave them back. He was still smiling. I picked my way back in the rain, now more like airborne dew. The mountains were scarcely visible but very present, at once rooted and wispy (like the driving instincts that show themselves as dreams) …

You can see in her descriptions the effect of the discipline of using every single grain of rice and cherishing every single worm and beetle. But what you would never guess, until the book's afterword, was how Maura was living when she wrote the loving pictures of her surroundings. She begged, for instance, in the snow in straw sandals in 20 degrees Celsius, her arms never lowered except when receiving an offering. She accomplished 1,000 days of Zen practice that included sleeping not more than three hours a night in an upright position, and spending the other 20 hours in work.

"Miss Maura," it says on the statue dedicated to her, "has been a real incarnation of Kannon Bohatsu to be loved and respected for ever." She was hardworking and courageous: those were the words that her teacher chose for his letter of condolence to the O'Halloran family.

The hard work led to her wanting to live her life "for other people," as she confided in her journal. "What else is there to do with it? Not that I expect to change the world or even a blade of grass, but it's as if to give myself is all I can do, as flowers have no choice but to blossom. At the moment the best I can see to do is to give to people this freedom, this bliss ... " And she would have brought her gifts and her skills to us. She was on her way back to Ireland when she was killed in the crash.

In all the world, how many statues are there to young Irish women? That itself might be an excuse for turning away, today, from public matters. Though a published book is a public matter. It is itself most elegantly and thoughtfully presented, and I hope that some people will seek out the pleasure of reading it.

Pure Heart, Enlightened Mind: The Zen Journal and Letters of Maura O'Halloran is in the shops here. And it has just been published in Germany, with a huge fanfare. The Germans quote some of the American reviews, especially the one in the *New York Times* which talks about the way this book approaches the Absolute through the everyday. The Absolute, I'm sure, can take care of itself. But it is a rare event to see the everyday made radiant.

The Irish Times, August 7, 1995

Don't Rain on My Parade

Well ... I don't know ... We're all supposed to be delighted at the tarting up of the Patrick's Day Parade. We're all supposed to agree that the one we've had all these years is old hat and an embarrassment and not "sufficiently imaginative" for the people who measure imaginativeness round here. But I felt for our glum little parade. I thought that in the absence of anyone knowing by instinct how to celebrate our national day – or even to agree on whether we've got a nation to go with our national day – the trade 'n' industry parade was quite a sensible way of handling things.

We counted our possessions in it, so to speak. We didn't have just one Downes' Bakery bread van (it was Downes, wasn't it, or was it Johnson Mooney & O'Brien that used to enter their entire fleet?). We had tens of bread vans. We used to have every single motorcycle in the army, if I remember correctly. In later years we've had all the frozen baton-twirling little girls in Greater Dublin, not just some of them. Granted, the parade may not have displayed any flair, or artfulness, or beauty. But then, we're not like that. We're not an artful and beautiful people. We're materialists, and that's what the parade was: a modest showing off of the modest things we've got.

Maybe down in the West they're all artful and imaginative and full of beauty. They say they are, anyway. But this was Dublin's parade, not some provincial town's. Dublin's and America's. It was quite magnificently true to the 1950s. Same as

Irish-America, actually. A place as small as Galway can afford to mess around with culture in the form of Catalan acrobats and Native-Indian mask dancers and so on. But here in the capital we have to be serious about business. And business equals lorries and vans and very, very cold groups of uniformed public employees. And even if it wasn't always numbingly cold on St. Patrick's Day, there's nothing Mediterranean about Irish transport, industry, and commerce. Now, I suppose, they'll have mime artists. Made-up things. Whereas we used to have ambulances. Real things.

We're just going to be like everywhere else, now. We'll have an imaginative, visually exciting, blah-blah parade. You might as well be in Rio de Janeiro or Barcelona. Whereas we in Dublin used to have what Marshall McLuhan would have called a cool parade. In other words, it wasn't "hot," not in any sense. It didn't do all the imaginative work for you the way television, say, does.

It was like radio. (Maybe hot and cool are the other way around.) You had to use your own imagination to believe that the parade was even meant to be entertaining, much less that it was entertaining. This is something that professional paradesters forget. It was never what was in the parade that mattered. It was going to the parade. Going into town on the bus. Wearing your green rosette. Town being different. Everything lasting for ages, because of the multiplicity of bread vans. Getting chips. If the parade had consisted of the entire civil service marching in platoons in their good Dannimacs, generations of Dubliners would still have hauled their kids in to see it.

They liked it. Marian Finucane for instance – a notoriously sound woman, formerly a sound child – used to go into town on her own to see it when she got too old to be brought. She'd squeeze her way through all the legs to the front. Mind you: she's tall. Small Dubliners have never seen more than swaying tops of lorries. Quite a few people must have enjoyed it, because they went to it of their own free will. The crash barriers are there to prove it. Admittedly they went to Macnas's *Gulliver*, too. But *Gulliver* was easy. Any old body can enjoy colorful imaginative entertainment. It took a real Dubliner to enjoy 25 bread vans followed by a flatbed truck with a frozen swing band on it.

Year after year, runny-nosed children in parkas were hoisted onto shoulders to admire the ATA Alarm: year after year it won. Year after year RTÉ's presenters met their Waterloo, as they shivered outside the GPO amidst the motley crew that represents the establishment on Patrick's Day, and ran out of things to say. There's only so much you can say about a lorry covered in crepe-paper flowers, even if you can legitimately say it in Irish first and then in English or, for variety, the other way around. The only absolutely unembarassed RTÉ parade presenter ever there was Bibi. But alas! Where is Bibi now?

There was a case for leaving it alone. This whole place is getting too twee and Disneyfied and professionally Wonderlanded altogether. Do you know what the traditional Patrick's Day Parade was like? It was like de Valera's post offices – lots of which are still around as their grand plain, sturdy selves. As buildings, they make a stab at a kind of civic impressiveness. But they don't insist. They don't suck up to the citizen by being charming or comfortable or anything like that. Take them or leave them is what they imply.

Same for the parade. If beauty and imaginativeness and a

good time is what you're looking for, you may take yourself off to Galway or Orlando or watch the telly. But leave O'Connell Street in an east wind to the real Irish. St. Patrick had it hard on the slopes of Slemish herding his sheep. He was no wimp. And his parade isn't for wimps, either.

The Irish Times, January 20, 1996

Schools and Sadism

There are straightforward historical reasons for the scandal of Goldenbridge. First, there were bound to be bad nuns. "Entering religion," as it was called, was an extremely difficult road to take, and many young women must have taken it for the wrong reasons. There were social pressures on girls to enter.

To the world, it was the height of respectability to have a daughter a nun. To a girl educated by nuns, as most of us were until the 1970s, to continue in that milieu often seemed a more plausible option than trying to get into the civil service or going to dances till you found a husband. Becoming a nun meant you didn't have to deal with sexuality at all; your parents would be pleased with you; you would be secure, and you would have much more status than most women. In the fervent atmosphere of the old convent schools, this might easily present itself to a girl as being madly in love with God. But if she wasn't, really, madly in love with God, she was stuck in a relationship calculated to drive her mad.

What's more, even if she was a fulfilled Bride of Christ, she might have to teach children or run an orphanage or nurse sick people to prove it. Even though having "a vocation" in no way qualified her to do these things, and she may have been grossly unsuited to her lifetime's task.

There was a concept, very popular when I was a girl, of "breaking the will" to make one worthy of God's love. It was a fascist's charter, of course, which is why it was so popular

85

with administrators. Lots of schools were keen on breaking the wills of bold, sinful, children. But the teachers themselves were controlled by this idea.

So if you longed as a nun to go on the missions, they made you teach maths in a suburb. If you were gifted academically, they put you in charge of a kitchen. Generations of young women went along with this, and humbled and disciplined themselves and confessed sins of pride when their perfect docility gave way. They flogged themselves and fasted and poured out prayers so as to fit the square peg of themselves into the round hole provided for them. No wonder some of them went mad.

There was a silliness surrounding vocations. A big, spotty, adolescent girl would come into class alight with excitement. She'd whisper to her friend; the friend would whisper to her friend; and finally the news would be out: "So-and-so felt a hand laid on her head and heard an unearthly voice saying 'Come, Follow Me!'" And soon after, so-and-so would be taken away for an intimate talk with a popular nun. How many of those girls eventually found themselves full of anger, and turned that anger to rage? How many of them used the strength of a thwarted personality to infect their communities?

Entering religion, then, could be done in bad faith. That's the first thing. But society as a whole was in bad faith towards nuns. By the 1950s, the great nineteenth-century orders of nuns had been reduced to serving the Irish patriarchy, the same as everyone else. The care of children, especially, was fobbed off on them. And nobody valued children, unless they were well-heeled children – a system then and now promoted by the priests who insisted on running expensive private schools so that there would always be an "us" and a "them." It was no wonder that a nun here and there internalized the cruel values of the power structure. You could do what you liked to ordinary children, and you could take any amount of frustration out on poor children. I don't know why the Sisters of Mercy are standing in the pillory alone. A great many of other "religious" should be standing beside them.

You cannot talk to a group of Irish men about their schooldays for two minutes before someone starts telling tales of brutality. An ear deaf from a blow; a stammer from constant humiliations; a terrible episode of incontinence in public from fear; and – over and over again – a brain never used because all the boy wanted from school was to get away from it. The kind of mad sadism many men remember didn't happen in respectable girls' schools. But physical punishment was common.

I went to schools run by four orders. One was the Irish Sisters of Charity. I was cast as St. Gabriel in a tableau when I was seven or so, posed at the end of the school concert, standing above the Holy Family with my wings spread protectively. But I saw my friend in the audience and waved my wings at her. The nun beat me around the room afterwards with the leg of a chair. Later, I was a pupil at a Sisters of the Holy Faith school. The nuns had a long leather strap as part of their habit – it was attached to their belts. But the head nun had a special, double-thickness strap which was kept in a cupboard. I was strapped with it many times, and it reduced me to a snivelling supplicant, squeezing my red-hot hands between my knees and begging for forgiveness.

This was trivial stuff, but it suggests a context for Goldenbridge. And the lid hasn't been lifted yet on the industrial schools, or on the runaways the farmers hunted – at £5 a head – and returned to those schools, or on the gardaí who put women who had children outside marriage into mental homes for life at a nod from their respectable families, or on the awful things done to "boarded-outs" – the slave labor of modern Irish agriculture. Almost everyone supported the regime. A man I met yesterday, for instance, told me that a Brother beat him so badly he was in bed for a week, after emergency treatment in hospital. As soon as he could walk his mother marched him back up to school, to the same Brother. She asked the Brother to continue to put manners on the boy, and said how grateful she and her husband were.

People are reluctant to face the truth. But I believe the truth is that what lay behind the cruelty perpetrated on children in care was Catholicism itself. It developed the concepts of sexual wickedness and maternal sin which were used to facilitate the expression of sadism. And the more general ordinary abuse of children was in part a consequence of more Catholic teaching, this time on contraception. It was known that almost all the children of large families – almost all children – would never have a stake in Irish society, never have children here themselves, never count for anything. Their eventual unimportance in London or Springfield, Massachusetts, was visited upon them early. Why would their minders or teachers value them? Their country didn't value them.

Why would you cherish the orphans in your care? What was their destiny? Well, one destiny was to become a skivvy in a convent. Every convent had a pecking order, and the skivvies, scrubbing the mud off tons of potatoes, in their poor broken boots, were at the bottom. Why would you lavish love on a child who is only going to be a skivvy when she grows up?

The burghers of the town came down to the nun and got a skivvy ...

Contemporary Ireland floats on a sea of grief. Many, many people are guilty of causing it. This isn't about one nun or group of nuns, though they have much to answer for. But they are scapegoats, too, for others still hiding.

The Irish Times, March 4, 1996

Little Blessings

Who shaped you, bore you? Who, with delicate skeletal passion, made you and started you singing. As you sing ... ? Michael Hartnett

They came and gave me tablets to dry up the milk. That's all I remember. I heard the baby cry once. But they took it before I even knew whether it was a boy or a girl. Years later, I was told that it was sent to America only a few days afterwards. I can't remember signing anything. I was only 15. I'm sure my baby went to a good home. But I would give anything to know. That baby is 50 years old now. How could I find that one person when there are so many people in America?"

Mary sits in her little room in Dublin, quite alone, except for the ghost of the lost baby. She is one of thousands of Irish women, now middle-aged or old, who were victims of the punitive attitude to sex outside marriage which dominated Irish culture well into the 1970s. Under the desolate rules of that culture, a girl unfortunate enough to get pregnant by someone who wouldn't, or couldn't, marry her had two choices. She could go to England, or, if she was sufficiently tough or fortunate, she might keep her baby – as the rock star Phil Lynott's mother did, for example.

But on Irish soil, the mother had to go as far as possible from where she was known, usually to one of the huge mother-and-baby homes run by nuns. There she had her baby. And then the baby had to disappear. Legitimate orphans went into Irish institutions. Illegitimate babies could, after 1952, be placed for adoption. The mother, usually very young, usually very confused, was sent by the nuns to a notary public to make a formal surrender of her rights. The memory of this can still make a woman, now 60, weep at the injustice: "The nuns had got a job for me as a maid, a few months after the birth. My wages were very small. I had to pay the nuns for the keep of my baby. Then I had to pay this man, to guarantee that I'd let my baby go. I can't walk down that street in Dublin where his office was. It is 42 years ago, but I can't forget the heartbreak."

The mother signed a document undertaking "never to see or interfere with or make any claim on" her child again. Sometimes, the baby was newborn when it was taken away. One woman, whose baby was put straight into a children's home, used to travel to that home for a long time, just to peer through the hedge at the children's playtime.

It was often worse if the mother and baby had had time to bond. If the baby was born in a County Home – formerly the workhouse – mother and child were allowed to stay together for two years. Catherine, who now lives in Ohio, went to look for her birth mother in County Galway. When she found her, 33 years after their parting, her mother said that the worst bit was that she hadn't been able to go back to her own life until her daughter was adopted – "but I didn't want to let you go." Catherine's mother had found a job in the same town as the mother-and-baby home. She had visited Catherine every day, she told her. "Then one day the nun told me to say good-bye. And you knew, though you were only two-and-a-half; you sensed that you would never see me again. You screamed and screamed. You knew." According to the woman who adopted Catherine, when she arrived in the U.S. she did not speak for months.

Almost every extended family in Ireland has had a girl give birth outside marriage. At one time it was inevitable, in a culture where dancing and courting were everyone's leisure activities, but where there was no access to contraception, and abortion was a criminal offense. The solution was adoption. In 1967, for instance, there were 1,540 births outside marriage and 1,493 adoption orders made. The nuns who ran most of the adoption agencies placed at least 40,000 Irish children for adoption between about 1955 and 1995. The birth mothers were not told where. The nuns ran things their way. They still do. Most of what records remain from that era are still guarded by the elderly religious. No legislation covers their actions when mother and child now seek to find each other. The nuns are answerable to no one.

Outside Ireland, attitudes have changed. Adopted people in the UK have won the right to see their birth certificates. In the U.S., adoption and immigration information – such as applies to babies brought in for adoption – became available under the U.S. Information Privacy Act. Enquiries from abroad began to trickle into Barnardo's in Dublin, the only independent agency to offer help in this area. On average, they were contacted every day by three mothers and six adults who had been separated from their families of origin.

The first letters from adopted children came from Britain, in the late 1970s; then from the U.S., in the 1980s. "My adoptive mother," went one, "told me I had sores on my face and I was always hungry when I came from Ireland. Could you please tell me what the orphanages there were like in those days? Was there no law to make sure that children were well looked after? It bothers me that I was in such poor shape when my adoptive mother got me."

And another: "Dear Sirs, please can you explain why the document authorizing adoption by my mother from County

Galway was not signed by her? Are there other cases where there is just the typewritten name and no signature? Could you tell me how to find her as she may not have known what she was doing?" It was some time before Barnardo's received a different kind of letter: "I cannot begin to tell you what feelings your reply to me has generated. The day I met my son at the airport was the happiest day of both our lives."

Barnardo's does not trace mothers or children. It can only counsel and advise. Until recently, it could cope with the demand for its services. But now their "adoption hotline" is almost overwhelmed. This is largely in response to an Irish television documentary broadcast earlier this year, which alleged terrible cruelty in a Dublin "orphanage" – although the children were hardly ever orphans. Only a few weeks previously, hundreds of Irish people had spontaneously demonstrated outside the Chinese embassy in protest against conditions in orphanages there. Now they heard that Goldenbridge, in Dublin, was worse than China in the memories of the women who talked about it on camera. Much worse. Women told of babies left straining on potties for so long that their anuses dropped, so that the loose membrane had to be pushed back in. They told of children forced to thread beads onto wire, hour after hour, in order to make rosaries for a nun, who beat them if they faltered. A child had smuggled a letter out, begging for help. No one had cared to interfere.

Stories tumbled out of numerous other "childcare" institutions in the Ireland of the recent past. Men who had been boys in homes run by religious men had memories as painful, and more brutal and sexual, than the women had of the nuns. And mothers who had hidden the fact that they had once had a baby had to deal with these revelations. They needed now to know that their child had not ended up in one of these places. The airwaves rang with pain. On one radio program, a mother described the circumstances surrounding the giving up of her son. The son, recognizing what he knew about his own beginnings, contacted the program. They had found each other. But, for others, the search is endless.

Maggie Butler is an American psychologist, a coolly competent woman who has reared two adult children, and whose career in the U.S. was full of vitality. But she moved to Ireland three years ago, and intends to go on living there in her search for her real mother. "I have always known my mother was Irish," she says. "But it was when I held my first baby, just after she was born, and I realized that that was my first time to hold my own flesh and blood – that's when I realized that I had to, some day, set out to find her."

She hasn't found her. But she has probably been close to the woman who gave her up 44 years ago. One trail led to an old nun who had worked in one of the busiest mother-and-baby homes, and was now spending her last days in the care of a rural institution. This nun saw an article by Maggie in a newspaper, and sent word to her. When Maggie went to the institution, the nun told her that she kept her article beside the chair she spent her days in. "Because I remember your mother," she told Maggie. "She was a beautiful woman. Her face had angles, just like yours ... "

But later she said, "Sometimes the women who came to the home to have babies gave false names, you know." "Why would they give false names?" Maggie asked, knowing she was being told something interesting. "Well, if they came of a wealthy background, if they had prestige." Maggie's mother may fear there will be a claim on her land or money: she may not want to be found. And, if this is so, she will not be. "But I must go on trying," Maggie says. "You know the feeling, when you recognize a face but can't quite remember the name? Well, I have the name, but the face keeps escaping me."

Maggie Butler spoke about this on Irish radio. The interview was heard by another woman, the director of the newly established National Archive of Ireland. Hadn't she seen some files lately, she thought to herself — something to do with babies and the U.S.? And so it happens that, in an office in a government department in Dublin, about 2,000 files are now being kept under lock-and-key while a committee considers their status. Each file bears the name of a child born in Ireland. Each contains the same few documents. They were repatriated, as a matter of routine housekeeping, from the Irish Consulate in Washington, D.C. They date, mostly, from the mid-1950s to the mid-1960s. They encapsulate stories of suffering in Ireland and joy in the U.S. They are the records of the adoption in the U.S. of some of the babies born in secrecy in Ireland. This is where at least some of the 40,000 babies given up for adoption are now known to have gone.

The only sign of the women who gave birth to them are the names on the "document of surrender." But a lot more is shown about the adoptive parents, because they had to prove that they were "good Catholics." The bishops of the Roman Catholic Church had laid the groundwork for that when they finally allowed Irish legislators to pass the country's first adoption law, in 1952. They had always opposed adoption, not least because letting a single mother "easily relinquish" her child might act as an incentive to promiscuity.

"A child's rights in respect of faith and morals must be protected by such safeguards as will assure his adoption by persons who profess and practise the religion of the child," they dictated. A U.S. couple adopting an Irish baby, therefore, had to provide a letter from their medical adviser, confirming that they were not, through the use of contraceptives, "deliberately shirking natural conception." The adoptive mother had to promise to give up work outside the home. The prospective home had to be vetted by a Catholic organization. The new parents had to promise to educate the child in Catholic schools. Evidence had to be produced as to the state of the parents' health and the size of their income. In comparison, the birth mother is a shadow and the father a nonentity.

The imbalance continues. The U.S. babies – now adult – can find the circumstances of their adoption. But their real mothers in Ireland have no legal right to any information about them. In the 1950s and 1960s, at least another 40,000 babies, along with the 40,000 legally adopted, were taken from their families. In the prevailing climate of contempt for poverty or failure, thousands upon thousands of children were fostered, "boarded out" to farmers, put into special schools, or reared by individuals, perhaps distantly related. Foundlings, about whom nothing was known, were kept in institutions and never adopted in case they were the children of a legally married couple: children of marriages, however long abandoned, were never adopted.

These children moved around from institution to institution until they were 16, when they could enter service or go to England. If they then wanted their records – say, for medical information – they discovered that there were none. Birth information was falsified, or lost. When the religious who had run the institutions died, all they knew died with them. In these circumstances, the American files are an exceptional hoard of potentially healing information. But they sit in the government office while civil servants attempt to work out the problems of confidentiality which surround them. "It is the Minister for Foreign Affairs' wish," the Irish parliament was told when the American files were discovered, "to be as helpful as possible in relation to the provision of information. But there is no clear-cut answer to the dilemma posed by the competing interests relative to information on adoptions. It is a dilemma posed by the sad circumstances surrounding the reality of adoption."

Barnardo's, often in the person of Norah Gibbons, who runs the adoption hotline there, is left to break to inquirers the news that there is no central register, voluntary or otherwise, to help them in their search. At present, about 200 U.S. citizens are trying to find their Irish mothers, and *20/20*, the U.S. television news program presented by Barbara Walters, is broadcasting their story. An embarrassed Irish government may have to respond to the new demands this will create.

Times have undoubtedly changed. Young Irishwomen are different now. In 1993, for example, there were 7,000 births outside marriage and only 648 adoption orders. But the old women who had their babies in the past have not changed. The values of that time were burnt into them. They will not come forward to be filmed, even for U.S. television. They still have too much to lose. For them, the stigma is still there.

The first two women to contact Barnardo's after news of the U.S. files came out were both in their sixties, both married to husbands they had never told, and both thought that theirs had been the only baby ever to go to America. Nothing can be done for them while the U.S. files remain closed. But at least they have grasped, for the first time, what it was they signed when they gave their babies up: "I undertake never to see or to interfere or to make any claim upon the child ... " Mothers often remember nothing but the approximate date of the child's birth. But that would be enough to discover whether the child went to the U.S., because the birth date would be on the passport issued to a baby.

The yearning felt by women who surrendered their babies is such that an Irish radio program discussing the U.S. files had to appeal to people not to go to the office of the National Archive. But, in the world they lived in, these women could do no other. They were as much creatures of their time as the clerics who assured themselves of the Catholicism of adoptive parents and not much else. The emotional well-being of women and children counted for nothing in patriarchal Ireland – less than nothing if they were also poor. And "outside the Church," as every Catholic child learned to chant from the Penny Catechism, "there is no salvation." There is a strong folk memory of Irish-Catholic children being tempted into Protestantism during The Famine. Even in this century, Irish mothers would have wanted their babies to go to Catholics, who would not have an evangelical motive for adopting. They would also have wanted them to go to the U.S., the home of wealth and glamour. Anne Phelan, a former air hostess with Aer Lingus, remembers the baby flights to America. On one particular night in 1952, she saw a manifest of a Dublin flight connecting with a Pan-American to Idlewild. "Stewardess x 2 x 10%," it read. A "10%" is a baby.

There was nothing secret about it. When Anne Phelan was working in the airline's office in central Dublin, an American officer in uniform came in and chatted to the counter staff. "I'm back again," he told them happily. "My wife was thrilled with the adopted daughter I brought her. Now I've come to buy myself a son." That's what Phelan especially remembers – the word "buy" being used quite unselfconsciously. No one at the time thought anything of it. "We all used to collect for the orphanages. We were delighted to think the nuns would get some money for the others and the babies would get wonderful new homes in America. We heard that Jane Russell was coming for an Irish baby. We were all dying to see her."

Couriers may have made a little profit. "Please book your transportation at your Pan-American office," a nun in Ireland writes to an adoptive parent in Chicago. "All our children travel thus. We group them in four, and four adopting parents share the expenses of one guardian for the children." But the nuns got nothing from the adoptive parents except voluntary donations, which were essential to keep the service going: the birth mothers, often servants or office girls, could not usually pay for the upkeep of their babies. Money was so tight in the homes that the first thing an adoptive or foster mother did was to buy the child clothes, then wash and iron the ones she or he had come in, and send them back to the nuns for the next child.

The state meanwhile has always stayed aloof from the whole problem. But Maggie Butler, for one, knows that the problems caused by fostering and adoption have been vigorously tackled in other countries, simply out of respect for mothers' and children's enduring need for knowledge of each other. She fears another evasion by "official" Ireland. "Ireland is a country that finds it difficult to take responsibility for itself," she says. "But this new information challenges the habit of burying traumas somewhere out of sight. What the country does about the files will be significant in lots of ways."

Meantime, the phones ring and ring in Barnardo's. "We're doing what has to be done," a weary Norah Gibbons says, after another morning of answering them. "We're listening to the past."

The Independent, April 27, 1996

Suffer the Little Children

On a hill in Jerusalem there is a museum called Yad Vashem, and it tells in pictures and words one of humankind's most terrible stories. It tells the story of the terrible fate visited on Europe's Jews by the ideology of Nazism. Tapes repeat the names of the murdered. Banks of candles flicker in memory of the children. The sepia faces of the dead look out imploringly from cracks in the sides of railway wagons, from the backs of lorries, from the tumbled bricks of ghettos. It is very hard to look at. And when you turn away from the too sorrowful images, you notice the people who are looking at them, and that is almost as affecting. When I was there I saw a new immigrant to Israel – a Russian, from his gray plastic shoes and baggy suit – in helpless tears in front of one old photo.

The Holocaust is unique. But it is the only event in modern history sufficiently grave to provide the tones in which we may speak of the spectrum of child abuse, if "abuse" is the right word for abducting little girls and wreaking your will on their terrified selves until they get too weak and broken to resist, and you can play with them as they die. What happened to the little girls in Belgium is too terrible to contemplate. Literally. I don't know how many people last week, reading the description of the prison in which their long-drawn-out suffering took place, were able to get past the word "soundproof."

And those girls are just the ones we know about. Every single week in this newspaper, details of men gratifying themselves through the rape and sexual abuse and terrorization and corruption and physical and mental destruction of children in this country – things done every day, and being done now as I write – are repeated. And that is just the witness from the tiny proportion of these crimes which comes to light and which reaches the courts. Until our times and the spread of mass media, all this was hidden. Now, the depth and extent of the ordinary, everyday, endemic evil done to children is coming out. This is not a holocaust, but it is like the Holocaust in at least one way. It changes everything. The state of knowing and fully acknowledging the reality of child abuse is a state utterly different from not knowing it.

About the children in Belgium, is there more we can do than bow the head, like the man in the museum in Jerusalem, and give way to grief? Can we somehow refuse to let evil defeat our human ingenuity? The EU Justice and Home Affairs Ministers, meeting last week, did their best to come up with a bureaucratic response to the intra-national aspect of the sexual exploitation of children. But, of course, the ministers are politicians. They're not artists, or moralists, or prophets. They can't begin their discussions with a howl of outrage. They can't dwell on the central fact of child sex abuse, which is that the abused are children. Children can't match their predators. They can't hope to escape. They are too small. They are not strong enough. They don't know enough.

The crime of child sex abuse is as gross as it is because the children are humans with human imaginations and human emotions who suffer just as adults do the vast pains of terror and abandonment. As the little girls in their cage in Belgium must have done. But unlike adults, they have no resources with which to outwit the designs of the people who hate them.

The ministers cannot but proceed as if everything is the same this year as it was last year except that some legislative and administrative changes need to be made. But everything isn't the same. A woman wrote to me about the picture of a little girl on the back of the Dublin telephone directory. "I don't understand the blond under-age girl wearing a sleeveless dress and ballet shoes," she says. "Today, when every teenager wears jeans and thick-soled runners. Every paper every day speaks of child molestation. What does this ad mean?"

You may turn to this image and say to yourself: "Ah, for God's sake, it's just a pretty picture of a little kid. You'd have to be sick to see anything wrong with it." But I feel for the woman who wrote in. The world is sick. I don't want to see little girls arbitrarily used as models. I don't care if this seems irrational. I want new rules about children. You wouldn't crack a joke about Abie and Solly to a Jew stumbling out of the Yad Vashem Memorial Museum. Neither do I want to hear a defense of using solitary little girls in woods while the cage in Belgium is still burning in our brains. If people are serious about protecting children, huge and wrenching changes need to be made within the cultures of the world, not one of which, as far as I know, protects children. Some of these changes will be on the level of general attitude. Some, especially in our law-based culture, will be on the level of crime and punishment.

About the latter – cherished notions, such as that an individual is free to do what he or she wants within the law, and is innocent until found guilty, and is purged of all guilt when punishment has been discharged, will have to be examined. Fashion photographers are free, for example, to use anorexic models in cowering poses so as to glamorize the idea of abused girl children. I think that such provocative cynicism should be actionable as accessory to child sex abuse. Anybody is free, at the moment, to gratify themselves with pornographic pictures of children. Why is possession of child pornography not an offense? Given that the pornography can only exist because the offense of forcing or coercing children into pornographic acts has been committed?

Why are known child rapists, like the one in Belgium, released back into the community without supervision? It is known that pedophilia is an all-but-incurable perversion. Is all this not enough to justify tagging? Is it not enough to justify a central register of child sex abusers' passports? Is it not enough to justify the setting up of a DNA database? Proposals like these may be light-years away from the spiritual revolution that is necessary to prevent what is probably the most commonplace evil connected with child sex abuse – that complacent male authorities turn a less than censorious eye to the "fun and games" men might be known to have with their own children or the children around the neighborhood. But in a way, the more dramatic sanctions are the easiest to put in place.

There would have been no Holocaust if people in general had stood by the Jews. There would be no child prostitutes, paint covering their hunger, there would be no small bodies broken by big ones, there would be no horrors behind soundproof doors, if we were entirely sensitive to children. And, however lofty that ideal may seem, we can all aspire to it.

A friend was telling me of a small but precious sign of a new consciousness. There is a man in her street whom the children love playing with and who loves children. The thing is, these days, he never plays with them in his house. He plays with them in the street.

The Irish Times, September 30, 1996

Temples to Trade

Dublin's little shops have been on their way out ever since the city center began to change a few years ago, when the people with big money went back into property. And they're being finished off by the Anglicization of the shopping industry. It is only a matter of time now till the last of the old leases falls in, and shops that sold lisle stockings or loose sweets or tinned peas or a few rashers or distemper brushes are turned into more lucrative operations. The streets on my way into town are gentrifying at speed. Crooked houses where mysterious old people lived behind gray net-curtains in bedsitters over shops are demolished overnight, and a billboard for promising, desirable apartments goes up over their rubble.

A "For Sale" sign has gone up over The Kilkenny Dairy and will soon go up over all the dairies, with their rows of cornflake packets on wooden shelves lumpy with years of gloss paint. Further on, I pass a shop that sells men's suits. The tickets on them are homemade – felt pen on cardboard. And farther on there's a shop that sells men's hats and caps, in orderly rows on their little mushrooms. Often in these old shops there is a smell of gas from the Superser. The lighting is dim. They still have money drawers with wooden hollows, instead of cash registers.

But it is not just the passing of variety that is to be mourned. It is that these shops were centers of the local community. Now, although the city is full of new housing, it is not full of new communities. Though maybe some restaurants and bars are creating new local tribes out of the young people who adopt them.

Shopping is the central activity of the First World. It is what the masses will enter the next millennium doing. And shopping used to have a human, and therefore a potentially moral, dimension. Increasingly, the way capitalism is organizing shopping strips it – without our even noticing – of that dimension.

Last week I saw a terrible thing. On O'Connell Bridge a teenaged beggar was sitting on the pavement rocking back and forward like a demented person. He seemed to be deformed. His legs were stretched out in front of him and his poor dirty feet were bare and blue with cold. I am hardened by the years of seeing children beg. But this was the worst I ever saw in Ireland. (And yet I'm glad that there are beggars everywhere at the moment. The guards must tacitly allow them to ply their trade where they can, in the weeks coming up to Christmas, when money is sloshing around the city. I hope, anyway, that that's what happens.)

No one paused beside the boy, because of that tunneling intentness, that fervor of Christmas shopping that makes people speed past everything else, muzzles down like greyhounds after hares, which is already infecting Dublin. I was on my way myself to the latest cathedral, the Jervis Street Centre. I'd heard breathless stories about it. Boots the Chemist simply could not keep the shelves supplied, so fast were the lines selling out. Security people were trying to control the crowds fighting to get into Debenhams. Traffic was stretching back half a mile from the car park, as it does from the Stephen's Green Centre car park. The tales about Jervis Street must be not unlike tales that swept medieval Paris, or Isfahan, or Benares, when another great place of worship came into use. "Have you been down to Jervis Street yet?" people are saying. Or, "Have you been out to Blanchardstown?"

Yet the interest and pleasure people expect from these places is completely out of proportion to what they deliver. They look shiny and spacious and luxurious. They play the same part that Victorian pubs played when cities were darker and colder and much more desperate than they are today: they are centers of light and heat. They make the visitor conscious of being sheltered from an inclement world.

But behind that brightness, they are mean. Try to find the Ladies in Jervis Street, for instance. There are no directions on the ground floor, presumably to discourage use. When you find it, it isn't altogether pleasant, because the buttons for the flushes are stiff, and the roll in the toilet paper dispenser is so tightly encased that a leaf can't be pulled out without shredding. Anyone could have told the designers these things, and got them to put a little more thought into such matters. But that would involve thinking about shoppers as people, not consumers.

In Blanchardstown, there aren't even any toilets in the Bewley's Café in the shopping center. And in Blanchardstown, there is hardly anywhere you can sit down for free. As in Jervis Street, the few seats are packed. The idea is to keep you moving, keep you shopping. Even when the shops are nothing much. The acres of shiny terrazzo distract you from noticing that the emperor has no clothes – that the most dowdy of English merchandise is largely what is on offer. In Blanchardstown the management appears to have put coins in the fountain water to manufacture a bit of magic. But magic isn't so easily conjured.

The distraught boy beggar, and the shortage of places for

shoppers to sit down, belong on the same spectrum. There is no room in a city given over to buying and selling for human altruism. One of the comforting things about shopping, even, is that you forget that you are a human. In a shopping mall, there are no humans. Whereas there were humans with power and responsibility in the old sweetshops, newsagents, and dairies.

Whoever owns all these chain stores isn't there, and no one cares if you're a pound short of the full price or your feet hurt or you can't read the labels because you've forgotten your glasses. No one cares about you. And yet your personhood is being exploited. The modern anonymous, ordinary person is never more valued and potent than when deciding to buy A rather than B, in X shop rather than Y. Everyone wants you when you're spending money.

I was so depressed by the Jervis Street place that I went in to the Ritz Café in Middle Abbey Street, a cavernous, family-run fish and chip café which is one of the best places in the city for a hot snack, and where there is that air of tranquil rest and reflection which used to belong to pubs and has now all but disappeared.

An old man had finished his meal and came up to the serving counter to fumble out the price of it. He should have paid in advance, of course, and he should have been paying down at the cash desk. But he was old. So commerce came to a halt while the old man was gently helped. I don't know the people who run the Ritz. I've never spoken to them. But I'm grateful to them for that small moment. Only how long will such values last? Down the street, there are plans for a "food court." Will family-run chippers survive? Will "food courts" help slow, old men? Or must we look around for new sources of moral vitality, now, as even the memory fades of how rich the interplay between individuals and the world of goods and services used to be?

The Irish Times, December 2, 1996

Violence Against Women

I was on Inis Meáin for a few days over the New Year. It got dark – very dark, to a visitor not used to the island – from about 4:30 PM onward. As you walked along the windy road people could be upon you, sometimes so invisibly that you only knew they were there by the sound of their breathing. Sometimes footsteps gained on you. Or the lights of a tractor showed a man and a dog coming along the road towards you. The stars burned brightly in the great black sky, and I realized why I hadn't seen the stars for years. Because I hadn't walked around in the dark, because I hadn't felt safe. I'd forgotten what it was like to move around at night, stopping to look up at the sky.

Two more women battered to death in the last two weeks. Nineteen women killed last year. And the refuges for women only battered – not, this time, to death – crammed with terrified and angry women. Something goes wrong: the man doesn't get what he wants, or perceives some other outrage, and the sleeping giant of his physical strength grunts into life. It can't be easy to batter someone to death. You have to be raging with hate and fury to do it. But there seems to be no shortage of men full enough of hatred to do it.

Men kill women because they can. But when things are equal – when everyone has equal access to handguns, and women have equal opportunities for murder – men still kill far more women than women kill men. The potential violence of men toward women – the readiness with which they will rape and batter and murder – is part of the context within which the equable and affectionate relationships between the mass of men and women take place. But as far as I know men rarely talk about male violence, or initiate debates on it, or introduce legislation about it, or form organizations to tackle it, or stand as candidates on the issue of it, or attempt to mount big attitude-changing campaigns about it as they have done about other life-threatening matters.

Men just do this sort of thing, we're told. If a girl takes a lift home at night in a car with two men in it – two low human beings, fellow creations, made like her of heart and mind and soul – she must understand what is likely to happen to her. No one takes responsibility for this fact, extraordinary though it is. Men don't. It is shunted on to the agenda of women's committees. Being afraid to go out the door because you are a woman is supposed to be a woman's problem. It is a woman's problem, but its solution is not. Its solution lies with humankind, but primarily with men.

We know more about violence than any humans before us have known. Soldiers have raped in war before, but only now can one sit at home in Ireland and watch on the television Muslim parents weep over their daughter, zombie-like in a German hospital, broken by months of gang rape by Serb soldiers. Children disappeared before, but before we can escape it, we see the photo of the anguished face of the child who was rescued from Marc Dutroux's torture cages.

One of the ways one can now imagine Ireland is as a landscape dotted all over with the sites where the bodies of murdered women have been recently found. Poor Mrs. Livingstone in her suburban house in Malahide. The beloved daughter who walked out of her warm bungalow in Portlaoise

111

and whose body was found out in the lonely bog, in a ditch of mud. The public toilets in Loughrea. The path from the bus to the edge of the houses in Blanchardstown. Another murder, and another flag in the map. A boreen winding up a rushy hill in west Cork. And the bright apartments of the new modern Ireland on Dublin's Liffey Street. Their initiation. Their first intimate murder.

Mass blame of men is useless as well as sexist, and deeply offensive to the majority of men who have nothing whatsoever to do with physical violence. However, the majority of men do probably consider women to be inferior to men, and therefore in their deepest hearts estimate women's lives as of lesser value. Such an attitude is enshrined in the religions and laws and social customs of the world. Men have never combined to assert the equality of women as they have combined against other injustices. The Taliban in Afghanistan are men, and the Islamic enforcers in Algeria are men, and the Pope and his clerical servants in Rome, blandly instructing the women of the world to defer to them in decisions about childbearing, are men.

It is hard for women who think of what has been made of the world not to fear men, and to hate their power, on the record of what men have done and do. One may not fear or hate any man just for being a man. But, as for men in general … I won't read Marilyn French's *The War Against Women*, for instance, because I don't want to know any more about what is done to the women and children of the world in the prostitution and pornography industries of the planet, to take one example. I wouldn't be able to go on believing that a real, visceral respect for women, which might affect the rate at which they are murdered by men, is possible. Is maybe possible.

A ploy that might lessen the anger involved all round on the subject of male violence would be to excise the word "male." We could attempt to ignore gender and to transpose the whole problem to the plane of civil rights. Relatively powerless citizens (who happen to be women) are being murdered by relatively powerful ones (men). It is in the interest of every citizen to make a determined effort to stop this, and not to write it off as part of human nature – to propose that half the citizens of this state are innately more violent than the other half.

In Canada, apparently, the government has not been ashamed to run a huge educational program calling for zero tolerance for physical violence. It is almost unimaginable that our hidebound and self-satisfied Dáil would do any such thing. But I suppose there's a chance. Another approach would be to ally this cause to other causes that hinge on the abuse of power, such as cruelty to children and to animals. Another would be to place the murder of women where it belongs, on the spectrum of the denigration of the female that operates at every level from the instant a girl child is born until the male priest officiates at her burial.

Another, of course, would be to bring up your daughters to be as wary of the opposite sex as they would be of savage animals. To switch on their security alarm every time a man – especially a man who has been drinking – comes in the door. But that's ridiculous, isn't it? And terribly insulting to men? But then – what are our daughters to be told?

The Irish Times, January 6, 1997

Questions of Relative Rights

For Christmas week I was stuck in a small, litter-strewn Bulgarian ski resort, where there was no snow, and therefore no skiing and therefore nothing much to do. The nearest town was a couple of hours away by bus. I would have gone to see it, but that a couple who had visited it said they saw dancing bears in the square there. The handler had a kind of bit going through the bear's mouth, and when he pulled it, the bear went up on his hind legs to try to escape the pain, and seemed to be dancing. Then the handler played his fiddle, as if to accompany the bear's dance. You were expected to throw a few coins to the handler in appreciation of this performance.

I didn't want to see bears being used like this. On the other hand, anyone who is trying to survive by begging in a country with as severe an economic crisis as Bulgaria has, is most pitiably poor. I have seen a bear and a bear master in the sleet in winter in Istanbul. Who knows where the two of them sheltered at night? The man was gaunt with cold and hunger. He was inflicting whatever it was on the animal because he himself was trapped and had no other way to survive. Perhaps he was keeping a family on his few coins. So I suppose.

I tried to think about the relative rights concerned. And whenever I do face questions of relative rights, the dialogue surrounding abortion starts up again in my mind. And I am back again among the uncertainties and ambiguities that surround my attitudes to abortion. Attitudes, in the plural: I have not got the comfort of absolute conviction on this or any comparably important matter. The society I am part of has made some interim decisions about Irish women and abortion. They are not very principled ones, and they do not represent a consensus, but they do allow for coexistence. But the 10 years or so we spent getting to those decisions didn't exhaust the subject. It will never be exhausted.

I thought of the women I have known who absolutely and utterly could not, as they perceived it, in the circumstances they were in, continue a pregnancy. And I thought of the things that constitute suffering – the apprehension of pain, and the memory of it. Does the bear suffer, or does it experience each moment of its existence separately? Can a very developed foetus suffer? I know it reacts to stimulus, but can we ever know whether it can suffer? And then, can animals be compared to humans? Can something unborn be compared to something born? The bear is only an animal, but it has lived within human society.

Is it the arrival into society that makes the difference to rights and duties, so that one would not kill a week-old baby but one would a week-old foetus? Or is it a question of when the foetus becomes not the mother? The unborn cannot survive as the bear would survive if it could get away from its master. Doesn't that make the choice of the woman's survival over the foetus's survival unique – it is the woman's choice not because of some entitlement, but because she literally chooses one part of herself over another?

I know how confused this is. But people do flounder when it comes to the deep questions, such as the morality of humankind's dealings with animals, and the morality of its dealings with unborn humans. You would think that the long debate about abortion legislation would have taught those who were not completely satisfied with either "yes" or "no" how to approach this complex subject. But the heat of the debate simplified it. You weren't supposed to think. You were supposed to see that all abortion is so self-evidently wrong that no thinking is necessary. And that nothing remains but to condemn. But I find that I have to go on thinking.

Abortion keeps coming up. The Pro Life Campaign people will never stop looking for another referendum. And you may have noticed that the Holy See Mission to the United Nations has withdrawn its symbolic contribution of $2,000 to UNICEF – the United Nations International Children's Emergency Fund. It said that UNICEF workers in various countries were "distributing contraceptives and counseling their use." I should hope they were, I may say. But I don't believe that that's the Vatican's real reason. I believe that another of its given reasons – that UNICEF "participated in the publication of a UN manual advocating the distribution of abortifacient 'post-coital' contraceptives to refugee women in emergency situations" – is the sticking point.

The UN booklet in question was about women – refugee women – who have been raped in war. I hazard the view that many people would find it acceptable that such women should have access to the morning-after pill, and that it is in the interest of their existing children and their future children (never mind themselves) that they should, and UNICEF is an organization that puts children first. I personally could not bear to add any prohibition of my own to the layers of prohibitions heaped on a Muslim woman, say, raped in Bosnia. Her life has been destroyed by a war waged above her head by men, her body has been violated by strange men who raped her in the confident expectation that this would lead to her rejection by her own men, and on top of that, remote men in the Vatican are prohibiting her from doing anything to prevent a child being born of the rape. I see a woman in those circumstances – and in the one Bosnian war alone there were thousands of women in just such circumstances – as tormented and outraged beyond what can be done to an animal. She is the bear, writ a million times large, and she is also a human, and a sister.

Those are my feelings. But the Vatican represents a different range of feelings. The Vatican holds observer status at the United Nations because of its territorial possessions in Rome. Its donations, like the $2,000 to UNICEF, are not serious contributions – they are symbols of its moral approval or disapproval. I myself approve of there being a body with such a role attached to the UN.

Or rather, insofar as the moral and spiritual dimension of humankind is organized into religions and philosophies and so on, I am glad that those organizations are accepted as influential in humankind's affairs. This leaves me in the position of supporting the Holy See Mission's existence and function, while passionately disapproving of what it seeks to do to the world's most vulnerable women in the matter of childbearing. It is as if I wanted the bear master to play his fiddle and at the same time wanted the bear to be free. How many paradoxes can one situation contain? And how can a person stop thinking and feeling while they remain to be resolved?

The Irish Times, January 13, 1997

Sinatra

There are other famous people in their eighties who aren't too well, but the one whose decline I'm alert to, the one it makes a difference to me whether death comes for, is Frank Sinatra. That will be some kind of concluding moment. He was a great figure, not so much in the events of my life as in the coloring of them, inside my head. I remember coming out of the Strand Cinema in Dublin in about 1956, transfixed, after seeing him in *The Man with the Golden Arm*. And I saw him for real on a wonderful, dreamy, misty night in Lansdowne Road, when he came here not long ago.

That's what? Forty-something years? And all that time, if ever I heard his name, I knew that it signaled something finely done, something excellent and beautiful. He was so good at what he did. His grave, precise voice shaped his half-century. First he sang a certain kind of song a certain way: then they wrote that kind of song. Then we felt the feelings to go with the song.

And it wasn't just that he was so good. It was that he was our pattern of elegance, back when there were so few exemplars. When he sang "All the Way" there was a dry, impersonal yearning in the tone that we learnt from him, and which then became one of the measures of how we truly felt about spotty youths with names like Decco and Shay. And we were spotty and ungainly ourselves, but we felt the passions that Sinatra's great torch songs elegized. We felt great splodges and wodges of desire and jealousy and disillusion and regret and hope. He put shape on all that. There wasn't a single elegant or world-class thing in any of our schools or houses. Except the elegance of his voice and the musical arrangements he commissioned for his voice in albums like *Songs for Swinging Lovers.* Sinatra sang "I've Got You Under My Skin" on that, and a certain driving vigor in it, a controlled excitement, was what we took – or I did, anyway – as how you should feel or would feel if you were perfectly suited to someone. His confidence with rhythm was the pattern of all confidence. And the way he swung into "You Make Me Feel So Young" was the very essence of exuberance – of being here on this earth, delighting in life and love. He was such a great musician until just recently that it is hard to imagine that his creativity will not survive the death of his body. We knew him, after all, in unbodily ways – he emanated from the disc of vinyl going round and round on the record player.

He was never young, or old. At Lansdowne Road he did the soliloquy "My Boy Bill" from *Carousel.* You try doing that – particularly if you're well into your seventies – and you'll find the measure of respect for him. He seems to be, by the accounts I've seen, not a particularly lovable man. But that doesn't matter now. What matters is that he could easily have got away with giving much less than he gave in his life.

But he wasn't content to be merely a star. He took possession instead of a seat among the minor gods. He was one of the guiding spirits of the age, an artist who took popular song as seriously as it deserves to be taken. He went to every length to perfect the modern art of singing songs in a recording studio with an orchestra. He moved from arranger to arranger, musician to musician, record company to record company, always looking for better, not easier, collaborators. And he never sang a phrase lazily.

Even when he did awful songs – I can't bear "Love and Marriage" myself, or the twee little one about the beaver and the dam – he contributed his full gift of intelligent pace, perfect diction, suppleness of voice, and always that ashy, dry tone out at the edge of his voice that somehow made what he said distinguished, as if he were an emissary for the song itself, not a performer of it.

That absolutely carried over to his physical self. From coming out on to the North Strand that day, the boys around were scanned for how much or how little they looked like him. Sinatra's looks weren't just a way to look: they were *the* way. The thing to be was thin, sad-eyed, all sensitive mouth, the face a feline triangle. And as Sinatra got older that lean face kept its weary beauty, even under the toupee, and it was always the face that mattered: for the rest, he might have been disembodied.

He was what was meant in my mind by a sophisticated man, a middle-of-the-night man, a man who'd been around. He was the pattern of a lover, not a husband. These are things you have to know, when you're growing up. Someone has to suggest to you the different relationships that are possible. Not that relationship was a word much used then, or that anything about Sinatra prompted thought of relationships. He was, rather, the solitary man, singing the blues in an empty nightclub, alone. The only way to insert yourself into the fantasy was to be the lost or unattainable woman who had broken his heart.

How were these things sorted out in the imagination of young people, in the eras before the mass media brought actors and singers into our homes? In the eras before print and photography? Sinatra – like James Dean, like Elvis, like John Lennon later – gave us concepts of the attractive. There was nowhere else to get them. Ireland in the 1950s or 1960s or – if it comes to that – until very recently, proffered few ideals of stylish self-presentation. Who were we to look to? Dev? The Clipper Carlton?

Today, I would seek out as desirable people of middle age who, say, speak Irish and take life seriously and care about the natural world. But when I was 14 and 16 and 18, a *Gaeilgeoir* hill-walking schoolteacher was more or less the only male ideal around, and with every fiber of our being we rejected that and wanted a Sinatra, all the way from here to eternity.

Since sex didn't officially exist, how were we to know, if it hadn't been for Sinatra, that there is a deadly serious sexiness, which his voice singing "All the Way" perfectly expresses? He was a cerebral example of the perfectly sexy, not an animal example. There's no poignancy in the decay of his body, as there was in Elvis. When he does die there'll be a few days of his songs being played over and over. And there he'll be, as achingly attractive as ever. "All or Nothing at All," he'll sing, and the time between might never have been.

I read somewhere he told his daughter that what he wanted for Christmas was to be here next Christmas. I wish for him what he wishes for himself, of course. But he is here – he isn't going anywhere – as long as I'm alive myself. I don't own any tapes or CDs of him. I'd never sit down and concentrate on him. It is as a treasure that suddenly flashes up out of the mediocrity of ordinary life that he best manifests himself. You stand in a shop, and his quizzical voice comes on the distant radio. All around you the imperfect falls away, and hearing him singing you hear one thing done, perfectly.

The Irish Times, February 3, 1997

The Robinson Presidency

Soon after Mary Robinson was elected President she gave an interview to a religious affairs program on BBC Radio in Belfast. After a few questions the interviewer could be heard gathering himself to ask what he thought the hard one. "And would you," he said, "describe yourself as a feminist?" – in the humorously incredulous tone of one inquiring as to whether the interviewee was willing to admit to an eccentricity.

"Yes," she said, simply.

She didn't amplify. She didn't apologize. She just took the word for the generally descriptive word it is, and calmly possessed it. You could say she purged the word, and started it off anew.

The point, after all, of her election was not that she is a woman – Mrs. Thatcher is a woman – but that she is a feminist. This means, at the least, a woman consciously alert to gender-based discrimination, and where this operates against women, consciously committed to bringing about redress. It means a woman interested in human and civil rights for those who are denied them – often enough, everywhere on the planet, women.

In that sense, Mrs. Robinson's next area of endeavor will follow on not just from the Presidency but from her work before the Presidency, where in formal constitutional cases and in informal help and advice she moved Irish women toward a footing of equality on the basis of the law. It was what she had done for women, and not her being herself a woman, that choked me with tears back then, seven years ago, when she took office. When I saw her on television from Dublin Castle, being treated at the inauguration of her Presidency with all the respect and honor this state can command, it was for that the tears came rolling down. Not that she was a woman, but that after all the gibes and the sneers and the setbacks, she was a "women's libber" – a woman who deliberately had challenged the status quo.

If she had never been President, she still, as a lawyer, had already made a huge difference to Irish women. So much so that many activists deplored her running for the office. If she gets in, she'll be lost to us, they said, just as Irish people are saying today that she'll be lost to Ireland. But she simply converted one role into a broader one. She could not, from Áras an Uachtaráin, do the specific things for women that she had done before. She did something different, and even more valuable. She lent her prestige to the womanly. She enormously broadened the standing of womanliness in her years as President. And she did this in two ways. One was by the valuation she placed on everything local and domestic and homemade and un-self-important, in utter contrast to the values of existing establishments. The other was in the role she gave to feeling.

From the very beginning she used her office as a source of comfort to individuals and as a means of reordering the agenda of what and who is important in this society or unimportant. She went on *Nodhlag na mBan* – Women's Christmas – to Mass with women prisoners. That was soon after her inauguration. Another Christmas – Christmas Eve, if I remember correctly – she went to Donegal to stand with the families of the missing fishermen. She was represented at the funeral of Brigid McCole and she had the family with her for Mrs. McCole's Month's Mind Mass.

I remember that when she was in Carrick-on-Shannon she called to the family of the girl who was murdered. She made contact with the shocked – the flooded-out householders in Galway, for instance – and she made innumerable private visits to hospitals, and to campsites, and to homes where there was unhappiness.

She was asserting, on our behalf, the importance of the emotions. She was saying that the state can be emotional, too. She went as us, and as his family, to the Mass in the Morning Star Hostel, for the family-less homeless man found dead on wasteground in winter. She had a genius for knowing where we would wish her to be. And when she broke down, in Somalia, and said that as a mother, her inner sense of justice revolted at what she saw, she was expanding the parameters of what heads of state may say in public. When she broke down again – the only other time – and said nothing, but just turned away – when on a visit to Cork, news of the end of the IRA cease-fire was passed to her, she was expressing our speechless pain, too.

The ideal of the stiff upper lip has dominated for centuries, as if at the level of diplomats and statesmen and great public representatives the heart had been transcended by a special, heartless, super race of people who are all control, all mind. She gave the lie to that lie. And it was all the more touching that she showed her feelings because she is, in so many ways, a reserved and formal woman. She actually didn't suit, by temperament and bearing, the cheerful, chaotic style of many of the little events she chose to attend. Any backslapping politicians would have been better at the required bonhomie.

It was always clear that she was there consciously, and on principle. The principle was an assertion of inclusiveness, the need for which could not have been so vivid to a man, however sympathetic, as it is to a woman. She stood with the tea-and-sandwich-makers so as to make a statement about the value of the domestic gifts – not because she herself has any apparent empathy with the domestic. And when she cried, we knew her tears were honest.

She wouldn't know how to do "I'm overcome that you've given me an Oscar" tears. She used the word "love" a lot, and was not ashamed: her palpable personal shyness was a guarantee of the word's meaning. May our feminist President take that care for small people and large feelings into a wider arena – may there be a global destination for her Ireland-forged feminism.

The Irish Times, March 13, 1997

That Backward Glance

The End of Hidden Ireland: Rebellion, Famine, and Emigration,
Robert Scally, Oxford University Press

What Irish-America has made of Ireland can bemuse
and amuse, especially around St. Patrick's Day,
when the history we play with is about as authentic as a plastic shamrock. But where have Irish-Americans been
able to form a true view of what the Irish part of their hybrid
name means? How open has anyone been about their distinctive heritage? How silent have they – and we – been about the
pain of their origins?

What were the Irish, in their own consciousness, and in the
view of others, when barefoot, half-naked, sick, heartbroken,
and knowing themselves to be despised, they broke from the
past and began their American lives? A myriad of questions
arises about the passage out of Ireland. One kind of person
was forced to become another kind: how did that process
unfold? And what was it like from inside: from within the
individual life?

These mysteries have recently been approached with respect and with energy by a professor of history at New York
University. Robert Scally spent ten years working on *The End
of Hidden Ireland,* yet it reads not like dry scholarship, but like
a novel, or poetry, unashamed of the pity and anger its story
cannot but evoke. Perhaps this is because there are differentiated people in it. Robert Scally centers his panorama on the

100 or so families hunted, finally, in 1847, from the townland of Ballykilcline, County Roscommon. He goes with them from their tumbled cabins in the bog to the square in Strokestown, where they were rounded up for the four-day journey to Dublin, and then he sails with them to Liverpool, and he accompanies them through their humiliations there, until he must leave them, where they fall out of history, as they huddle into steerage to cross the ocean to New York.

It was a terrible journey. On the road to Dublin most of the ragged band were "debilitated from at least a year of hunger, and some probably still suffered from the fevers and dysentery that were rife in the townland during the previous winter … With hordes of others from the townlands trekking the same route and thousands dying along its sides, the roads leading from the interior to the outports in the spring of 1848 were a sight that nearly all observers carried away as their most lasting 'memory of the Famine.'" The sight – not the sound. Scally remarks that "in contrast to their history before and after the journey, the demeanour of Irish peasant crowds in transit during the Famine years was almost invariably described as passive, diffident and quiet." We know the aversion the sight of the emigrants aroused in the people of the towns they passed through on their way to the ports. We know very little about their own feelings. "But nearly all descriptions note their silence," Robert Scally says, redeeming their sensibility from the silence of history.

The End Of Hidden Ireland does draw on a wealth of historical sources. But it is above all through the exercise of imaginative sympathy that Robert Scally brings these people to life. And the sympathy is born when he follows the ragged band back to their lost townland. This is where they briefly enter the record when – foolishly, vaingloriously – they began a rent strike against their Westminster rulers in 1834. That was the true beginning of their journey. They were evicted and forcibly emigrated in the end. But the transition from village to urban slum had begun much earlier than the actual time of eviction and emigration, "reaching them in small, imperceptible increments, disguising the fates that awaited them."

The Ballykilcline families were just a dot in the huge picture of Famine migration – at its height 150 years ago this year – a migration which, with what Robert Scally calls "its special quality of fleeing," and "the odour of racial hatred surrounding the emigrants' treatment … bears more resemblance to the slave trade or the boxcars of the Holocaust than to the routine crossings of a later age." Driven from the deep secrecy of their settlements, and fleeing hunger and disease, those who survived the horrors of Liverpool took the early ships, the "coffin ships" to the New World. In steerage "the families of farmers and cottiers died inches apart, within each other's intimate reeks and pleadings below decks." The steerage was a form of captivity, of absolute powerlessness "that even the poorest had not known before and that reduced many who once thought themselves strong to the level of their children. If seen as a separate, temporary nation afloat it might be said that the inmates of the emigrant steerages were suffering a second famine, one that was quite blind to the name or history of its victims." The Ballykilcline people, like most of the Famine migrants, must have arrived in the New World quite stripped of particularity – quite anonymous.

But that was a fertile anonymity. Back in Ireland, they had long endured an inhuman anonymity. Their individual names and histories had always been a matter of indifference to the people with power over them. In return, they did nothing to assist their masters to comprehend them. The "incoherence" of the townlands and their settlements was their protection. The rent strike in Ballykilcline was never quite understood, even by His Majesty's Commissioners against whom it was directed. "A tangle of evasions, dodges and fluid identities often defied the order that colonial rule required everywhere."

The peasant Irish had their own, secretive system, "and with that system, ruinous as it was, also went all the essentials of their way of life. Their means of resistance – conspiracy, pretence, foot-dragging, and obfuscation – were the only ones ordinarily available to them, 'weapons of the weak' like those employed by defeated and colonized peoples everywhere. The destruction of the townland community, whether by improvement, eviction, or emigration, inevitably threatened the survival of their language, their family and community systems, and the authority of tradition, including the distinct form of Christianity peculiar to moral Ireland before the Famine. The tenacity with which the peasantry held onto all this, and the catastrophic force of events eventually needed to pry them loose, attest to the value they placed on the life the townlands contained."

They were quite bare of material possessions, these people, and none of them owned any of the land. The local notables didn't know their names, and could hardly distinguish them from each other, and never knew how many Irish were living on a given piece of land, or understood the working arrangements between those people. Even the piece of land – far more important than the people who lived off it, though the people had lived there for centuries – didn't have a name assuredly known to the rulers. The first eviction notices ordered the people "to quit possession of the Crown lands called or known by the name of Ballykilcline, otherwise Killytullyvarry, Bungariffe, and Aghamore or by whatsoever other name or names the same or any subdenomination thereof maybe called or known ... "

Because they were distant, both geographically and psychologically, the landlords needed middlemen to execute their wishes, such as the wish to make their land "perfectly untenanted." When the Ballykilcline people tried, in the 1840s, to assert that they were not tenants of the Crown and did not have to pay rent to the Crown, the threat of eviction was brought down. It was hanging over them when the hunger began and title to the land became an academic matter, because the only future on the land was death by starvation. The threats were made, and the punishments administered by a hierarchy of middlemen, in descending order from the landlord's agent down to – in this place – "an ambitious opportunist and casual profiteer" by the name of Cox.

"The qualifications for this detested role were few but well suited to Cox's talents, cunning, indifference to scorn or threat, and bilingualism. In the midst of the turmoil and misery of the 1840s, he browsed zestfully on a variety of opportunities that presented themselves in the gap between the lower deputies of the landlords and the subtenants of the townlands, subsequently establishing himself as a comfortable farmer in the area, still remembered for his shady dealing during the Famine."

A whole range of Irish people did very well out of the Famine. But the ones Robert Scally cares for are gone – though not very long ago. Their traces are visible. The boggy, empty, rushy land you can see from the road into Rooskey is where

Ballykilcline was. Archaeologists, connected with Professor Scally, are working there, on the eloquent physical fragments of the hidden Ireland. And the townland went on existing, in memory. Professor Scally himself met a descendant of one of the families who crept back to live in that bog after the Famine, and he could recall the names of all its inhabitants, and the exact extent of their holdings.

They are close to us in some ways, the people who went on to become Americans. Yet in other ways they leave even our most penetrating imaginings behind. They suffered shocks unimaginable to us today. They had never been outside their known 10 or 15 miles. Their livelihood came from within their community. Even the education sought in the town schools by the favored small farmers left them lettered, but innocent of the world. And then, they were offered a lavish bounty to clear out. Some of them could no more go than the water or the grass of the place could have gone. A Patrick Connor, for instance, was one of "six heads of family who refused the emigrant bounty after all was lost, knowing that he and his many dependants would be ejected, starving, and in fever, in what he called 'the land of their nativity.'"

Robert Scally, and now his readers, knows something about these obscure people precisely because they were Crown tenants, and because they attempted a mild and legalistic rebellion, and the bureaucracies in Dublin and London preserved the petitions addressed by these people to the Crown Commissioners. The petitions are increasingly desperate. "That on the 26th of May your petitioners were turned out of their houses and dwellings ... That your petitioners if they are deprived of their crops and tillage will, with their families, be thrown on the world, and doomed to ruin and starvation ... "

But there was no response or even reply to the petitions. "Though most of the petitions begged for an early reply, few offered a 'return address,'" Robert Scally says. "It was possibly because no replies ever appeared that many other of the petitions bore resemblance to prayers, to which no answer was expected." In these hopeless petitions, "the false and resentful humility that would become a permanent part of their demeanor as emigrants was already visible."

The people of Ballykilcline became, through the actions of the Crown, what they had feared – "strangers in the land that gave them birth." They could not have envisaged these ruptures. As Scally says, "The time when nearly every family would expect to lose some of its members to emigration had not yet arrived, and the forced removal of whole townlands was a sight that none had yet seen." But 1847 was the end of all that. The emigrant ship or the poorhouse were the only options left to the blameless poor. A passage in this beautiful book describes it thus: "In their profoundly localized mentality, the intimately familiar spaces and shapes of their everyday surroundings, more than any abstract idea of Ireland as a nation, contained the meaning expressed in their petitions as 'the land of their birth.' What would later become 'the myth of exile' was an emigrant nationalism, suffused with bitter hindsight. But as they took the first steps on the road out and in the preceding months of distressful waiting among the emptying cabins, the sensations of loss were of their only place of belonging, a living grief not yet abstracted by time and distance."

They crossed the Irish Sea to Liverpool, sharing the boats with the cattle and wheat and pigs they had failed to raise in sufficient abundance to justify their own existence. "Peasants who had never seen seagoing ships of sail or steam now saw hundreds in motion at once. They had just left a world in which a few cabins of piled stones and turf were the center of life and now saw gigantic geometrical walls of granite, thousands of multistoried buildings lining the shore, crowds more numerous at a single glance than all the strangers they had seen in a lifetime ... "

The Irish were venomously hated in Liverpool. "The Irishman's squalor was thought to be as contagious as the diseases he carried with him." Scally's chapter on what was done to the Irish in Liverpool, and said of them, and how they internalized the bigotry directed at them, is all but unreadably painful. Melville was there in 1847. His account of a woman "in a dark alley dying for days with her two daughters in a vault 15 feet below the street, her blue arms folded to her livid bosom two shrunken things like children, her soulsickening wail known to all around," epitomizes the dehumanization of the city at this time, says Scally. "When the young American appealed to those nearest by, an old woman rubbish-picker said she had 'not time to attend to beggars and their brats.' Asking another where to take the woman, he was told, 'to the church yard.' When reminded that they were alive and not dead, the old woman replied, 'Then she'll never die. She's been down there these three days, with nothing to eat; that I know myself.' Finally approaching a policeman to help them he was told, 'There now, Jack, go on board your ship ... and leave these matters to the town.'"

Ballykilcline did not utterly disappear as a community until the Roscommon peasants had become American workers. But it did, then. And before that — of approximately 396 men, women and children recorded in Ballykilcline in 1846, 172 are missing by the time they arrive in New York. Some would have crept into another identity. But most must have been dead. "Their will and not mine be done," is a quotation from James Connor of Ballykilcline. Scally uses it as an epigraph.

Those first emigrants could actually see the coast of Ireland as they sailed past from Liverpool. They were on their way to a life of utterly unforeseen challenges. They were going to a democracy. "But with no experience of citizenship," asks Scally, "did their idea of freedom consist simply of being left alone?" And who did they think they were, anyway? Now that self-consciousness had been forced on them? "Peering from the stern rather than the bow of the emigrant ship," this unforgettable book ends, "that backward glance at the incongruous palms and gaily painted houses along the shore near Skibbereen was not only their last sight of Ireland but the first sight of themselves."

The Irish Times, March 15, 1997

Bloom's Dublin

Today being Bloomsday a motley crew of people will be trying to make out, in the Dublin of here and now, the lineaments of the Dublin Joyce was making out in his memory when he wrote *Ulysses*. But I think that in the last two or three years that Dublin finally disappeared. The Ulyssean way of life isn't there any more: this is in spite of the period of *Ulysses* being so close. Lady Gregory's granddaughters are very much alive: so are W. B. Yeats's son and daughter, and so is James Joyce's charming nephew. Strange, that Joyce's world should be remote as the Forest of Arden.

Joyce is alive in the flesh and blood of his descendants. He's alive in the physical fabric of Dublin, in that there are stones you and I can touch that he probably touched, too. We can be in exactly the spaces he was in. In Pearse Street, I look with trepidation, every time I pass, at the derelict former Academy Cinema. You can see the older walls at the back. This was the Ancient Concert Rooms where Joyce gave a song recital even though the accompanist had abruptly departed, where Nora formed the view, which she held for life, that he should have stuck to the singing and left the writing alone. I watch the building for fear it will disappear, knocked down, like 7 Eccles Street.

Still, much of the material world of *Ulysses* is intact. Glasnevin Cemetery is there and the Martello Tower and Sandymount Strand (by a miracle) and the National Library and, up to a point, the house of "The Dead" on Usher's Island. As long as Belvedere College stays in Dublin the streets to the north and east of Parnell Square will have a somewhat Joycean character. Stephen's Green is still there, Dollymount Strand, a version of the Ormond Hotel. Overall, and broadly speaking, the Dublin of *Ulysses* still stands.

The landmarks and seamarks of Dublin also still stand. But that's not what gives the city its feel. Until very recently, Dublin was a city of the poor and the scraping-by. Such people live out in the open. The center of Dublin used to be as inescapably sociable as a Travellers' camp. That sense of a condition shared is gone. Dublin was a city not only of the unemployed but of the underemployed and the evading-employment employed. This made it a city of people – well, men, mostly – filling in time, moving unhurriedly from place to place. Pub to pub, usually, but also pub to office, office to pub, pub to other man's office to get back a loaned fiver or part thereof, other man's office to other man's pub, and finally, even, pub to home.

It was a city full of people on not particularly urgent errands. The pubs were its piazzas and oases. Each had a personality respected by all. They were distinct, the pubs, except that they were all arenas where the most elaborate rituals of personal, group, and community drinking were performed. I wish a few anthropologists had come among us while we were still like that, to record our ways. Because the middle classes – and the heroes of *Ulysses* are middle class – have stopped moving around drinking like that. They have stopped, at least, in the city center, which as far as I'm concerned is the city. Serious drinking on the part of talkative adults has retreated to cavernous lounge bars in postal districts whose numbers are in double figures. Or it has retreated to the dining table, where people drink wine. The very mention of dining tables shows how far we have come from *Ulysses*. People have homes, now, who used to only have places to sleep. The Joyce family was at the bottom of a long decline on the first Bloomsday. It had been downhill for a long time, for them and Dublin.

This Bloomsday, Dubliners, used to shabbiness and making do, find themselves caught in the glaring light of undeniable prosperity. Suddenly, for example, even people who haven't earned or inherited a penny have property, because they are being left valuable houses by their parents, whereas till the 1970s the great majority rented, as the Joyce family did. And when you have a stake in the suburbs, your heart is there. You want to get out of town. Why would you wander the streets all day?

Up to 20 years ago respectable if penniless schoolteacher/ writers like Stephen and cultivated gentlemen in the advertising business with delightful wives, like Leopold Bloom, might be found living in basements and cheap flats and bedsitters or in sets of rooms in old buildings. Those places are all offices and nightclubs now. Flats have become apartments, and they shelter playful ways of life, not self-consciously momentous ones, like Bloom's and Dedalus's. Young people loll on their futons in them and watch MTV. They're comfortable. They don't wander.

What would be in it for them? They don't know anyone except the people they know. Opportunity will not come their way at random on the streets as it did for Bloom and Stephen. Spending a whole day wandering has stopped seeming natural. The continuity of experience of a walking-Dublin-at-random day has been broken, though there are a few people – effectively single people – who still know the highways and byways of the city well enough, and know enough people to create personal Bloomsdays.

But most *flâneurs* now are merely students. Or they're visitors, cast out of their B&Bs after the big fried breakfast. The thing about Bloom and Stephen Dedalus is that they were serious, grown-up men, in the business of earning a living. It was incidental to what they felt were the real purposes of their lives that they were scholars of the city, constantly commentating on it, and themselves contributing to its complexity. Such men don't commit themselves to the bosom of the city of Dublin any more.

The people of *Dubliners* and *Ulysses* are as true to life as ever. Social change doesn't do away with lonely spinsters or bullying fathers or sensitive artists or edgy husbands. But the public world those people inhabited which Joyce depicted with naturalistic fidelity has become archaic. Drunkenness itself has changed. Central Dublin pubs were the real homes of men like Joyce's father, who was drunk on an average of 3.97 days a week, according to his son Stanislaus's statistics. But intellect was on display in pubs, too. You could be educated in a pub. Now, security men loom at the door to keep out the English stag parties, and there are lots of other places to be educated.

No one but Dubliners ever knew, of course, that *Ulysses* was a meticulous slice of life. To foreign readers, its setting was imaginary in every sense. But I myself witnessed that exact Dublin. It was alive until money killed it. Today we are confined to enclaves, but Bloom walked wide and deep, using all the city there was. We are provincials, compared to their urbanity.

The Irish Times, June 16, 1997

138

As for Love

You never hear anybody getting all excited when all four of those waiting on tables in a café are women, or all four of the cleaners late at night in the office are women. Oh, no. The usual woman-haters have been having such a field day with their sneers at the Presidential candidates that you'll forgive me if I say something serious that I mean. I look on the feminist project as the great project of my time on earth, and I'm happy that I've lived to see it have some success. A baby girl born in many parts of the world, including Ireland, has a much better chance today than she would ever have had before of using the whole of her unique self's potential during her life. There are many comic aspects to this Presidential campaign, and I hope to laugh as much as anybody over the next few weeks. But it will play its part in the liberation of women.

Women candidates in themselves are not ridiculous. The self-esteem of the candidates and what it says to other women is not ridiculous. But it is not all that significant either. Especially when the candidates were put in place, on the whole, by powerful men. When the day dawns when Ms. X, the leader of Fianna Fáil, and Ms. Y, the leader of the Labour Party, and so on decide who will contest the Presidency, that's the day I'll get excited.

Still, competent women in public life are the kind of thing that the heroines of Irishwomen's liberation – only 25 years ago – wanted to see. They had great faith in the idea that substituting women for men in existing institutions would transform the institutions. This turns out to be hardly ever the case. You can have substantial legislative change, as we have had, and you can open up opportunities to girls and women. And still women never get their hands on real power. Still they're out there on the margin. The culture in which women themselves and what are thought of as women's pre-occupations and women's values are sincerely believed to be self-evidently inferior to male values can remain quite untouched. That is why the most stunningly unexpected news in the contemporary story of women's liberation is not this Presidential election or any other, but the huge shift in values signaled by the intense mourning for Princess Diana.

The British people, and many others, came out and said that from their hearts they valued her. Her. That girlish woman, so often light and lost. Her admirers were not marshaled by anybody and did not come out as a mob. They came out individual by individual, couple by couple, family by family. They asserted their identification with what she had lived for. And what had she lived for? Why, her children, she said. And love. And these are what young women all over the planet live for and have always lived for. The mourning for her indicated, amazingly, that these values are now held by men, too.

Yet the girl on the bus reading a Mills & Boon novel, or the single mother on welfare defying society by having another child because she loves children and thinks she's a good mother – no living adults could have been more despised by the men who run the world. Such women aren't even thought of as having values, or as being capable of meaningful choice. They're thought of as outcrops of the organic world, the barely animate. Nobody cares how well they do the job of motherhood they undertake, and nobody cares how well they give and receive love.

Yet, unexpectedly, those nobodies found a laureate in Diana. Out of the peculiar accidents of her uncommon life emerged a doughty champion of the most common woman's destiny. Shop girls' values you could call them. If you were full of contempt, and slightly old-fashioned, that's what you might call the values that Princess Diana stood for. But you wouldn't say that in public. Not now. They agreed with what she thought of as the good and the right. They understood the terms in which she justified herself to herself. The answer she returned to the question "What is my life for?" was the same minimal but intensely powerful one that humble young women the world over would make, too, if anyone asked their opinion.

She believed that she had been a good mother. Most of the women on the planet have no other sphere to shine in: it's be a good mother or be good for nothing. She validated their work. "I'm as thick as a plank," she murmured in her graceful and self-deprecating way, because women aren't allowed to say that it takes intelligence and vigor to make a good mother, even if the world never recognizes those qualities. It is thought to be a small ambition, to be a good mother. But is it small? Is motherhood brainless? Are brains what the Hillary Clintons have, whereas all the Dianas are just wombs on legs? Or are there several kinds of brains, though the world hasn't begun to distinguish them?

As for love, it is the determinant of you and your children's destiny. Who you get, and who gets you, and what he's like, and how you get on, is the event of your life. (It is a huge event in his life, too, but he is not so dependent on it.) The precondition, almost, of loving your children is being loved yourself. Diana felt perfectly entitled to look for "love." She'd given the conventions her best try. She'd married for "love" and in good faith. If her husband didn't love her – the modern rule goes – she was, morally speaking, free to try James Hewitt or Dodi Fayed or anybody. It is somehow assumed that she wasn't looking for love, just for personal gratification. But you look for love to make you loving. Love is now about nurturing, not passion. A woman's version of love is in the ascendant.

I went to Kensington Palace Gardens the day before they took away the flowers, when the park, on a hot autumn day, had become an Indian scene, with gray dust covering the great swathes of bouquets and candles and balloons and night lights. As I began to read some of the many written outpourings, I felt that almost anything could be argued from them. It was necessary to be simple, to open my heart, almost. And, at its simplest, what the tributes to Diana had in common was naked, unashamed emotion. They were offered with pride to a woman who never did anything qualitatively different from what women have always done (even if her opportunities for caring – like hugging AIDS victims, or campaigning against landmines – were more dramatic than most).

I remember once writing about the Irish language and the surprise of finding it surviving in the most unexpected way, among completely unregarded people. Similarly, the advance feminization (if not feminism) has made in the culture of our time has been revealed, as a complete surprise, by the response to the tragic death of this young woman. Compared to that revelation, our sudden gender consciousness here in Ireland is a small thing. It is fun, and it is interesting. But it isn't, as the claiming of Diana's values, as the people's values is, a profoundly important event.

The Irish Times, September 22, 1997

Consequences of Disempowerment

Last week, at a moving and charming occasion, a group of women and girls from the Travelling community presented a booklet of pieces, written by themselves and others like themselves, to an enthusiastic audience in the training center where they'd learned to read and write. St. Basil's in Tallaght was bright for the special day, and the big table in the kitchen was covered with trays of wonderful savories and scones, hot out of the oven and heaped with jam and cream. The women who read things out had big hairstyles and jewelry, and high platform shoes on bare legs, and shy smiles. Seventeen children, one of them had. Fourteen, another. "What happens in the Travelling community if you can't have children?" "Oohhh," they shook their heads.

What happens to the 13-year-old Traveller girl in the news if she has an abortion? They shook their heads, grimly. What happens if she doesn't? They shook their heads, equally grimly. These splendid women have great power in the home, and they serve those homes with unremitting labor. But they had never said one word in public before last week's little event. They have absolutely zero social standing, and they have neither influence nor power.

Read what they write – the simple accounts of humiliations endured at the hairdresser, in the pub, in the shop, at school, in the launderette. Read their descriptions of living among rats and mud. Then ask yourself, how is that these wrongs persist? The answer is: we have power; they have none. All it would take to transform the Traveller problem is for settled Ireland to allow 3,000 units of accommodation to be built. Somewhere. Fat chance. The sudden lavishing of attention on one Traveller child because she is pregnant is enough to make you sick. Where were all of us when she was born herself into absolute disadvantage?

The Traveller women accept, in their world, a role for women that I wouldn't accept in mine. But there's far more of them than there are of me. Among millions, if not billions of people on the planet, things are organized between the sexes as they are by the Travellers. The men go out. The women stay in. They rear the children. They are estimated according to their fecundity. So I think, anyway. I know very little about being a Traveller.

One of the consequences of being powerless is that the powerful don't need or want to know about you. This applies to all the powerless. The faceless Egyptian gunmen who suddenly from out of nowhere jumped on the tourists and pumped bullets into them and slashed them with knives and violated the women even as they killed them – they seem figures of nightmare to us. There's no explanation for them. That's what we say.

Maybe the assassins were all mad. But perhaps they were driven mad. There were a few books for sale in Luxor airport, the once I was there. Most of them were about ancient Egypt, because that's what the tourists are interested in, looking blandly past all the real, living Egyptians to the time of the Pharaohs, the same as we look past the Travellers and weep for the dispossessed who are safely dead. But there was one book by an American who had spent several years living among the stone-poor peasantry almost exactly where last week's massacre happened – across the river from Luxor, on the way to the tourist sights.

If you read that book, and take in what it says about lives of incessant toil unchanged for a thousand years, about the violence and frustration and hopelessness that are the condition of fellahin life, you might begin to understand how the passion of fundamentalism is aroused. You might see why other people can become unreal to people who know themselves to be invisible in the large world, and despised within the small world around them, and who have been made savage by this knowledge.

The details that are beginning to emerge about the world some Irish Travellers inhabit are as exotic to most of us as if they'd come from the edge of the Sahara. They show what is universally true: powerlessness is bad for people. It stupefies them. The children's allowance book is handed over to a moneylender. A child is raped and beaten. A woman is raped lying beside her disabled husband. Children are living in a heap of mud, ostracized even by their own.

No outside writer, as far as I know, has ever spent four years with Irish Travellers. The settled community wants to see and hear as little as possible about Travellers. How much have the objections to an anonymous but altogether eloquent photo of the miserable caravans which were home to the raped child have to do with not wanting to know? How much privacy have we granted to people who live in the mud on the edge of the road without toilets, or water in any case, that suddenly privacy is so precious now?

The attention lavished on a Traveller family now is an item on someone else's agenda, not their own. The small children in the family of the raped child suddenly have color photos of foetuses to play with on their cold and muddy roadside. They were brought to the caravan by antiabortion activists. "Don't kill the baby," the small children have learnt they are to say to their pregnant sister. So someone who was with them last week told me. You have to laugh: Muslim fundamentalism is mad, and potentially bad, we assume. Christian fundamentalism, however, is just fine.

The raped 13-year-old is an emblem, not a person. Let her stand for all Travellers, all people at the bottom of all societies, all the multiply disempowered. The baby grows within her whether she likes it or not. And as for her self – her thoughts and feelings and sense of her own position – she is, as a consequence of the helplessness which allowed a rapist to overpower and violate her, more a site of battle, and a provider of opportunities for others, than a person.

If she gives the baby up for adoption it will be held against her in her community. If she doesn't, the baby has a feared and hated father. It will be held against her that she was raped in the first place. The Travelling culture is very strict on women. They must be virgins when they marry and they must have children. Youth Defence is a partner in this world view. They say she must have the baby.

Last week was a good time to be with the Travelling girls and women in Tallaght. They were born into nothing. They have addresses in fields. Yet there they are, doing voter education, driving lessons, numeracy. I met one who has a responsible job: she is housekeeper in the house of a woman she met in – guess what? – her meditation group.

There they were – smiling, but always reserved. If we knew more about them we'd fear them less. We'd see how richly they respond to even the smallest crumbs from our table. It is we, the powerful, who will not change. We set up the society in which this defenseless child was raped into motherhood. We did it, not them. We passed by their broken caravans with the unseeing eyes of tourists. And we will again tomorrow.

The Irish Times, November 24, 1997

Heading North

I don't know whether this new year is going to be happy for me, but it is certainly going to be new. As soon as I get accommodation I'm going to live in Northern Ireland. I'm going to go on writing the same kind of thing for this paper as I've done up to now, but from a slightly shifted perspective; at least, I assume the perspective will shift. I assume public affairs will look different from a spot on the island that isn't Dublin.

They'd look different if I were living a Michael-Viney-life in the countryside somewhere, so how much more when I'm actually in another jurisdiction and in the middle of cultures that for all their seeming familiarity are very different from mine? There isn't anywhere in the Republic, however hidden, that I wouldn't have some kind of grasp of after living there for a while. But the North? Although I've been there tens of times, I know almost nothing about it. I'm not at ease there. I've always felt a flush of relief recrossing the border.

I know why I'm making this move, even though I don't know how to organize it. Needless to say, I didn't think up the idea myself. I doubt if one person in 10,000, living a comfortable and busy life in southern Ireland, would dream of upping and moving North. But journalism is an interesting trade. Newspapers quickly fossilize if the people who direct them aren't exceptionally alert to change. So my editor talked to me about his sense that with the violence passing, and a new political deal in the United Kingdom, there's a process of fundamental change happening between both parts of the island. There is a demonstrable growth in contact, yet at the same time North and South are worlds still largely unknown to each other.

He talked about what this newspaper did when the Soviet Union was suddenly there to be revealed to the world in 1987–88. In a way, that was easy to handle, since there was no possible threat to ourselves from people so distant. What's more, readers were interested in everything about the former Soviet Union. But Northern Ireland is a greater challenge because it is so near: the people there live their lives much as we do, and many Southern people claim it bores them sick.

On the level of customs and instincts, values and mores, North and South are perhaps as lacking in understanding of each other as ourselves and the Russians. Yet Northerners are not exotic foreigners. Conor O'Clery can make getting a haircut in Moscow or dealing with the mosquitoes in Beijing interesting. But is anyone going to be interested in the detail of getting a haircut in Dungannon, or in what you do about a plague of flies in Kilkeel? My editor feels that there's an opportunity now (maybe, even, a responsibility) to bring the daily life of unremarkable people in the North into the understanding of the South. But how can that be done? And what possible difference can a few occasional words from one ordinary journalist make?

Yet where do you start changing the information available within a culture, or the tone of certain kinds of information, if not with small things? The extraordinary in Northern Ireland has been well served by journalism. But very few journalists that I can think of, from the South, have ever gone there just to be there. Not to find out anything in particular, or become expert on anything, but just to be: and by being there, understand a little how things are viewed from there, instead of reporting them as seen by a hit-and-run Southern visitor.

But what frightens me is that the effort might lead to nothing. I might move my clothes and books and the dog and the cat and make arrangements to live somewhere in Northern Ireland for – say – six months or a year. I'd go out to the shop in the morning for bread and it would be a Northern shop and Northern bread; I'd bring the dog for a Northern walk, I'd read the local papers, I'd watch local television; when I had to go to such-and-such a place I'd be interested in local weather, the local security situation. I'd get to know a few people – I hope – and they'd be Northern people. But what if that made no difference? What if I still instinctively read everything in a Southern way? What if I still assessed everything in terms of Southern interests? If I fail to get under at least the outer layer of a Northern skin, will the failure be just mine or will it be representative?

Where to live? I sit here with a map of Northern Ireland, and conjure up the little I know about it. I don't want to live anywhere very extreme. I don't want to live in an apartment in Belfast like some young person in financial services. I don't want to live in one of those mega-rich villages in North Down. I don't want to live in Derry, because the Republic would feel too close. I'd like to live somewhere beautiful, beside a lake, or in an orchard, or near the sea, or down an old lane. (Who wouldn't?) I'd like to try to be part of a community – a village, or a village within a town or a city. I obviously don't want to be shot in a pub. But I'd try anywhere. Would somebody out there like a nice discreet *Irish Times* journalist for a tenant?

There has always been great writing from the North about

war and politics. But maybe the story that really matters now is right there in the thoughts and feelings of dog-walkers and people buying bread. What does it mean, after all, to say "the ordinary people want peace"? What silent acceptance piled on silent acceptance have allowed Republican and Unionist leaders to go to talks?

But also, leaving aside local issues, will all-island things, things like Princess Di's death or the BSE scare, look different viewed from Northern Ireland outwards? These questions are too big, it may strike you, to be answered in a commentary on the ordinary experience of living an ordinary domestic life. Maybe I'll only be able to write about very simple things. Everything will interest me, anyway: the problem is going to be making it interesting for you. I may be going to get lost in a journalistic no-man's-land, but the decision is made. I'm looking for a home.

The Irish Times, January 5, 1998

On Sectarian Hatred

The overwhelming majority of Belfast people do quiet, respectable, mildly sociable things, like everybody. Everything looks absolutely normal: the bakery, the post office, the park where the old ladies walk their dogs. And then this curtain parts and a glimpse is caught: sometimes of the merely bizarre, sometimes of the blackly awful. A soldier with a rifle cocked walks backward out of the bushes of the park. You come home and your little street has been cordoned off because they're going to blow up a car which has been left there without number plates. Someone tells you that the bright-blue wheelie-bins in the next borough are a political statement: the council had to withdraw dark green ones.

You spell out a word to someone who's filling in a form and she looks up and smiles. "You said 'haitch' instead of 'aitch,'" she says. "You must be a Catholic." With that, you realize that she must be a Catholic or she wouldn't have risked the remark. And that's the oddest thing of all, the way the word "Catholic" rises from the general din. "Another Catholic has been shot … " "A Catholic taxi-driver escaped death earlier today when … " A newcomer from the South, almost completely unaware even of being a Catholic, is astonished, stunned even, trying to imagine a class of people called "Catholics." Some little thing inside you shifts.

I met a young Dublin man in Belfast. I had just been to Mass and I was telling him how surprised at myself I'd been – at how very much I'd wanted to go and how much it had meant to me. He said it was one of the main things he had noticed: none of his friends at UCD bothered about religion one way or another, but the same kind of young people in the North really cared. "Protestants too," he said, "they take it seriously too."

I wonder how seriously they take the murder of fellow-Christians. In their sermons and so on, what do Dr. Paisley and his like say, if anything, about the recent murders of Catholics? Murdering Catholics is something you'd expect a Christian pastor to have something to say about. The priest had something to say at Mass. I'm entitled to listen to him, even though I don't belong to his suffering community. The name "Catholic" is not the same on me as on the dead men. All the same, I was born into a Catholic culture and I would describe myself as a female Irish Catholic if I had to start describing myself from the beginning. (Belief is a separate matter.) I go to Mass in foreign cities for the comfort of its familiarity. I would look forward to going in Belfast, even if Catholics were not being murdered for being Catholics.

Of course, Belfast Catholics are not being murdered because of transubstantiation or the Virgin Mary or anything else to do with Catholicism as a collection of beliefs and practices. "Catholic" is shorthand for a politico-social entity and it is a word for "other." I don't know what vague image goes through the murderer's head when he and his friends bend over some table in some Loyalist drinking-club somewhere and say: "Isn't that guy in the paintspray shop a Taig?" and begin to plot a murder.

The image can't have any relation to the quiet and ordinary people coming along the Sunday-morning, seagull-invaded streets to the church at Clonard. They took their places in the old pews amid the profusion of Victorian frescoes and lamps and stained glass and statues and shrines the same as anywhere – the same as people who look like that have walked into churches like that and knelt and then settled themselves like that, all my life.

The difference was in what the priest said when he began his sermon. "What are we to do?" he asked. "What are we to do?"

He began with the slogan the murder gangs announced they were using. ACAT. All Catholics Are Targets. When there are demonic forces abroad, he said, using slogans like that, what are we to do? I found myself leaning forward to hear the answer, straining to hear what he might say, longing to be advised – "Oh tell us, Father, what are we to do?" Of course, the priest doesn't know anymore than anyone else what Catholics endangered by unbridled sectarian hatred are to do. The preceding week, three Catholics had been murdered for being Catholics. That happened to be Christian Unity Week.

He urged us not to lose faith in Christian unity and not to stop praying, and he told us with real joy that there was a Presbyterian in the congregation who had come to Clonard to share in our worship and lead us in the Prayers of the Faithful. Indeed, this was a striking thing, for me at least, but even if it is the long-term answer, it isn't the short-term one.

I understood from that movement of my body – leaning forward to be told what to do – one of the reasons why Northern Ireland is such a patriarchy. If you're just one of the common people, you're vulnerable. You need a protector. The virtues attributed to women – communality, collectivity, the construction of shared spaces in which the young can grow – are impossible to value when the argument comes out of the barrel of a gun. When a man going about his ordinary work can be shot for no gain to the murderer except, presumably, the adulation of his Catholic-hating peers, you need something stronger than him to stop him.

You need, in fact, the power of the state. You need the benign and impartial patriarchate called the police, but when you come out of Clonard monastery and walk up the Falls Road you are walking through a modern town where there is no police. The RUC is not assented to. Not at all. On the lamp-posts it says: "RUC OUT" – and this is passionately meant.

A completely noncontroversial group who happen to be from West Belfast had an office party in their workplace at Christmas and it was interrupted by a bomb scare. The RUC came to search the building. The group wouldn't let the RUC in. As far as they're concerned, the RUC will take note of who is in which office, where the entrances and exits are and so on, and will use the intelligence themselves to oppress or will pass it on to the very Loyalists who made the bomb threat. The group wants extra security after the bomb threat. They won't accept it from the RUC. They're trying to get government help to meet the cost of using a private security firm.

Meanwhile you go on with your quiet respectable life with your notion of the abnormal changed. It isn't the murder rate. That is "acceptable," as they say. It isn't even that it is Catholics who were murdered, exclusively, that particular week. It is that a Southerner has no experience of absolute alienation from the very bases of civic life. Can it be that Clondalkin during the worst riot is a society and Belfast at its most peaceful is not?

The Irish Times, February 2, 1998

The Vanishing Border

The turn in Ireland's fortunes is summed up for me by the border itself. I mean the actual, physical border where it is at its most formal, on the main road from Belfast to Dublin. I remember my father furtively turning away his face, while the car waited at the border there, because he didn't want anyone to see the distress it caused him to cross on to British territory.

And wait is what cars used to do, because there was a piece of paper called a triptych that drivers had to have and there were slow bureaucratic maneuvers to do with customs and excise. This was even before the Troubles. When they came, the customs situation was simplified because the customs hut was blown up or burnt down. But the road-crossing became increasingly difficult, what with military and paramilitary exactions.

You never knew how long you might have to wait in a queue before bumping over the ramp and through the army post where your number was scrutinized, at best, and where you might well be detained for hours, at worst. Well, that wasn't the worst. People were killed or were wounded on that stretch of road between Ravensdale Forest on the Dundalk side and Newry in the North. It was one of the most stained places.

You should see it now. Its no-man's-land used to be the epitome of the difficult, unlovely landscape of Ireland. It was a stretch of small, marshy fields, haphazardly marked out by gorse and briars and meandering ditches. History had left crumbling two-room cottages dotted all over it, hardly seeming to belong to the same era as the dun steel of the British Army surveillance posts up on the lumpy hills. Now, that old land, that somebody must once have hopelessly tried to farm, is being infilled at speed. New ramps lead to a fuel farm where the huge lorries that keep this First-World island in luxuries gather to exchange behemoth signals.

The hotel at the border gets bigger and bigger. There's a health and leisure center there. The petrol stations incorporate shops, coffee bars, information centers, telephones. It is true that the road itself is still narrow, but work has begun on widening and straightening it. The furze bushes topple before the JCBs. And new houses with PVC gables and patio extensions and dormer windows are rising over the ruins of the old cottages. This border is on the move into suburbia. Soon it will be one giant motorway service station.

The British Army is still there, but not so that a passing motorist would notice. The memory of its looming presence has faded. There used to be a big corrugated-iron encampment through which traffic going North and South was funneled. Then the encampment went, but the road was still diverted through its ghost. Now they've straightened out the road.

Up on the bank there are two little stone memorials, with flowers in front of them, to British soldiers who died here. Above those again there's a watching-post. But soon you will be passing by too quickly to notice. Last Thursday, in the tense hours leading up to polling day, soldiers had set up roadblocks along the routes to Belfast and were checking licenses. But that's abnormal, now.

All this will soon be a highway. Cars will whiz from Dublin to Belfast, and the sight and the feel and the memories awoken by particular places like Balbriggan and Drogheda and

Dundalk will be forgotten. The variations in the texture of Ireland will disappear. Belfast to Dublin will be like Antwerp to Lille or Stuttgart to Nancy. You'll speed along on top of the history. Lidice. Huesca. Poyntzpass. They'll all equally be names on signposts.

This is what is going to happen. No matter how long it takes. The money changers on the border will abandon the old farmhouses and cottages they so incongruously use as their offices, and red-brick villas with conservatories will rise on their sites. In five years' time – if Britain enters the EMU – there will just be euros, North and South. It will be more and more difficult for the smugglers along the half-forgotten border to make a living, much less enough to supply their families with the statutory 20-room haciendas with gold-plated bathrooms. In any case, their sons and daughters will all be studying fine art in Florence or aerospace design in Dresden on Euroschemes. They will not be interested in the ancestral skills of filling in the tag-holes in cows' ears with paste, or injecting badly made growth hormones into young pigs.

Maybe there'll be casino ships or floating liquor supermarkets moored in Carlingford Lough, staffed by Kurds and Moldovans. But probably there'll be nothing to tell that two sovereign jurisdictions abut along this line. It will be like going from Holland into Belgium. There is nothing to mark a border there. It takes a while to know you have left a country with such-and-such a name and arrived at a place with a different one. Eventually, of course, the cultural differences show up. In Ireland there will be much better bread and cakes in the bakeries in the north of the country, and the breads will have different names than in the southern part. Humor will be blacker in the North. Cars will be more washed. The South will be more sociable and much more ready to have fun. Little things.

Before, when I was growing up, Ireland was at peace, but it was the peace, North and South, of perfectly achieved repression. This new peace – the coming of which is now inevitable, let who will stand in its way – will be more life-giving. There will be space to move in it, because the big contentions that filled all the space between us will dissolve with each passing year back into the blur called the past.

The walking wounded from the Troubles will move among us. They won't even have each other to talk to: there are going to be different rates of recovery from the last 30 years in different parts of the island. On the Loyalist estates in Portadown or in the alienated villages of South Armagh, or in east Fermanagh where one community felt itself the object of a planned campaign of extinction, the inner life of the people will be very slow to change.

Change it will, however. The alder and willow scrub in the low fields in the pass between Dundalk and Newry will be covered over with the sheds and loading bays of an entrepôt. Where now Spanish broom has escaped from old gardens, satellite dishes will be planted in concrete yards behind security railings. The emotion that filled my father and so many others will wither in the neon glare. Whatever the passions of the new Ireland will be, they won't be the ones that once rose from the land itself. "What border?" visitors will say, glancing out from their speeding cars at nothing much.

The Irish Times, May 25, 1998

Prayer Is Political

I f anyone had predicted what I would miss the England vs. Argentina match for, I wouldn't have believed them. The thought that I might be in the company of a group praying at Drumcree – outside the church itself – and then walking along the bit of country road which leads to the Garvaghy Road, and then walking along the road through the housing estates, never crossed my mind.

What is involved at Drumcree is a complex sociopolitical situation bred in a conflict over economic resources and still expressive of the property and power relationships between the two communities in Northern Ireland. That is the unspoken analysis behind respectable commentary on Drumcree. If a few people want to go there to claim the place for the Lord, in the sure expectation that His grace will in some way enter the situation, that's their, so to speak, problem.

If respectable commentators ever have to mention such people – and they very much don't want to – they dismiss them. As sweet but dim. As dupes of a self-interested Christian patriarchy. As needing their heads examined. So sure is the contemporary commentating establishment that everything is about money and politics, that it never occurs to it to ask whether there might not be other forces at work which also have power.

The assumption is that the people on both sides of the conflict at Drumcree – and throughout Northern Ireland – are mere actors of the roles laid down for them by economic history. Yet that is not at all how people experience themselves and their lives. And like most people, the people of Northern Ireland have views on what is right and wrong, and would prefer to do right in their lives, if only because it feels more comfortable than the alternative. And in Northern Ireland, the prevailing concepts of right and wrong have been shaped by Christianity, often in the form of direct and vivid relationships with Christ hardly mediated by institutions.

This conscious Christianity of so many of its people has had an effect on the Northern Troubles. It has been on one level malign: the local streak of popular anti-Catholicism, made evident again in last week's burnings of churches, has been fomented to increase aggression. But Christianity has also had a benign influence. Something, after all, stopped the place from becoming one huge Drumcree. Something stopped it sliding towards being a Bosnia. People with faith, such as the people I was with at Drumcree, would see that something as being the work of the Lord.

I don't have that faith. But I certainly do think that the deep seriousness with which certain Christian imperatives are taken by faithful Christians – imperatives such as forgiving those who trespass against you as you hope to be forgiven yourself – has counted in preventing total civil war and will count in making the peace. Of course, it could hardly be more unfashionable to say so. But then, how good a guide is fashion? I have been listening, for instance, for a long time to socialist doctrines, such as that what needs to be done to combat sectarianism is for working people to come together, workplace by workplace, to bring about the overthrow of the unjust capitalist system which depends on sectarianism.

But socialist ideologies don't seem to have had much influence on the course of events in the North. There has been very little expression of cross-community workplace solidarity. Yet it is virile to talk about socialism. Whereas it is wet to say that the same workers would readily call themselves Christians. They would identify Christianity as the ideology of their choice. They would listen to what it says to them about sectarianism sooner than they would listen to any secular socialist thinker.

A week ago, I went to a Sunday evening forum in East Belfast run by "a group of ordinary people who have come to know Jesus Christ as Lord and Savior." Usually, I'd feel more skeptical than ever in the presence of ecstatic certainty. But the evening turned out to be a keen discussion between men and women from all kinds of religious and social backgrounds of a very difficult relationship – the relationship between individual conviction and the wide sociopolitical realities with which it must deal.

They talked about how close a view of good as righteousness is to an excessive attachment to "law and order." They talked about the difference between forgiveness and not bearing ill will – with particular reference to Gordon Wilson and to a woman at the forum whose husband was shot dead in front of her. They talked about the limits of the influence of personal sincerity. Even the jokes led to useful discussion. They talked, in no warm terms, about the media.

One of this Christian Fellowship Church's commitments is to unity. "It is difficult to see," its literature says, "how God can honor the Church in Ireland while its divisions, exposed to the whole world, bring such dishonor to His name and cause confusion among those who are genuinely seeking the truth … As a church we must seek to respond to the Holy Spirit's impulse to love our brother, be he Catholic or Protestant, Unionist or Republican … "

The woman whose husband had been murdered mentioned

that she was meeting some friends from Catholic and Baptist prayer groups during the week to walk and pray at Drumcree, as they had done last year. And so, having met up in Belfast and prayed, right there on the pavement, for God's blessing on the enterprise, a small group of us went down in the gray evening to Portadown.

Someone had painted this message on the road just down from Drumcree church: "F*** Off Dickheads Go Home." There were men and boys guarding the church. A car ostentatiously followed us when we were near the church. Yet it was just an ordinary evening on the outskirts of an ordinary town. Through the windows you could see the images of the England football match. An old man coming away from the chip shop gave my dog his sausage roll.

The houses off Garvaghy Road are no tenements: they are neat homes, with bedding plants out the front and elaborate curtains upstairs. Like anywhere. It even seemed ordinary that the people I had come with almost inaudibly talked to the Lord as they went along. Opposite the filling station, one of the Catholic men sang a Taizé hymn under his breath. It is nothing to those people to talk about miracles. It seemed to them that a miracle might happen, and violence be turned away from Drumcree.

It seemed to me that they and their like are miracle enough to be going on with. In the face of a history designed to make them hate each other, the vast majority of people in Northern Ireland do not hate each other. They believe that hatred is wrong. The personal is political. In the end, prayer is political.

The Irish Times, July 6, 1998

On Northern Ireland

The Omagh bomb draws a line under the long years of the Troubles. That's it, now. That's the end. But it is only the end of the big violence. Even if, as I firmly believe, there is never another bomb on Irish soil, small violences will go on day by day, because history has created in Northern Ireland a society full of grudge and disdain. It is a society that does not yet like itself enough to relax its sectarianism. And my impression is that it does not feel liked. A small but very bitter aspect of the Omagh atrocity is that it dirtied the name of Northern Ireland worldwide, even though the people of Northern Ireland had nothing at all to do with it, except to grieve for their dead.

Last January, when I was going to live in Belfast for a while, I talked about how I felt about that on the Gay Byrne radio program. Now, I have a date with the show to go back soon, to talk about how the little experiment went. And the first thing I've learnt is to respect the very wounded sensibilities of Northern people.

I hope to talk differently: not to assume that an underlying seriousness will be understood no matter how flippant the surface. I identify much more now than I did then with Northerners. I can hear now the smug received opinions in other people's voices when they talk about Northern Ireland. I can hear, here in the South, how at ease everyone is with remarks about the North full of a contempt and revulsion. We forget that the people who live there belong there, and have as much need to be proud of their own place as we have to be proud of ours.

An atrocity like Omagh is so huge that it dictates the terms in which Northern Ireland, or indeed the whole of Ireland, is thought of. It wipes out the ordinary, peaceful, daily experience of 99 percent of the people. That goes unreported. Yet there are many ways of experiencing Northern Ireland which are not only normal but delightful. Take the lovely coastline, all the way around the northeast from near Derry to near Larne. You could drive for miles and miles through villages and small towns and well-kept farmland and seaside resorts and upland bog and ravines full of woods and you'd see no sign of the Troubles because all this corner was hardly troubled at all.

If you got out where a beautiful sweep of hay meadows goes down to cliffs and little coves, opposite the bulk of Rathlin Island, you'd be in the village of Ballintoy. If you probed a little bit under the tourist surface you'd find that the area is half-Catholic, half-Protestant. It is in Ian Paisley's constituency. But apart from the odd bigoted individual, it is a contented place with a strong sense of community.

Talk to any old farmer there. "We turn the hay for each other and we always did," they'll say, Protestant or Catholic. A Catholic says: "There's a wee Orange band there but you'd never hear it play a bigoted tune. The whole village turns out to see it on the day." Similarly the whole village, in the shape of the community council which is chaired by a Protestant, is involved in a scheme to train the kids in Irish dancing. Everyone takes an interest in the hurling. People intermarry, go to each others' funerals, drink together. They don't need integrated education because they aren't fighting with each other. It is true that one of the village pubs was blown up some years ago, but that wasn't because of tension in the village, because there is no tension. The place is turning from farming to tourism. It has a little harbor and a little beach, an excellent hostel, two cafés in cottages with fine home-baking, pubs, and B&Bs.

Yet the fate of places like Ballintoy has been in the hands of people with bombs and guns. Its people have had to cope with the kind of ignorance that leads my own people, here in the South, continually to say to me, about living in the North: "You're very brave to go up there. I wouldn't do it." It is a very hard thing to belong to a decent and friendly, if two-sided, Northern community and know that you are judged by the worst that happens in your country, not the best. Particularly when the passions that have animated violent Republicanism and Loyalism are unfelt. The motivation for an atrocity like Omagh is actually much clearer in Dublin than in Ballintoy. "It is people from the cities who do all that," they say about the Troubles in Ballintoy.

But when you drive away from Ballintoy you reenter a more normal, edgy atmosphere. It would be untruthful to just concentrate on the Ballintoys. There are also places you can't go to if you have such-and-such a name. All along the east coast of County Down, for example, there are caravan parks covered with Loyalist graffiti. These are holiday places. They're for enjoying yourself in. But a Catholic couldn't venture into those places. That's true, and it is a measure of the North's abnormality. What is more, it is almost impossible to imagine the day when Catholics will be at ease there. And this is in spite of the fact that the last six months have been a time of the most inventive peacemaking. The caravan park is as much part of Northern reality as Ballintoy. Still, the sectarian basis of the Northern state is everywhere evident.

What can we do to help? Well, we can approach the subject

of Northern Ireland with more care and more humility. We can make a better effort to understand the place. I was privileged enough to be given the opportunity of learning on the ground. It has changed the clichés in my mind. But I know I only barely scraped the surface of the assignment. It was too big. Even if I were young, starting out as a journalist, I don't know that I would be subtle enough and patient enough to commit myself to Northern Ireland. Yet the fact is that Northern Ireland has been the most important thing about Ireland in my lifetime.

Living there for a while was a right thing to do. When I heard about the Omagh bomb I thought "Oh, poor Northern Ireland!" among the first things I thought. I didn't have that perspective before. And I take what I've learnt about Northern Ireland, good and bad, with me with thanks, now as I go on extended leave. I'm going to see if I can write something that is not an opinion column, something with people in it, and a plot.

All around me there is change. I'm going to try to change myself. It may not work; but the thing about trying is that at least you move on. You start again in a different place.

The Irish Times, August 31, 1998

2000-2008

On Teeth

Let us turn away, at the start of this wonderful New Year, from all the things that make us despair because we don't know what to do about them, to something we can do something about. Teeth. Anyone young enough to have never given their teeth a thought can stop reading, now. Anyone of the real old school, when Irish women got all their teeth extracted before marriage so as to assure the oul' fella that they'd never cost him a penny, can also stop reading.

They solved one problem that way, though I daresay they landed themselves with another. In my childhood, if you howled with a toothache for long enough to extract a grudged half-a-crown from your mother, you went into O'Connell Street and climbed the stairs over the Kylemore Dairy, and they put some rubber bondage stuff on your head and the gas machine panted like a dragon and next thing you woke up, *sans* tooth, in a daze. I have a feeling child dentistry is a bit more sophisticated now, though who can say that such experiences didn't toughen us all up and turn us into survivors?

New York dentists can and do advertise, and they more or less promise these days that you need never lose a tooth. You need never have teeth that stick out or teeth that recede. Above all, you need never have discolored teeth. The practice I go to in Manhattan is a sight to see every day at lunchtime. There is a long corridor with kind of open cells on each side, and in each cell, reclining and watching television during lunch hour, is a man or a woman with a tray attached to their face. They

171

have dropped in for an hour of bleaching. Bleached teeth are a near-necessity when it comes to looking like a winner. Anyway, Americans love that dazzling white. It is the end result of technology mastered, of effort chosen, of money expended, of actions taken. It is a visible sign of having acted in the face of destiny: not just lain down and fatalistically accepted the hand that nature dealt you.

I got teeth capped and veneered in that luxury place. Talk about coming full circle from O'Connell Street. The dentist phones a prescription for a few Valium to my local pharmacy and I take one or two an hour before my appointment and wobble in, full of goodwill. The assistant lies me down and wraps me in a soft, heated blanket. He asks me which of the CDs they keep for me, personally, I'd like to listen to today. I don't really know what happens next except that the dentist breeds canaries and we often talk about canaries and, indeed, he lent me a canary at one point but all it did was kick birdseed at my bed. I leave the office, feeling wonderful. There is some serious business with my Visa card on the way out but I barely notice.

Then I come home to Ireland, and every time I open my mouth someone starts staring at my new teeth. A too-candid friend said, "In the name of God, where'd you get the teeth?" Other people just laughed. See, I'd forgotten. You're not supposed to improve yourself, here. You're supposed to assert your gritty authenticity by a display of yellowing, crooked, brownish bits and pieces of teeth that have the amazing merit of being untouched by the twentieth century.

Well, believe me, my dears, you get no thanks in the United States of America for fidelity to natural decay. You see someone shudder about someone and say, "Ugh! Did you see those British teeth?" It is out of the question that you could have any career in the entertainment or commercial world, not to mention any erotic career, with the kind of teeth that walk around Dublin.

The philosophical difference is interesting. Does our attitude to our corporeal selves derive from our past as an oppressed and pauperized population, indifferent to our bodies except as they will be transfigured on the Last Day, and placing hope of perfection in the next world and not in this one? Does the American attitude have to do with Protestant self-respect in the here and now? With individualism? With materialism at its best? Is it all to do with money? What would English novelist Martin Amis (whose gnashers were well-publicized) have done if he'd had no money? What would I have done if I hadn't unexpectedly made the price of my bits of porcelain?

All I know is that the whole world is in the debt of the American drive to control what of our natural selves can be controlled. The contraceptive pill has been a boon to the human race of such importance that I'm convinced we have what is known as God to thank for it. The present Pope doesn't believe that, of course, but he might if he were a woman who'd had two children instead of twelve, and consequently had teeth in her head instead of pustulant gums.

Because I need hardly say that our deepest self-image, as well as our physical well-being, is connected with our teeth. We judge our time of life by our teeth. Some day I will give in and admit that I am old and that I must retire from the human race and share my bed with mongrels and cats. When I do, it will be because there's nothing more I can do about my teeth.

The Irish Times Magazine, January 6, 2001

A Cultural Patriot

When I read last week that the great cultural patriot Dónall Ó Móráin had died, I was unexpectedly reminded of a few remarks made to me recently by a cool, wealthy young Irishman who owns two state-of-the-art Irish club/pub/cafés in a very fashionable part of New York. They're doing fantastic business, his places. There's live Irish music and literary celebrations and various kinds of performance, and these bring in the most hip of the Irish kids – the Wall Street ones, and the ones in second-generation Internet commerce. And where the young Irish go, the other young people follow.

There's no question about it these days, the Irish are considered winners, out on their own when it comes to enjoying themselves. They're different from the other English-speaking kids because they have, and they're proud to have, a culture of their own. They are variously committed to, but all know they have access to, two literary traditions; an ancient and still vital musical tradition; both an old and a nineteenth-century dance tradition; a language, Irish, which is still spoken and written in, and increasingly and unselfconsciously quoted, referred to, and used, for example, in contemporary song. They know that these things are some of the visible signs of the distinctiveness called "being Irish," which men and women have fought and willingly died for, which is about as far as commitment can go. There are a great many other factors which go to make up the confidence of the successful young Irish. But their cultural specialness is fundamental to their pride.

When Dónall Ó Móráin set up Gael Linn I was a child at school in a typical convent in a typical small town. The nuns who (like a great many people at the time, I now see) were involved in defining an ideal of the respectable and the genteel looked to nowhere but England. They entertained no native model of excellence, and they respected nothing that came from themselves or anyone they knew. They bowed and scraped, of course, to rich people, to professional men, such as doctors; and to bishops and heads of orders and priests in a descending order of importance down to curates. But that doesn't mean that they respected them. They respected England. They sat every girl in the school down in the big hall to listen to the coronation of the Queen of England on the radio. "Girls," the music nun said to us with such reverence in her voice that I can hear her still, "always remember that 'God Save the Queen' is the most noble melody ever written in eight bars." It was intimated to us that the Irish language was a horrible obstacle put in our way by the Department of Education. Irish, if it belonged anywhere, was for "the Tech" at the other end of the town, where ungenteel men who smelled of whiskey taught the town's losers metalwork before they went to England.

I used to see Dónall Ó Móráin having his lunch in that little survival of 1970s Dublin, Alfredo's Restaurant in Lincoln Row. Everything about the place had once been innovative but had long been culturally naturalized. Scampi. A decor of Chianti bottles. Alfredo's attracted the most loyal of regular customers – most of them, like the ambience, no longer young. And some of those regulars had pasts more important than the passerby would ever guess from the modest place. Dónall Ó Móráin never made any money and was never what you'd

call famous. But he was one of the middle generation of patriots (now, to our impoverishment, dying off) who, by using every
stratagem, in the book and out of it, kept the Irish language alive
in urban Ireland, and kept traditional music alive, and kept Irish-
language publishing and journalism alive when they were as near
death as in the town where I went to the snobby convent.

Lots of ventures failed. But how movingly those Gael Linn
people tried, in meager and frightened times, to make even the
maddest ideas work! Someone used to call to the door of our
house collecting money for the Gael Linn pools; my mother
won a sum once. Children who hadn't otherwise a chance of
getting to the Gaeltacht had a chance through Gael Linn schol-
arships. Recordings of Irish music, now so commonplace,
were thrillingly new and precious when they were issued by
Gael Linn. Bingo was played in Irish by hundreds of oul' ones
who could hardly say "*slán*." Newsreels, oysters, fish farming
... Ó Móráin's Gael Linn tried everything. And it had to, because the drive towards creating an Irish bourgeoisie (as in my
nuns), where anti-Irishness would be the very badge of
respectability, was very strong – and was greatly strengthened
by the association of patriotism and cultural nationalism with
the IRA, after 1970.

One big thing. Had Dónall Ó Móráin emigrated, or suc-
cumbed to the temptation of a life at the Irish Bar, I don't know
who could have risen to certain national moments as he did. In
the 1970s, when Conor Cruise O'Brien was the Minister for
Post and Telegraphs, and had responsibility for broadcasting, he
put forward the idea of rebroadcasting BBC 2 television to the
Republic instead of having an RTÉ 2. This was in the interest
of our understanding the British point of view on things better than we did (I presume; O'Brien doesn't mention the

episode in his autobiography). But Dónall Ó Móráin and Séan Mac Réamoinn are two of the people who crisscrossed the country arguing the case for what I'll call – I don't suppose they did – a more self-respecting view of Irish broadcasting. And in the end, as I understand it, a national opinion poll found the minister's idea rejected by two to one. It is out of the question that such a proposal would be met with anything but incredulous laughter today. That is the legacy, not just of that one campaign of Dónall Ó Móráin's, but of what he stood for and worked for all his life. I hope he knew before he died that what he did is remembered, and with a rare and profound gratitude.

The Irish Times Magazine, January 20, 2001

Landscape Transformed

There are tattered bits of planning application notices stuck to plywood boards in every second field in rural Ireland. Several of them are nailed to poles along the lane that I look on as home myself. I couldn't have hoped that my corner would be left untouched. When I heard a bulldozer on Christmas Eve I tried to think positively – to be grateful for the nearly nine years I've had, during which only two new houses went up and only one of those slap-bang in front of me. I said to myself that other people deserve the benefit of this place as much as I do. I said everything positive I could think of to myself. But I lament, and it is not just personal. I'm watching the transformation of one Irish townland from an ancient agricultural settlement into a middle-class suburb.

The fact is that the small farming that shaped this place is finished. And there's no way of keeping a farm landscape meaningful without farming. My area is still held in thrall by the mud-covered, agile little cattle who are the living beings most at home on this island and who I can imagine surviving here after humans are gone. But eventually we may have to conceive of an Ireland without cattle. What will become of all the Irish men who have few skills or little conversation outside the same beasts?

There are slatted sheds and calves and slurry-spreaders and chewed-up lanes, fields and burst silage bales and all that all around where I live, and mavericks are forever smashing through hedges and getting out on the road, providing a primitive kind of entertainment. But those tools to making a living are not going to last. There isn't a living to be made from cattle and REPS (Rural Environmental Protection Scheme) subsidies. A hard worker in my part of the west could probably make a living for one person from 30 acres. But you can get more than what you'd earn in one year of extremely hard work for one small house site. The farmers around here – where planning permission can be got – may have small incomes, but they're sitting on fortunes. On the other hand, a lot of small farmers don't want to sell land. Land and its management is their heritage and their culture.

When a field has gone for a bungalow with dormer windows (and seven or eight bedrooms, to set the place up for doing Bed & Breakfast), it is gone for ever. Suddenly the field's ancient furniture isn't relevant: the stone walls, the stiles and steps, the windbreaks for animals. Most of the new walls are breeze-block. I think there's a Clare County Council guideline about facing breeze-block walls in stone, but if there is, it certainly isn't enforced around my place. But then, it is impossible to guess from the new housing around what the planners want West Clare to look like. The only policy that would have made a difference to the visual aspect of this area was never even tried: that is, that the refurbishment of existing houses and cottages would be vigorously preferred to new houses. Everyone goes for a new house, and they all seem to be off the same plan. A planner's plan: it is inconceivable that absolutely everyone, for miles around, wanted dormer windows.

There is a community around here, of course. The old families have known each other forever. There's a further community of people who are not from this exact townland but are in the know about it. Anywhere in Ireland, the local garda and doctor and estate agent and teacher and solicitor and hardware merchant and county councillor and TD and property developer, roughly speaking, know who owns what land, what problems they have, what their characters are like, whether they'll sell, to whom they'll sell, how much money will be upfront and how much hidden, what effect the sale will have on the seller's life, etc., etc.

People like me don't and can't belong to either of these communities, even if, like me, they've been coming to the area for 25 years. In fact, if I were ever shown the inside track, I'd view the invitation with the greatest suspicion. There is one last generation of small farmers still with us. They go into Saturday-evening Mass on their tractors and they might take a pint afterwards and the supermarket gets their messages ready in a cardboard box and they go to the mart and they can play traditional instruments – many of them, this being Clare. If they were at a wedding, they might dance the figure of a set for fun. They believe in God and Mary and the GAA and funnily enough, around here, Fine Gael. Their nephews and nieces aren't going to turn into those old men. The courteous and witty and highly individual personalities that were somehow nurtured in the hard world of small farming are dying out.

Large parts of the country are still shaped to the old men's ways. The new communities haven't formed yet. Will they ever? We incomers have no task in common in what was a farming landscape, and nothing else to share. And this period will leave wounds. The etiquette and ethics involved in the changeover from land-for-farming to land-for-houses are by no means agreed upon. I myself do not approve of my own nostalgia for a way of life that was so hard on men, women, and children and that led to so much self-destructiveness.

Maybe it will be a healthier Ireland when it is, effectively, a series of housing estates interspersed with towns. The feel of a landscape, however, shaped to a communal purpose by long experience, will be gone.

The Irish Times Magazine, February 17, 2001

Different for Girls

I noticed recently, in an interview with a woman who works in the arts, that she counted it in her career that she was from the same village as poet Brendan Kennelly, because when she was a child, that fact had raised her awareness of the arts. Role models really do matter. How is it, then, that the mothers and fathers of girl children don't raise a peep of protest at the limitations imposed on girls' dreams by the pervasive, indolent sexism of Irish life? How come they accept every insult to their daughters as if that's just the way it is?

Take the following random examples from a recent week: new ambassadors. Eleven new ambassadors, we're funding. I happened to notice that all 11 were men. And I thought, doesn't this government have a barefaced nerve, all the same? Wouldn't you think they'd have snuck one woman in there just to take the bare look off themselves, the way, say, *Questions and Answers* goes to the trouble of doing? If there were no women applicants for the posts, why didn't the minister or the Taoiseach or the appointments board or somebody say so, and pretend to regret the fact? If there were women applicants but they were all unworthy, why not say that the government hopes that the gender balance will improve over time? And if the men were appointed without application, then I want to know why. My taxes and yours pay for our diplomats abroad – people, who, incidentally, are meant to be representative, to reflect the variety of the people of Ireland. Some variety!

The present Taoiseach did once make all the usual noises about aiming for a tiny improvement in the gender ratio when it comes to publicly paid-for appointments, but nothing will come of that rhetoric until people at large – mothers and fathers – ask for a level playing field for girl children, so that no one dare come out with a list of 11 plum appointments, in no way dependant on physical strength, publicly paid for by women and men, representing Ireland, and all going to men.

I was sorry to find myself noticing the gender ratio in another news item. A list of the lucky recipients of awards for scientific research, it was, a few weeks ago. There were umpteen of them, and there were little pictures on the page of all these interesting-looking men who are going to pursue interesting research projects in our universities. A great life, by the way, research. A true privilege, in this difficult world, to be paid to do it. I was actually reading the piece wondering where UCD had got to, because I noticed it didn't figure. Then I'm afraid I noticed that half the human race didn't figure either. Not a woman to hand. I'm driven to the conclusion that they're an inferior type of being, women. In scientific research circles anyway. The twenty-first century, this is, and not one of you sisters out there is worthy of getting a nice grant? Shame on you.

I have no interest in becoming a gender-counting obsessive, I can assure you. But look at the Dublin Theatre Festival. Women don't figure much in classic drama, of course. But the three new short plays are also by men: two men are doing a thing on Kurt Weill; *Woyzeck* will be done by a man with music by a man; there are two correctly named one-man shows; the invited director is a man – oh, this is as boring for me as for you. Anyway, that's not what I'm talking about at all.

What caught my eye was the "pre-performance talks and panel discussions" on the work of Tom Murphy – a man whose plays I go to, often with women. Our money is good enough to get us in, and we understand the words and all, and we talk among ourselves about them afterwards. The plays and, by the way, his novel, often contemplate womanliness as well as masculinity, not to mention their interaction. I imagine, for example, that *Bailegangaire* would not have been written in an all-male world.

But the speakers mentioned – Colm Tóibín, Dominic Drumgoole, Fintan O'Toole, Tom Kilroy, Jim Nolan, Conor McPherson, and John Waters – while all of them most interestingly involved in writing and performing and talking, do not cover the entire range of genders. I suppose there wasn't an actress capable of joining them? No? Would someone such as, say, Rosaleen Linehan, one of the most intelligent women in Ireland, have had nothing to say? What about women directors? How do they feel about doing Murphy? None of them with anything to say? Pity.

By coincidence, after I'd done a bit of expostulating about this around the town, I myself was asked to write a note for the Tom Murphy program. But if I or any other woman wasn't good enough to be announced to the press with the A-team listed above, how do you think we feel about being asked to do the sandwiches?

I don't want to be stuck with this sort of sensitivity. It upsets me – and for nothing, because if things are good enough for all you parents of girls, then of course they have to be good enough for me. But I genuinely don't understand it. I don't know any father who doesn't love his daughters as deeply as he loves his sons. But when it comes to gatekeeping –

choosing ambassadors, conferring research grants, picking discussion panels, and anything else with status that you care to mention – the same good fathers block women out. And they neither feel, nor say, they're sorry.

The Irish Times Magazine, September 1, 2001

A Love Letter to Manhattan

On Saturday, if you live near Houston Street in the Village, you might as well not try to sleep. Until near dawn the kids drive along the street, east to west, west to east, whooping and hollering and beeping their car horns. They're partying, for no better reason than they are where they are. In Fun City.

I know, because I spent the past three winters in various rented rooms in lower Manhattan, writing my first novel, and then trying to think of a second. Writers can live anywhere, but I chose there as the place to attempt a late career change, because New York is a city created by the optimism of generations of immigrants, and I hoped the optimism would rub off on me. I chose it because, to my mind, it was more than fun – it was a joyous place, the Paris of our time, stylish, frivolous, affordable, and wonderfully hospitable to dreams. It is the one place I know where personal transformation is the general goal and applies to everyone of any age and gender and class, from the boy from a dusty crossroads in Guatemala who delivers the groceries, to the face-lifted and tummy-tucked women who cruise Tiffany's efficiently while their husbands wait at the bar of the Harvard Club. Manhattan is not monumental and self-important, like Washington, and it doesn't manufacture, like Chicago, and it isn't intellectual, like Boston. Its industries are the light ones – publishing, fashion, advertising. It knows it is light, and it sends its own light New Yorkness up.

Twice when I was there the place indulged itself in mass hysteria: when first a hurricane and then a blizzard were forecast. It is true that the pedlar streets around Chinatown were weirdly empty of fake-Prada handbag sellers for a day, and the sky went black, and a hot wind whipped along buildings I had never seen barricaded before. But that was as bad as the hurricane got. Afterward, there wasn't the slightest embarrassment at the over-reaction to the weather warnings, or any apology. Manhattan had been playing a game called frightening itself. It never seriously believed the Apocalypse was coming. But now, butterfly Manhattan is pinned under the nets of vicious forces, though viciousness is wholly alien to its spirit.

The island narrows to the width of three fields, down where the Trade Center towers stood. It has a unique atmosphere, that district, where you can almost touch one side of the city from the other, and there are glimpses of vistas as watery as Venice, and the stocky buildings are lightened by brisk, marine breezes full of sparkle and light. At night its narrow streets are taken over by dimly gleaming seabirds who come down to scavenge the fast-food wrappers the office workers leave behind when they pour out of their offices and hurry home. The beginnings of the city are here, at what was once the tip of a scrub-covered peninsula, where the slow sheets of water from the East River and the Hudson River succumb to the bright expanse of the great harbor. I lived down there for a while: a block from the ferry to Ellis Island in one direction, two blocks from the World Trade Center in the other. I was lent a place high up in an ornate building which was once offices and is now apartments for singles working across the way in Wall Street – a short, curved street that follows the line of the log wall the first European settlers put up to defend their settlement against the people they had dispossessed.

Their native enemies slipped up and down along the trail they'd made in the wilderness – a trail that the Dutch settlers called *Burgh Weg*, which became the word, Broadway. On the floor above me, young men and women in expensive sports gear toiled on the treadmills in the gym, where clerks in celluloid collars once stood at their ledgers.

Investors were trying to make the financial district into a neighborhood, but it hadn't really caught on. The place lost all its urbanity in the evenings. The bars and cafés closed when the offices did. Even the sex club closed early. Chauffeurs dozed in their limos outside expensive drinking clubs waiting for the last broker or banker to come out, wiping his lips, to be driven to the suburbs. The streets were empty and very quiet. But because the island is so narrow at that point and so many subway lines enter Manhattan there, just below the surface, the moaning and clanking of the trains filled the air all night long. It was as if huge demons were trapped down there, under the earth on which the skyscrapers stood.

There was a notice in the bookshop at the foot of the World Trade Center building one day – a man who'd written a book on the birds of Manhattan would lead a bird-watching tour from there, all welcome. The ten or so of us who showed up were a typically motley, eccentric, socially inexplicable group of New Yorkers. One old man had a sola topi on, and some of the others wore sturdy shoes and carried binoculars, though we were following the walkways and piazzas directly under the towers, and looking for our birds in the plantings in pebble-dash troughs and dank beds that divided the expanses of concrete. Several of the bird-watchers had water bottles fixed to their belts, though I don't suppose we were ever more than a hundred yards from refreshments. But the repartee was loud and funny, and as we mooched along towards Battery Park we actually did see more than a dozen different kinds of bird pecking at the thin grass, or going about their bird lives under the municipal laurel bushes, behind the roller skaters and cyclists and baby buggies and the courting couples entwined on graffiti-covered benches.

"What bird," someone asked, "is the official bird of New York?"

No one was sure.

"It should be the bluebird," a woman said dreamily, "because the bluebird is the bird of happiness."

"Don't you believe it, honey," a woman in full makeup, wearing a long lace dress and a huge backpack, said. "No one ever came to this city to be happy."

But they did. Where we were walking – a stone's throw from where bloodstained dereliction now begins – is tear-stained land, but the tears were tears of joy. That's where the immigrant ships tied up, before there were entry controls. That's where the blacks and the Irish fought it out for waterfront jobs – tough jobs, but better than anything they could have had, ever, where they came from. Europeans escaped the limitations they had been born into, when they walked down the gangways and out into the pullulating, raucous, no-holds-barred city. I went to Manhattan for that – to be an immigrant. I wanted to try something new in a city that was created by wave upon wave of adventurers trying something new. I lived most of the time in a bedsitter on 3rd Street. But I used to go back to the bottom of the island because I loved the way you can see the layers of experience the city is composed of down there. I might have been in the vicinity of the World Trade Center towers to use the central

189

post office beside them, or to mooch around Century 21, the greatest designer discount store in the world. There were always Irish voices in there, calling to each other about La Perla bras in an unfortunate red, or Moschino jeans for half-nothing but only in dwarf or giant sizes. Walking home from south to north I would be following the immigrant trail again, towards a new life, a welcomed future.

I have two sets of friends who live very near where the towers were – lived, they've been evacuated now. On the night of the last presidential election there was a party and the windows were open onto Chambers Street because our hostess is English, so smoking was allowed, and our cheers and laughter must have disturbed the druggies and the homeless having a sit-up sleep in the all-night burger bars. At some point, the exhausted presenter on one channel announced that the whole thing was a mess and it might be days before we knew who had won the presidency.

"OK – I'm going home," I said, finishing off my wine. "I'm happy, and I want to stay that way." And I walked home, humming.

I set my course so as to keep in view the Chrysler building, ahead of me in Midtown, because its scalloped roof is so beautiful. Just as I always kept the WTC towers in view when I walked south. Often, the clouds were lower than the top floors. At evening time, especially; the ranks of lights high up in the dark, behind moving shreds of cloud, were lovely, glimmering, silver things. And there was a pink-neon furled umbrella on the facade of the second tower. It was vaguely amusing. I have friends who have a newsstand/café on Hudson Street. The husband strolled out his door and looked up after he heard the first bang. He is a gentle man, a music lover, a man who agreed that the two of us could leave the Met after just one act of *Tristan and Isolde* because it was so overwhelmingly moving. He stood on the pavement outside his building, and witnessed his fellow human beings as they jumped to their deaths. They jumped past the pink umbrella. When will he be whole again? When will my friend who works in J.P. Morgan in Wall Street be untroubled again? She can't ever go back there, she says: the smell of death got into her that day. My friends in publishing are mainly Jewish. How long will the U.S. protect Israel, they must be asking themselves, if this is the price it is asked to pay? And is there anywhere at all in the world they can be unafraid? My best friend asked me a few months ago whether I thought it was safe for her to go to the Jerusalem Book Fair. Now, Jerusalem is everywhere that beautiful, formerly sanguine, young woman walks.

I made some money from my novel, and with it I arranged for semipermanent access to the innocent high spirits of Manhattan. For the price of a house in, say, Crumlin, I put a deposit on a space in a warehouse just beside the Holland Tunnel. The idea was that by next year, maybe, the warehouse would be turned into apartments. Whenever I thought of the winter months I might be going to spend there, I imagined walking the lively streets and hurrying in from the sharp, blue-skied cold to talkative meals in restaurants, and then the payoff – being able to do hard work because of being so carefree. Now, I can imagine nothing.

My plan, of course, doesn't matter at all in itself. But I mention it because it matters that the gift of hope, which has been Manhattan's gift to millions throughout its existence, and was its gift to me, has been snatched from its grasp. It matters that the spectrum of intangible things I valued Manhattan for is the very spectrum that has disappeared. The myth that Manhattan had of itself has been murdered. Its harmless obsessions with fashion and celebrity and being where it's at have been massacred along with everything else. A society that never imagined itself being anything but envied – that could not imagine being hated – must now find dark and uncertain ways of being.

I take it that there is dust everywhere on the building I was going to have my space in. There must be dust all over lower Manhattan. Consider what must be in that dust, since hardly any whole bodies have been found. If ever I look down at a smudge on my hand there, I'll know what I'm looking at. But – leave Manhattan? Turn away from it? Would you turn away from a beloved woman because she had been brutally raped? Wouldn't the love still be there, though now it accommodates pain and division and sadness? I'm an old hand – I knew that here we have no abiding city. I knew that there are really no Fun Cities. But it is sorrow of a new kind, for those who loved Manhattan's sassy self-belief the way one would love it in a child, to see that suffering is turning the child, even as one looks on, into a wary adult.

The Irish Times Magazine, September 22, 2001

A World of Indifference

One of the most suggestive statistics I ever heard was this – that when researchers went back to ask citizens why they had not voted in a U.S. presidential election, a significant proportion said they didn't know an election was on. Although the election absolutely dominated television, these hundreds of thousands of people hadn't allowed it into their heads. They hadn't bothered listening to people talking on television. They heard news bulletins but they didn't attend to their content. They switched off when workmates brought up the subject of the election. They never gave the thing a thought. They must have been so sunk in their personal lives that the whole public world passed them by.

You may think this is an unimaginable state of affairs. But it exactly describes how comfortable citizens of the First World such as ourselves relate to reports of injustice in the world as a whole. None of us really pays attention to the overall picture of what humankind has made so far of its stay on planet earth.

This reality is brought home by a certain kind of rhetorical question I'm now sick of. It goes: how come the world sat back complacently and allowed a massacre such as, say, Sabra and Chatila or, say, Rwanda to proceed, but jumped into action when a fraction of the number of Rwandan dead was massacred in the U.S.? As if the speaker had been worrying about Rwanda all along.

How come the world was quite content until September 11

to allow the men of Afghanistan to trash their country to the point where the Taliban were welcome, and then to allow the Taliban in the absence of any other enemy to assert their maleness by defining girls and women as dangerous animals, but not after September 11? As if the Taliban's attitude to women had all the while been weighing on the questioner's mind.

But let me join in — how come the world was indifferent to the plight of the refugees from Afghan virility who have been living wretchedly or dying in camps in Pakistan for the past 15 years? How come the spotlight rests on Afghanistan and not on the endemic horrors of the world — on little girls with painted faces kept in wooden cots in Lahore for the excitement of men; prostitutes chained to the beds in their workplaces in Thailand; small children breaking stones in quarries everywhere; half-starved children passively enduring their fate in North Korea; half-starved men picking over garbage dumps; laboring men holding themselves out for hire on wintry streets before dawn; simple-minded men waiting on death rows in U.S. jails; pauper alcoholics howling for vodka in the hell-hole towns of Siberia; miners who toil like beasts in Bolivia, chewing narcotic leaves against the pains of hunger; the homeless, muttering under their blankets in the porches of churches in Washington, D.C. ...

Do you think I couldn't go on?

All these "how come?" questions are designed to make us feel bad by pointing up the inconsistencies we live with, and the narrow limits of our compassion, and our self-interestedness. But that's all they do, apart from making the people who ask them feel morally superior.

In ordinary life, no one behaves much better for being made to feel guilty. "How can I feel for the whole world?" people mutter to themselves. How can I even know enough to know whose side to be on? And even if I had all the information and all the moral courage and all the resources I wish I had, what good is one person against all the evil out there? The problems of the planet are simply too big to be tackled.

And they're right. There is no effective way of feeling for the world. And it is a dreadful place, infinitely worse than we bother to recognize. We obscure, in a cloud of diversionary "how comes?" the simple truth that what humans have made of this planet is horrible. Although the events of September 11 and the craziness of what has been happening since may have lifted a corner of the fog we habitually stumble about in. The world is savagely unjust, and the only respite from injustice is won by force.

States have no goodness. They suppress these villains here and promote those villains there, with no aim but self-aggrandizement. They foster testosterone madness, inside and outside armies. Whole cultures, including Hollywood, glorify violence. War wonderfully distracts from injustice. We look at the photos of suffering children – huge eyes in bony heads drooping from little, frail bodies that will pass through life without ever knowing what it is like to feel full. And we watch the billion-pound missiles fall. And we pass on.

There seem to me three things we can do in this situation. We can support the United Nations in every possible way. If we get the chance to provide soldiers to "peacekeep," or indeed to fight, people demonstrably as foul to each other as to their enemies, we should grasp it, and forget the old guff about the moral example of our Irish neutrality. And the last one is to be as good as we can in our own lives. We have to believe that in spite of what humankind does, individuals can – inter-mittently – achieve personal goodness.

Though God knows there are times when it is hard to muster up enough self-approval to get out of bed.

The Irish Times Magazine, January 5, 2002

Whose Life Is It?

Imagine wanting to die. Everywhere and always we see the most powerful and inextinguishable attachment to life, even after years chained to a radiator in Beirut, even deaf and blind and palsied, even after years of loneliness, abandoned on an island, even reduced to a suffering human husk.

Every so often the plight of some poor person who actually wants to die crosses the public consciousness and I, for one, turn away from contemplating it. It seems to me worse than any torture I have ever tried to imagine – to long to escape from the body to peace, and to be prevented by the same body from doing that. But our population is aging. And surely in a more elderly Ireland certain themes will begin to arise, as power and influence and articulacy in public life are wielded by people who find themselves old. Some day soon there will be an argument about being allowed to kill yourself or get yourself killed that will have more of an air of personal intensity than the "forced feeding" case heard in the Supreme Court in 1995.

What has always impressed me is the seriousness – the full mind – with which people ask for euthanasia. They could nearly always arrange to die in private, but the cases they bring to court assert that they want to die as members in good standing, so to speak, of the human community. It is as if the people who want assisted death want us to know that they, more than anyone, recognize the gravity of what they want to do; they want us to give our blessing, they want us to see them off.

197

In this, euthanasia couldn't be less like abortion, even though, for obvious reasons, the two are often lumped in together. The babies Irish women do not carry to term are not an absence, except on a poetic level. Whatever else you may think about abortion, the life it ends does not have the same social resonance as the life euthanasia ends. There are no friends and neighbors. There is no history. The unborn child has not known the challenges of living and having flexed mind and body and spirit to meet them. The person trapped in some awful disease may be again, toward the end of their lives, as incapable of autonomous physical action as they were before they were born. But the two phases are in every other respect incomparable.

The death-seeker has a mind left – that's the seat of the torture. I saw a doctor who works in this area argue recently that people who have to all intents and purposes lost their bodies should not despair and seek to die. They should look to the likes of Stephen Hawking, the brilliant mathematician, and make their brains the place where they express their personality and their joy in being alive. That's a tough one, isn't it? The values of our time consign a huge class of people to a tabloid culture – Pamela Anderson and the Premiership and meeting your mates to get legless. As such, there's something a bit repellent about a middle-class doctor offering a blue-collar kid the consolations of the intellect.

But it is worth thinking about. You never do know how your self will be changed by circumstances. I've known a young couple who seemed altogether shallow rise into sustained, awe-inspiring heroism when their two children turned out to have a rare disease that requires constant care. I've seen people near suicide from insoluble money worries get money out of the blue.

But what is so terrible about most of the euthanasia cases I've heard of is that it really would not be reasonable to say there are no permanent traps, and a year from now today's impossibilities may well be possible. Death does have to come, in the end, but it is hard to see how to make this a cheerful fact for someone who wants to die and who believes that this time next year they won't even be able to indicate that they want to die.

It must be the most awful situation in the world, to see someone signaling you with their eyes that they want you to add the lethal bit to that dose of morphine. When life itself is the great and mysterious gift, far beyond us! Would you shake your head slowly, mouthing the word "No"? Would you find it in yourself, if it were left to you, to deny someone else their choice of dying over living? Whose life, as they say, is it? Whose? God's? Society's? The individual's? No wonder the human race has found it necessary to invent Supreme Courts.

Don't imagine that this issue is addressed by your issuing a pious bulletin about your own position, which is what happens in discussion about moral issues here. Even if we assume that a great many people in Ireland are capable of rising to the highest challenges, and would never in any circumstances themselves demean the gift of life ... still, still, there will soon be those among us who want to bring forward their deaths.

If you're the one who's asked to help – what will you do? What do you want the Supreme Court, on your behalf, to do? And would your views be the same if pain and despair meant that you were doing the asking?

The Irish Times Magazine, January 12, 2002

The Cliffs of Moher

I note with misery that Clare County Council has given itself permission to build a multimillion-euro tourist processing plant at the modest spectacle provided by nature herself: the short stretch of not-very-high cliffs at the Cliffs of Moher. I had hoped that the difficulties local farmers raised when asked to sell their land to the bureaucrats would last long enough for fashion to change around again, and that by the time they gave in, proposals such as the present one for a ludicrously inflated visitor center would not be tolerated. But no such luck.

If any reader cares to head for the Cliffs of Moher now, they will find there the original attraction – the stretch of cliff which the County Council can do nothing to enhance or diminish. They will find about six wind-blown and very happy winter tourists wandering about the simple Victorian pathways, which are all that are needed, as a matter of fact, to walk a hundred yards so as to look back and duly note that you have been walking on a cliff. Go up to the visitors and ask them whether they feel the need for an audio-visual theater. Guess what: they don't. They made their way to the cliff to be in a relatively unspoiled part of Ireland that is easily accessible and on a tourist route. They have not gone there to study cliffs, with the aid of audio-visual props. Nor, I take it, have they gone there to see an exhibition.

The exhibition and theater the council wants to build are pure gigantism on the part of the council and the people with a stake in the thing getting built. What the visitors would like is something hot to drink, something to eat, toilets, and a souvenir shop. Those are there already. They are also available, in lavish abundance, in a radius of one to three miles in cafés, pubs, and restaurants. Oh, there are so many places to have a bowl of soup within five minutes of the Cliffs of Moher that to build a restaurant there is whatever the opposite of a priority is.

Of course, a lot of places are closed in the winter. That is because – Clare County Council, are you listening? – there are few tourists in West Clare in winter. Your theater and exhibition space and restaurant will be closed for at least half the year and you – we – will be left with the maintenance of your white elephant. If you were not bureaucrats – if you were people venturing your own money and needing to repay loans or make a profit – you wouldn't dream of building a visitor center that needs to be as big as you've planned it, for only two months in the year.

Has anyone, by the way, ever bothered finding out how much money is made or lost in visitor centers, such as the one in Kenagh in Longford, or the one in Dunquin, or the one not 20 minutes from Clare County Council's headquarters, in Coole Park? Almost all visitor centers should be temporary, dismantleable structures. However, once the boys get their teeth into a nice expensive plan they all want to build Croke Park.

The Cliffs of Moher are, in themselves, to put it at its strongest, mildly exciting. They became a tourist attraction because they were near enough to Lahinch for the nineteenth-century ladies to be driven out there for a healthy blast of air. And because they're just a few steps off the main road. Also because they're a handy stop-off between Killarney and

201

Galway. Like, they're not a destination. But the reason I send visitors there, and the reason that I'm so upset at the council's plans, is that they're in a lovely, unspoiled setting. Because the landowners held out, there are only low and unobtrusive buildings beside the existing car park. Beautiful old fields edged, still, with the flagstone of the region, surround the present visitor center. The road is the old one. The slope of fields down to Liscannor is a miraculous patchwork quilt in shades of turquoise green.

Now the council's "traffic management scheme" – designed to cope with the crowds coming to the audio-visual theater and the exhibition space, no doubt – will involve further car parks and, I suppose, road-widening and -straightening. Nothing more instantly makes Clare ordinary. Its landscape is one of small effects, made by the work of humans over centuries – walls and fields and winding lanes and farm buildings and houses. It is small-scale and domestic. It is utterly unlike the wilderness around the Céide Fields, in County Mayo, just as the availability of restaurants in tourist Clare is utterly unlike their availability in Mayo west of Ballycastle.

None of the Clare attractions – not one – needs a Céide Fields–type visitor center. The most they're going to need in the foreseeable future is a way of managing cars and coaches so as to unclog the roads in high summer – preferably a small-scale, unobtrusive, eco-sensitive transport plan involving one-way systems down back lanes and something like the horses-and-buggies of yore or electric mini-buses. Something from this, the twenty-first century. Not, as this proposed center is, a grandiose leftover from the past.

The Irish Times Magazine, February 2, 2002

Dissenting Voices

I came across the estimate the other day that, in response to the killings in the U.S. on September 11, the Americans have killed about 8,000 to 12,000 Taliban fighters and about 1,000 Afghan civilians. That's about four times more people than the September terrorists killed. The writer – a right-wing columnist in the *New York Times* – was making the argument that the Afghan deaths were worthwhile, not, as you might think, for whatever retaliatory or exemplary power they might have over other terrorists, but because of the benefits they had brought to Afghanistan.

Besides counting the dead, he had collected other statistics, such as the number of children vaccinated against measles who would not have been vaccinated while the Taliban were *in situ*, and the number of women who will not die in pregnancy and children who will not die pitiably young, because the aid agencies have got back into Afghanistan, and social and health programs are getting off the ground.

The writer claimed that people who object to American bellicosity should reflect on those gains. Above all, he said, an accelerated teacher-training scheme will lead to more than a million children receiving an education who, previously, would have had none. People should recognize, the writer said, that there can be humanitarian gains from military intervention.

I was thinking about this as I walked past the local high school here in Brooklyn, where a sign beside the front door tells you that firearms are forbidden on the premises, and all visitors must understand that they may be randomly scanned. It's not that I doubt the value of the education provided in even the most embattled school. But I think there's more than a mote in our American writer's eye. You can see the superficial logic of his position, but the powerful have a duty to be self-conscious. How would he like it if Russia bombed the U.S. into doing something about its disadvantaged people? Because, in fact, there isn't an American hospital without its distraught suppliants at the Accident & Emergency entrance.

More than 41 million people in the U.S. don't have health insurance, and although health-care provision is highly local and in some places excellent, in other places it shares a standard with Kabul. In Texas, a homeless pregnant woman, for example, is in dire straits because almost all the hospitals will turn her away. Nor is there a bit of wasteground in the cities of this great and wealthy country that hasn't its population of lost souls wrapped in cardboard and rags. We in Ireland fail in the same ways, of course. But we're not, I hope, so familiar with our failure that we don't even see it any more.

The writer who is so pleased with America's actions belongs to a secure consensus. He is cocooned within a majority view. The element of thoughtful doubt that was part of the initial media discussion of America's response to September 11 has disappeared. Susan Sontag and Noam Chomsky have, it seems to me, been taken out of the dialogue available to the masses here. And even at home, voices such as Niall O'Dowd, wildly accusing us of anti-Americanism, have stifled discussion.

It may be that everything the American government and military have done and are doing is better than any of the alternatives. It may be that history will applaud. It is true that the Taliban regime was vile and that its values – which are widely held – need undermining at every opportunity. But we are not much better than zealots ourselves if we do not allow the articulation of views critical of the majority view.

In the same issue of the *New York Times* there was an article about the compensation offered by the religious orders to Irish victims of institutional abuse. Several people over here asked me, in shocked voices, to explain. Which I did, I hope, in a measured way, with emphasis on the range of thankless social tasks that Irish governments left to the religious, without whom the history of the powerless in Ireland would be even more painful than it is.

But privately I was thinking that the worst abuses came down to the facts that individual women and men let themselves go in callousness and sadism, and that the groups of which they were members allowed them to let themselves go. The religious orders were unchallenged on their territory in their day, and what is not challenged from outside is open to corruption from within.

This is the infinite value of the dissenting voice: that wherever it is not allowed to flourish, an institution – a school or an orphanage or a government or a media consensus – begins to slide toward allowing its worst energies into play. And the slide begins with the kind of blindness to nuance that, it seems to me, is displayed in the argument about the humanitarian value of sending destroyers and fighter planes and missiles to Afghanistan. What was to stop America from sending the Afghans the price of them long ago? Are not the intelligence and patience that should have gone into American foreign policy the true alternatives to despotism? What's so great about being the better-armed despot?

The Irish Times Magazine, February 16, 2002

Feeling for Ireland

You may remember a man called Tom Hayden who was famous in protest and progressive causes in the United States in the 1960s and 1970s, and perhaps more famous as the husband of Jane Fonda, when she, too, was politically engaged.

He was the only child of what sounds like a sad, outwardly respectable Irish-American marriage – a mother who was a lifetime sufferer from sclerosis, a father who visited mother and son at weekends and drank too much. But the young Tom's energy and organizational gifts were suited to his times, and since his student years he has been a busy, and often successful, leader of antiwar, civil rights, and environmental movements. His latest book is called *Irish on the Inside: In Search of the Soul of Irish America*, and it is a kind of memoir-essay about his own dealings with contemporary Ireland, mainly in connection with the nationalist cause in the North and in the U.S., and with President Clinton's peace initiatives. In it, he tries to assimilate the story of the past 30 years on this island to the confessional genre – he does operate in California, after all – and to make bridges between what he understands of the thinking and feeling behind the "armed struggle," and his own experience of civil struggle in the United States.

This is a highly original thing to do: we usually treat the Troubles as though they were unique and meaningless outside themselves, but his personal approach leads us out of that claustrophobia. A certain kind of resolution is arrived at when, in the end, Hayden perceives himself as "an American rebel, not in spite of being Irish but because of being Irish." But his journey is much more compelling than his arrival.

The book was scathingly reviewed in this paper by Eamon Delaney, whose own book, *An Accidental Diplomat,* about his years as a wonderfully watchful and clever junior in the Department of Foreign Affairs, got a rocky ride when it was published last year. But the review could have been even less sympathetic. Delaney did not stress the slapdash way with facts, and above all the sentimentality, which characterizes Tom Hayden's book.

There are few Irish readers who will not wince at the metaphor with which the book ends, to do with Irish immigrants returning home, each carrying a sod and a stone which become "a field, which in time becomes a field of flowers, a hill, a graveyard, an oak grove, a mountain, a place to bury pain and grow our history until memory surpasses forgetting and the sod of the dead becomes the fertile soil of awakenings." To Delaney, who was schooled in the skepticism, the cunning, and the discipline which has been brought by our governments and diplomats to the problem of Britain, Northern Ireland, and ourselves, Hayden's tone of the vague ecstatic must be near-intolerable.

Yet part of the value of this important book is that such a tone is one we have to learn to understand and yes, to accept, if we native Irish are ever to come to terms with Irish-America. As we should. Any reader who gets past Hayden's rhetoric to what he actually did and wanted to do about Ireland will find a story on two levels, full both of heart and of energetic commitment.

One is his personal yearning to make emotional connections with the Irish past so as to place himself in history and to pass our culture on to his own children. To this end, for instance, he visits a Famine death-pit in County Monaghan, where ancestors of his own may have been dumped. But before you start sneering at the Yank for doing such things, ask yourself how come none of us ever do them, or if we do, are embarrassed by them?

The other question Hayden asks is more problematic for many people in the Republic, including me. "How should the Irish-American soul be grounded?" he asks, and the asking represents a new Californian influence on the frozen, 1950s attitudes of East-Coast Irish-America. But the difficulty is that Hayden looks to Sinn Féin for his own grounding, and is relatively starry-eyed about Gerry Adams, Martin McGuinness, the hunger strikers, and so on – by our sour Southern standards anyway. The problem of coexistence with Unionism is simply not faced. "Brits Out!" substitutes for analysis.

But Tom Hayden has clearly been one of the more welcome and hard-working celebrity visitors to Derry and Belfast and South Armagh, and a lot of Republicans talked to him. And precisely because he is a person from a touchy-feely culture, he was as interested in what the activists felt about what they were doing, as in any other aspect of the "armed struggle."

To me, this is the great distinction of this book – that it cares about feelings, and for homes and wives and children, and dreams deferred, and regrets daily lived with. In our demonizing of Sinn Féin, politically necessary though that may have been, we denied our fellow-Irish in the North, on both sides of the divide, such feelings. But the book also draws a map of the reading and talking and thinking this Irish-

American did, so as to enlarge both sides of his identity.

You may object, as Delaney apparently did, to the sources Tom Hayden found. But you cannot object to the ardor and generosity of his search for them.

The Irish Times Magazine, March 2, 2002

Everyday Ireland

A Tragedy Waiting to Happen: The Chaotic Life of Brendan O'Donnell, Tony and J. J. Muggivan, Gill & Macmillan

On the outskirts of many an Irish town there is a building whose windows open only a crack, which gives off sorrow. This is the mental hospital. Sometimes you see a person for whom that building is home come out and, hunched in against the walls, make their way down the town, whey-faced, in trousers that are too short, to buy cigarettes in little sweetshops for their shaky, nicotined fingers. Brendan O'Donnell might have found a home and sensitive treatment in one of those places and, if so, he might never have lived in such anguish, tested and tortured his community, and finally murdered a young woman, a little boy, and the priest, Father Walsh, who went into the woods with the by-now savage Brendan to bring the last rites to the bodies of Imelda and Liam Riney. That is the thesis of this sad little book.

One of the brothers who wrote it, Tony Muggivan, was a neighbor of Brendan's, whose family took him in when Brendan was 14 years old and living rough in a derelict shed in the freezing sleet and snow of February, starved and in a suicidal state. Almost the first thing Tony did – after consulting his brother, J. J., who is a clinical social worker in the United States – was to take Brendan to one of these mental hospitals. The two of them waited for many hours in the hope of getting Brendan admitted.

"We were put into a large room with about 12 men in it,"

writes Tony. "Brendan sat in a corner. I stayed standing, watching these 12 men who were all staring at us. A big man stood up and slowly made his way across the room towards me. He was over six feet tall and was looking at me very seriously. He put his hand on my arm, very gently, and asked me, 'Can I go home with you?'"

One doctor interviewed Brendan and said he must be admitted at once. For a brief while – an hour maybe – there was hope that the boy might receive from the psychiatric so-called service of this state the shelter and therapy that might in time have turned him into just such a poor old man: broken, certainly, but no trouble to anybody. But another doctor turned up and took the first one aside, and Brendan was turned away. And in the years that followed, during which the Muggivan family made heroic efforts to help Brendan – even fighting to foster him – he was regularly turned away by the institutions and individuals who make up the network of state care, funded by the taxpayer, to which an Irish family or community at the end of its tether can supposedly turn. Amateurs, however well-meaning, cannot handle a person as bizarre and cruel and wounded as Brendan became after his mother died when he was nine. Goodness doesn't do it; what is needed is a well-funded, honorable, hard-working, intelligent professionalism.

J. J. Muggivan, the second author of this book, adds a kind of clinical commentary to Tony Muggivan's homely and heart-breaking narrative. He clearly believes that there was a point when an informed therapeutic response to Brendan's growing violence would have been effective – he thinks the boy was probably neurologically damaged, and that the drug regimes he was put on from time to time made his condition worse. For all anyone can say, he's right. But this isn't the U.S.; this is Ireland. At the end of Brendan O'Donnell's trial, the then-Minister for Health, Michael Noonan, ordered an inquiry into the way the psychiatric services had dealt with him. The inquiry was never carried out.

Inquiries into the treatment of such as Brendan have no urgency. And what, in any case, would an inquiry find? That the gatekeepers who saw no reason to take him on themselves came from the Ireland that accepted and still accepts the physical abuse of children in the home, that is still unsure that a child is worth saving from sexual abuse if the abuser is someone important, and that has no concept of emotional abuse? There was a priest in Brendan O'Donnell's locality who everyone knew was a child abuser; he fondled Brendan in public. Tony Muggivan and his wife, Mary, accidentally left Brendan alone for a moment with the priest and both heard him say: "I love you, Brendan." The glare turned on this hapless community by Brendan's lurid life illuminated other tragedies besides his own. Such as this priest's. Such as the tragedy of the local authorities who allowed the priest to flourish.

Actually, four people died, in this story from everyday Ireland. Brendan O'Donnell himself died at the age of 23, one day after he'd been administered 200 milligrams of a mind-stunning drug called Thoridazine and two days after he'd been administered 100 milligrams of it. This state does not keep a record of prisoners' prescriptions, but they are given a lot of drugs – drugs for Irish prisoners, apparently, cost four times more than drugs for English prisoners. It would ill become those of us who've never had to deal with a Brendan to criticize anyone who wanted him stunned. But if a population of murderers-become-zombies is the end result of a process that begins with bland reluctance to take in a difficult 14-year-old, it is not a process to be proud of.

The old man in the room in the asylum wanted to be taken home. But even with his personality almost extinguished by sedation, it is hard to imagine Brendan O'Donnell saying "take me home." Blame it on the psychiatric services if you like – author Tony Muggivan has to find somewhere to put his enduring anger. But some tragedies that unfold in the intimacy of family relationships can only be prevented by the care the rich get, and even then they can't always be prevented. Better, perhaps, at least for the two of them, if it had been his own mother and Brendan himself who had been taken into the woods by a madman and shot – as he on some psychic level knew. Only we in Ireland would not then have had to face what this book asks us again to face. Think of the castes in our society that are looked down on. Then sink even lower to a group even less respected. You will arrive at the mentally ill poor.

The Irish Times, November 13, 2004

On Old Age

There is hardly a topic I want less to write about and you want less to read about than old age. But a few comments are provoked by the recent outburst of government-funded attention to old people. One part of it was a poster campaign on the theme of "say no to ageism." I got involved with another part – a nationwide "celebration," as these things are fashionably described, of "age and creativity," a subject which a moment's thought will show is quite as likely to be tragic as anything else.

I hadn't read the e-mails about what I'd agreed to do with proper attention, and I thought because I was going to talk with people in libraries I was doing something connected with reading and writing. I was taken aback when I realized that I was involved with the "older age" thing. I'm not good at accepting the passage of time. Being the age I am feels absolutely untruthful; it feels like the first charade I have ever had to keep up. And there's nothing I can do to shake the role off, whereas anything else I ever disliked as much I could do something about.

I don't know who exactly the poster campaign about saying no to ageism was aimed at, apart from brutal nurses, of whom there can't be that many around. But I'm sure I'm not the only one who's as ageist as they come, not because I have anything against any or all old people, but because I don't want to be enrolled with them. Even as a kind of junior trainee.

Being treated like dirt isn't the worst thing about being very old. The worst thing wasn't mentioned by the campaign. I've known old people who wished they were dead. I've known people as good as dead from boredom, nervousness, anger, and a keen dislike of other people. I've known people who can't be consoled for the death of old friends. And what of the fear, for many, of what is approaching? Can we be helped in this most testing of all the stages of life? Can we help other people?

If the recent media campaign avoided the negative, it even more definitely avoided the positive. The night before my little library events I got panicky and I rang a librarian to ask what to talk about. "Ah, don't bother talking about anything," she said. "Just shock them." And that reminded me of the way we sanitize the existence of people whose bodies are no longer young. Did any part of the recent campaign about older people touch on sex? How do people, when the time comes, get information about sex and the aging body? Or do people lose interest in the sexuality that all their lives has been central to pride and self-liking just because they're old enough for the free travel? Are there special physical issues? What do studies show about physical expression within relationships – married, unmarried, gay? Is there much tenderness about at all? More and more I come across couples who after years of trouble seem in old age to love and trust. What is it that happens with age?

Will it have secret blessings? Older people know more than anyone else around, even if they can't always be bothered to point that out. Time or ill health may reduce their bodies to a helplessness comparable to a baby's, but inside they are highly experienced. The first rule of a campaign, then, that holds our senior people up to attention, should be that it will be conducted at a high level of intelligence and discrimination. But what, for example, did the recent campaign mean by "old"?

How can one word cover someone of 66 and a necessarily more frail 80-year-old at the same time? Nobody thinks that 13-year-olds are much the same as 19-year-olds.

And if it was vague about its subject, it was equally vague about what it was trying to change in us. What older people are likely to need is not to be dependant on private charity. They need access to doctors and hospitals and nursing homes. They may need somewhere to die at whatever pace fate allows. They may need their passing-on to be a scene invested with feeling and dignity. What the government spends money on is a signal of our communal priorities, and the steady and deliberate diversion of some of our national wealth toward providing these things would express respect on behalf of all of us.

But I don't know that we're capable of respecting people who have little and diminishing material power. The truth is that it's not age itself that makes the old unrespected. The truth is that the wealthy old can buy respect – or the fruits of respect, which is just as serviceable. This raises questions of the most complex kind. That's why I criticize the words of a campaign that was, of course, well-meaning. "Say no to ageism" strikes me as a wasted opportunity to be serious about serious things – a Disneyfication of issues that we haven't yet addressed, either in the shaping of the new Ireland, or in ourselves.

The Sunday Tribune, May 29, 2005

About Justice

The woman-haters have won the PR battle about feminism, in that they've made the word itself a turnoff. On the other hand, they haven't won the war. There are no people in Ireland whose lives have changed more for the better in the last half-century than women. An Irish person born female is now, social circumstances apart, in a position to use all of herself – her heart, her brains, her body, her spirit – in a life she has chosen for herself.

How can anyone who remembers the way things were not be deeply moved by, for example, the crowds of lovely, laughing women who run the Mini-Marathon? Most of the women, probably, are wives and mothers, or would like to be. If something goes wrong with those great life projects they will not find themselves alone and without resources, as so many of the women who have gone before us did. They can work now – not, if they're in the public service, be made to retire. They are full citizens – not casually treated as inferior, as they were when, for example, they weren't called to sit on juries. They can choose to make love without fearing pregnancy, or they can choose to accept as many children as lovemaking sends. They are allowed to like themselves now. Remember how it was? Remember, for example, that the Catholic Archbishop of Dublin instructed the government of the day to ban Tampax when it first came in? Can anyone not be glad that all the fear and contempt implicit in that tiny detail of our history has almost had its day?

I see, however, that *Irish Times* columnist John Waters for one is tormented by a fantasy of a worldwide feminist conspiracy apparently directed at his good self. I want to say – yes, there was and is an Irish feminist agenda. It is contentious, because power for women does mean less power for men. But it was and is about justice. Does he grudge other humans who have advanced towards justice – the working class, for example – their gains? Men were once serfs, but the patient achievement of advances allowed them to lift their heads up. Women's liberation is a continuation of that same advance.

His latest complaint is that reading too many books by women is bad for Leaving Cert students. I've never seen any evidence that he has a feeling for dispassionate inquiry so there's not much point in discussing with him what difference it makes to literature whether it is the work of a man or a woman, and whether imagination when it is verbal can be beyond gender, as it is, for example, in music. This is an interesting question, but *Liveline*, for instance, rounded up the usual suspects for a fake discussion in the hope – fully realized – that it would descend to shrillness. Good questions are often posed by John Waters, but in an atmosphere of anger and sourness that prevents them from being taken seriously.

What really hurt, recently, was a radio interview with Emily O'Reilly which I listened to precisely because I greatly admire her. Her gifts of mind and character wouldn't have got her to where she is if there hadn't been a concerted fight by feminists to open the way to educational and economic and professional opportunities for women, yet she went out of her way, in public, to disassociate herself from women as such. I heard her – the Ombudsman, of all people – tell the world with a little girlish laugh that she just can't stand being addressed as a woman – that when *The Women's Programme* on television called its audience "sisters" – humorously – she recoiled, offended. I can understand not wanting to be enrolled in a club you haven't joined. But has anyone ever heard a man imply that he feels contaminated by being associated with men?

That day another woman, a columnist with *The Sunday Times* called India Knight, who's usually a voice for common sense and good humor, took the opportunity to misrepresent feminism by saying that it downgraded her life because she loves being a housewife. The fact is that she writes as a privileged, upper-middle-class woman from a moneyed background with a life full of love, well-rounded between paid and unpaid work. Of course she likes being at home in the kind of home she has. She knows as well as I do that that's not the kind of confinement within a life of housework that feminism said wasn't a sufficiently ample destiny for any human. She must feel very secure, to so casually repeat the slurs of the enemies of activist women.

But if she lived here, she wouldn't feel secure. I keep myself going with a private competition. Which commentator, this week, has said the most insulting thing about women? Do join me. Send in your entries, any time you like. Maybe we can give a prize to the Irish Misogynist of the Year. It'll be a close-run thing between a packed field and we might get too sick of the whole thing to go on.

But frankly, it's either laugh at them, or lie down on the floor and weep.

The Sunday Tribune, June 19, 2005

Spirit of Africa

If you allowed yourself to contemplate the state of the world, your heart would never stop hurting. Children breaking stones in quarries and hauling carts in mines and huddled in doorways, watched by predators. Young girls chained to the beds in brothels. Innocent animals tormented, clear rivers polluted, whole villages – whole territories – in such despair that the men will be drunk from boyhood to death. A child half-dead from hunger – I saw a photo of this and can't forget it – crawling along a road in Sudan searching for grains of wheat that might have fallen from lorries.

I don't blame us that we hurriedly fade these pictures to black. The combination of pity and impotence is too hard to bear. I don't blame us for grasping at the relief of conscience the Live 8 project offered us. But I blame us for laziness in such thinking as we do about places like Africa. I think there are two extra efforts we should make.

The first is that instead of putting Africa out of our minds by declaring that it's too far gone for anything to make much difference, we should adjust our time frame. It is very important to remember that Europe was Africa once, and not so long ago. We "did" sixteenth- and seventeenth-century European history in school, and in those times, this continent – which now holds itself immeasurably superior to Africa – was a farrago of small states forever involved in irrational feuds and wars, a place steeped in what we now call superstition, a place where children, as a rule, did the jobs of beasts of burden and the great majority of women and men were treated as we now treat animals – a dark place where life was, as the philosopher put it, nasty, brutish, and short.

Even in this century and in our lifetime, Europeans have inflicted incalculable suffering in the two wars which became world wars. I've always been struck by the fact that workmen were still building the memorial, near Arras in France, to the Canadian dead of the First World War when the Second World War broke out.

The point is – all that has changed. The physical conflict, the in-turned savagery, are things of the past. Drive from one end of Europe to the other now, and though the towns and cities are full of human flotsam, the landscape is entirely at peace. And if you change your time frame about Africa – if you give it the same hundreds and hundreds of years to work through to the same state, handicapped though it is by what the colonial powers did to it, and by the destructive messages imprinted on it by the colonial experience – you can have hope for it.

That's the first thing to bear in mind.

Secondly, we need to take on board, profoundly, that the cultures of Africa are different from ours. It is not appropriate for First-World solipsists to lecture African countries on electoral democracy and good governance, as if they would all be Iowa if they pulled their socks up. We have an electoral democracy here, but at the height of the Haughey era, several of his favored barons, as well as he himself, were doing a Mobutu on Ireland. Every "gift" and bribe that led to unpaid tax was money looted from this country. Northern Ireland was a peaceful electoral democracy when the Catholics were being herded into gerrymandered slums to preserve Protestant rule.

If it comes to that, President Bush governs a country where millions of citizens cannot afford health insurance and die prematurely, not from photogenic famine, but from powerlessness in the face of the U.S. health system.

And think; if the Land Acts and the Land Commission here hadn't begun the job of distributing the land that formerly belonged to the ruling class, wouldn't an independent Ireland have done to the Anglo-Irish what Mugabe did to the white farmers? You have to hope, when you see Mbeki of South Africa reject criticism of Mugabe, that there are native and local ways of proceeding which we do not yet understand. Perhaps he knows, as we do not, that Mugabe's Zimbabwe is in transition rather than decline – as it turned out Ireland was, in the bleak 1950s, when it looked as if self-government had comprehensively failed the Irish.

You have to stand back before the mystery of the mind and spirit of the peoples of Africa – not look at them as the same as us, only victims. I spent time once with a woman who lived with her family in a room in Mbare, a poor people's housing project in Harare, going around the beer halls with her while she sold bowls of stew. I don't know whether she has been evicted, and I hope and pray that she has not. But if she has been, she'll survive, and she'll drag her family into survival. She was truly indomitable. When I think of that woman and of people I've met in other parts of Zimbabwe and Africa, it makes me want to hurry history on so that the strength and humor and goodness of the people can find expression. More difficult, even, than helping with aid is divesting ourselves of the patronizing ways we've learnt from the imperialists. If we respect, we'll find hope.

The Sunday Tribune, July 10, 2005

A Surplus of Social Capital

I think it was a great idea, at the recent Fianna Fáil think-in, to have outsiders address the troops. It is a good thing to peer out from the cave of what you already know at new things. But what in the name of God is all this "social capital" nonsense? Was Bertie consciously trailing a red herring past us when he conjured up problems of alienation and lack of social connection and community breakdown in this country?

Does he not know as well as anybody that the place is coming down with social capital, that it is practically handicapped by the intense sociability of daily life, and that the density of social connection here in fact swamps the individual and sidelines anything in the nature of abstract, intellectual discussion? The entire population of this country would fit into one, medium-sized American city. It is so intimate a place that, as I have long complained, it is impossible to have an illicit affair without being caught. It is impossible to run away from home; the person beside you on the bus will have been to school with your sister. On the whole, it is impossible to hurry social transactions for fear of being rude. It is impossible not to stand your round. It is impossible not to offer a caller a cup of tea. It is impossible not to offer a lift to the old bachelor on his way back to his tigeen from spending the day in the pub.

Today, for example, is a Sunday between the all-Ireland finals. The professor who addressed the Fianna Fáilers – an American – chose as an image of the unconnected individual a person who goes bowling alone instead of in a group. Is there a single inhabitant of Cork or Galway or Tyrone or Kerry who even contemplated going bowling alone since the semifinals? Sport flourishes here, providing hourly, daily, annual opportunities for bonding, for conversation and argument, for the expression of local identity and for the vociferous, exuberant expression of collective emotion. And as for the GAA – if you live in most places in Ireland outside south Dublin your problem is not that you're excluded from it or choose exclusion from it: your problem is how to get away from it. How not to buy raffle tickets, how not to go up to the club for a drink, how not to watch the kids being coached on a summer evening, how not to care whether your home place wins or loses their next match.

Declining church attendance. That's another thing that worries American commentators. But though it is a problem for clerics, I don't see that it's a problem for the rest of the community. The figures had nowhere to go but down: 30 years ago 91 percent of Catholics in the South and 95 percent in the North were Mass-goers. Now that their mammies don't beat them out of the bed to go, people in the 18–30 age bracket from all religious denominations are falling away from attendance. But the new churches are thriving, and so are do-it-yourself spiritual experiences based on meditation and healing and the like. If you count their adoration for certain kinds of music and certain performers as worship of the ideal – and they themselves do – young people today are far more into a spirit-acknowledging life than we were when we sat in churches letting it all wash over us. The alternative, in any case, to going to Mass or to divine service is not playing bowls alone. It is the wonderfully thriving weekend culture, which the kids, now that they have money and mobility, have embraced – a culture strikingly more collaborative and social than hanging around the churchyard after Mass.

Worrying about social capital is a load of cobblers here and a dangerous load of cobblers. Because it obscures what's really wrong. There are indeed lonely individuals – widows and widowers and isolated single parents and young mothers at home in new estates at the beginning of marriages – though I don't think Bertie had them in mind when he invited the party to think about alienation. It is the obdurately antisocial groups that are our society's biggest challenge. The handful of postal districts from which most of the inmates of our prisons come are alienated. Travellers are alienated. The housing estates where everyone's scraping by on inadequate social welfare are alienated. But it is not social capital that the people in these places are lacking in – they are each other's constant and generous resource and the warm hugger-mugger of their communities is their consolation for other defects.

It is privilege they lack. And opportunity. And self-belief. It is from us that they are alienated. This government has not tried very hard to break the cycle of transmission of no-hope lives from one generation to another. For example – in the face of resistance from its developer pals and of middle-class paranoia about their neighbors, it has failed to enforce its own provisions for affordable housing. If the Fianna Fáil conference was going to turn its attention to a social problem, it might have had a session on housing, house prices, and the institutionalization of inequality. But safer by far, the organizers must have sensed, to avoid the problems we have and concentrate on whipping up concern about the one social problem we don't have.

The Sunday Tribune, September 18, 2005

Our Irish Heritage

When I was so young that what I learned in school was all I knew, fragments of a picture of peasant Ireland floated around my head. There were old ladies who spoke Irish and had a very hard life, and people fell about in fields thinking they were pursuing whatever a corncrake was, and people drowned. There was such a gap between establishment literature and the ordinary experience of a young person from the east of the country that I could not hear what the Department of Education was saying.

That gap was nothing compared to a gap that has opened up since. It is a gap about suffering. There have been a number of memoirs written in recent times and their descriptions of childhood are as fine and powerful as descriptions can well get. And it would be a poor educational system that didn't try to feed some of that writing into the imaginative knowledge of young Irish people. I've no doubt that John McGahern's *Memoir* is of classic stature and will be prescribed in schools and colleges in time to come, not only for its beauty but as part of a report from Ireland's past, recalled in almost hallucinatory detail. But I don't know who could encounter it without being washed by the sorrow in it. Listening to him read it on the radio, in his voice which has always been plangent, was hard. Harder still was the impact of the last few pages, where he returns to the beloved mother whose death delivered him and his siblings – good little children, still hopeful at that stage – into the power of his capricious and sadistic father.

What are modern children to make of a heritage so dense with unhappiness? I don't know how anyone can read *Angela's Ashes* – a memoir of a very different kind from McGahern's, but one that was immediately understood all over the world – and not weep when the family is let down over and over again by the father, their love for him and their dependance on him over and over betrayed. The fathers, in that patriarchal Ireland that was sick with a piety divorced from both moral behavior and emotional intelligence, were themselves half-mad. They themselves had not been sufficiently loved. They must have raged at the responsibilities laid on them.

And who knows how much the behavior of men and women, in the Ireland before contraception, was deranged by a sexuality almost impossible to express with joy or respect? Ireland was so poor and so firmly in the grip of a body-hating Church that people struggled in ignorance their whole lives through. Who did gay men and women think they were, for example? How did they survive being clamped into hetero-sexual roles? And society itself mirrored the cruelty, since it shared the values, of an unhappy home. I paid a quick visit to the village of Hollymount, east of Ballinrobe, not long ago. I wanted to pay my respects to the plaque erected there in memory of the mother of Noel Browne, the social activist, fighter against the scourge of tuberculosis, determined anti-cleric, conscience of an obsolete political Left and survivor of a lacerating childhood. His memoir, *Against the Tide*, is also an Irish classic of childhood, though whether any teacher has the courage to use it – cautiously – as a text I do not know. His mother lay dying in Ballinrobe of the same TB that had killed her husband. No one offered her any help. She was sur-rounded by her half-starved children. She set out with her last strength for England, where she could hand the children over to their eldest sister, and then die. The pathetic family group passed through Hollymount, where she was born. Again, the pain and anger of seeing a mother in despair all but overwhelmed the writer.

It must all seem as foreign as the Blaskets to the blithe young of today. I see boys and girls, perfectly at ease with each other, heading off to rock concerts or taking their fake tans and highlighted hair to sun 'n' sex holidays abroad or buying panini and coffee for their lunch in country towns or chatting away on their mobiles and I think – is it all over? There are all kinds of other sufferings now and the young feel them, I know. But the primal one – being trapped in a brutal family – can it be the same as it once was? There must still be harsh and un-loving parents, but are the kids absolutely helpless before them, now? Aren't people watching, now? Irish children swim, for example, now; the teachers who take them to the swimming pools must see the bruises. Children have means of communi-cation. If they run away, someone will ask them why.

And they can learn from the anger in books like this. John McGahern didn't write *Memoir* to help us, but it does that all the same. This is what our society was and still in ways furtively strives to be. Historians of mid-twentieth-century Ireland can throw some light on how the instruments for making a child unhappy came to be formed, but here is the experience of a child's unhappiness, described as if by a candid child. An unforgiving child.

After such knowledge, what forgiveness?

The Sunday Tribune, September 25, 2005

Memoir Is Artful

A television program involving me and the family I come from went out on RTÉ a few nights ago. I saw an advance mention of it which made out that it was going to be all about my – long-ago and relatively un-exceptional – sex life. But if anybody turned it on expecting sex, they must have been sorely disappointed. I saw the program on DVD this week and I'm not entirely sure what its main theme was. But whatever it was, it wasn't anything to get titillated about.

I thought it was going to be one in a series of programs about the family – anybody's family – and the important things that happen within families. One unusual thing about my relationship with my family is that I wrote a memoir which I thought no one would read, but which in fact exposed my family's flaws and sorrows to a wide audience. Not many fam-ilies have to put up with that. But many families do have one person who breaks a silence, or speaks out in some way, or in some way describes and defines a family which up to then had no agreed-upon identity. But a family hangs together by remaining undescribed, so that each member can see it and themselves in relation to it in whatever way suits them best. The member who disturbs this comfort is asking for trouble. It's not even a question of keeping a family's secrets – though that's what's on most people's minds when they think about getting their life stories down on paper.

In a couple of months, I'll be leading a writing-in-the-first-person workshop at Listowel Writers' Week and I bet that topic comes up in the first hour; how do you tell the truth about what happened to you without hurting or betraying other people? Should you change names? Should you leave the worst out? But even if you say nothing but good things about the people in your memoir, even if its tone is positive and humorous and sweet – like, for example, *Thank You for the Days*, the book of autobiographical sketches by Deirdre Brady, who is a sister of my own – you can still get into a kind of trouble.

The writer can hardly give more than a small bit of attention to this person or that. But the person in question has always felt themselves to be large, and has a sense of their relationship with the writer as having been both large and vague. It shocks them to see themselves encapsulated. What's more, reading personal material by people you know is an uneasy business. The author doesn't seem a bit like his or her self. The author seems, frankly, a bit phony. The interesting thing is that if you read some of your own old letters, you'll get the same impression of your own self. You yourself will seem faintly phony. And that's because experience is too complex to be completely described in writing, and writing is a matter of picking and choosing, and the person who's doing the writing is an abbreviated version of the whole person in real life. Memoir is artful, however simple it may seem. Memoir edits both what it writes about and the person who writes it.

Lots of people, therefore, have a quarrel with the memoirist. But when those people are family members – siblings, perhaps – there is rich potential for further offense. Let's say the author describes a long and loving relationship with his or her parents. Well, that's going to stir up demons in the brothers and sisters who feel themselves to have been less loved.

Let's say your story is the story of a determined climb to the heights of a brilliant career. Will the stay-at-home siblings feel judged by that? And what about the family habit, unconsciously designed by the group to keep everyone in their box, of designating one member as, say, a show-off, and one as a joker, and one as authoritative maybe because they're the eldest, and another as childlike because they're the youngest. On the page, these callous but handy abbreviations, used by the family for its own smooth operation, lose all the irony and nuance they have in conversation.

I could go on. What about the fundamental fact that no two people remember any incident in exactly the same way? That never happened. It did. It didn't. So-and-so never said that. He was my boyfriend, not yours. She never really liked you. Et cetera. And what about the reputation of the family? What about the fallout for the others, facing their neighbors and friends and in-laws and colleagues, if one member of a family strips it bare in public? Memoirists seem so selfish to the people they drag in their wake. This, no doubt, is because they are selfish – though that itself is only shorthand for their having a need to be heard and to shape how they are heard which is really deep and imperative, or they wouldn't risk their relationship with the most important people in their lives.

All over the world people are sitting quietly writing their memoirs as if their stories are their own. They're wrapped up in themselves. It won't dawn on them for a long time that a family is a collective property, as well as an individual one. This is hindsight on my part, of course, but I see it now. And I see why there wasn't a television program on this subject on RTÉ last week, and why I doubt there ever will be. Recklessness can only go so far.

The Sunday Tribune, March 26, 2006

A Life of Heroic Honesty

The way country lanes are in Ireland at this time of year came into my head when I read that John McGahern was dead – such a beautiful time, with life bursting out through the flowers of the blackthorn and the vigorous singing of the small birds, and the earth and ourselves moving forward, the great round starting off again. Except for the dead, who have to stay behind. John's funeral procession made its way through a landscape of newly green little fields. He'd have known every detail of them. He was one with the place where he lived as few people are. And he was a man, to paraphrase Hardy, who used to notice such things.

Yet when I think of him, I think of the rainy, shadowy, dark-gray Dublin of his youth and mine, where the golden light from pubs was almost the only light along the quiet streets. And I have been thinking of him lately. There was an article in the *New York Review of Books* recently by Professor Denis Donoghue – a kind of general look at John McGahern's work on the occasion of the publication in the U.S. of his memoir. A whole generation was introduced to English and American literature in UCD by Prof. Donoghue – I was myself – and remember his magisterial teaching with a mixture of awe and heartfelt gratitude. He left Ireland, of course, and ascended in the U.S. to the heights of critical authority. But a cat may look at a king, and I thought his piece on McGahern disfigured by various kinds of snobbery. For the first time in my life, I wrote a "Letter to the Editor," to the *NYRB*. I hinted at the snobbery by referring to Prof. Donoghue's tone as one of "metropolitan hauteur," and then I addressed a couple of specific points in the review. I don't know whether the letter will be published.

I don't care. The only person I would have liked to see it was John. Not that I was any kind of friend of his – I've been in his company only about once a decade since he was a young teacher in Dublin and I was a student. I don't even know whether he remembered, when we bumped into each other, that we did know each other well for a while. I have a memory of him showing me, in an ice-cream parlor in O'Connell Street, a telegram from T. S. Eliot at Faber & Faber enthusiastically accepting *The Barracks* for publication, and I know he told me a sad anecdote about the day he met Eliot. But I don't altogether trust my memory. Those days were such a chaos of emotion and learning and having no money and ignorance and drinking and falling in love and missing buses and always having wet shoes. I got things wrong back then. And I was so wrapped up in myself, I hardly saw other people. But I knew that John was extraordinary, though he was only a National School teacher who taught, among a huge class of boys, my own young brothers – keeping order, I may say, not a bit more delicately than the other teachers.

He didn't seem to me to be good-looking or attractive. And he was nearly as poor as I was, after he paid for his lodgings. Once, a man from his own part of the country, who was a manager in the Adelphi Cinema, gave us a free meal in the café there. I remember the little lamp on the table and that we had bacon and eggs and tea in a silvery pot. It was a red-letter day, that. I remember that we went out to Skerries on a bus one weekday, in summer, and walked along a headland, full of light-heartedness. We walked on Howth Head too, and we walked miles and miles around the middle of Dublin. Or we went to the afternoon movies, or we sat in pubs, eking out one drink. The pub we used to meet in in Fairview turns up in his great story "Sierra Leone."

There was no emotional connection between us. Yet I valued every hour of our awkward friendship. I respected him, then and always. He had come out of childhood and youth a formidable person. He wasn't finished with suffering – he had been rejected by a woman he was mad about, and I remember how it used to hurt him when an ad came on that ran in the cinemas then – an ad for Mystic nylons, where a witchlike woman ran nylon stockings through her long hands. But he had already made himself. He was already embarked on a life of heroic honesty. He already knew what he meant by being a writer. He gave me, what he could ill-afford, a copy of Rilke's *Letters to a Young Poet*. Now, I see that John, for all that he was shabby and provincial-looking and unregarded and about to incur the hatred of the deathly Ireland of that time, had already absorbed Rilke's advice: "that you may find in yourself enough patience to endure and enough simplicity to have faith; that you may gain more and more confidence in what is difficult and in your solitude among other people."

There should be sorrow today, that that passage ends – "And as for the rest, let life happen to you. Believe me: life is in the right, always." No more life for John. But there was a distance from experience in him from the start – the distance he used, I suppose, in the making of his art – that prevents me from pitying him even for his death. John had pieced his broken heart together after he lost his mother. He had made himself into a true stoic. I don't think I've ever met anyone who so fully accepted the way things are. In the simplest way, he was always ready to die.

The Sunday Tribune, April 2, 2006

Your Cheatin' Heart

The highest achievements of thought, art, and religious feeling translate themselves, over time, into homely forms where ordinary people are perfectly comfortable with them. Take suffering, and failure, and then being saved by love so that within your own life there is something like a resurrection. That's the story of the movie *Walk the Line*, about Johnny Cash and his relationship with June Carter – a movie which, I read somewhere, has been many percentage points more popular with audiences in Ireland than in any other country. It's not exactly an Easter movie, but maybe it's about a form of salvation we can all identify with.

It's no surprise that it did so well here. Drive across this country, tuning in to one local radio station after another, and you'll hear songs about states of emotional loss and gain – as if they were the easiest things in the world to discuss – sung by local stars in accents borrowed from Tennessee and Arkansas. This is traditional Irish music just as fiddle music is – these songs, like Johnny Cash's, with their jog-jog beat and lurid plots that evoke summer nights in marquee tents and the smells of canvas and grass and perfume, and drink on warm breaths, and the sensuality of doing something in unison with another person's body.

Couples don't talk. They sing along with the melodies as if everyone, irrespective of gender, age, or circumstance, can fully identify with the tough but lovable bad guy who killed a man in Reno or the golden-hearted poker player or the long-married couple who, just because they're married, haven't lost the desire to fool around on a blanket on the ground. That's an important thing about country songs – everyone always knows the words, including people who under torture would not be able to remember the words of the National Anthem or "Danny Boy." But then, "Danny Boy" is an art song, compared to the likes of "Your Cheatin' Heart." It is bourgeois, not blue collar. Danny Boy never walked out on a good woman in Amarillo or took a gun to an overseer. And the tune goes up too high at the end for dancehall singers, not to mention that the speaker in "Danny Boy" is a woman, and country is par excellence the music of men.

Of course, the reason we all know all the words to country songs is that they could hardly be less demanding. They're as near monosyllabic as verbal communication can get. They rhyme. They are repeated over and over. The problem, in fact, is trying to get them out of, not into, your head. They are simple because they are chronicles of a simple world, where good is good and bad is bad and men are men and women are sweet and helpful angels whose main task here on earth is to stand by their man and help him through the night. Not that the ladies don't display a certain sweet feistiness – if her guy goes off to Jackson, see if she cares. And not that he doesn't love her: she may well be a yellow rose who is the only girl for him. But in principle, he has been working very hard – at shovelling 16 tons, killing guys, doing time, playing poker with a broken heart, et cetera – and he has enough on his plate without having to treat women as equals.

June Carter did all the right things for Johnny Cash in the movie and he was saved, though – in keeping with the general refusal to lend women the same importance as men – it wasn't June or his wife or his mother who was the cause of Johnny's problems: it was his father. You wouldn't call it a complex plot, and if it had been complex, single-expression Joaquin Phoenix would have been even less convincing than he was. To my mind, he never captured what makes Johnny Cash seem like a heroic everyman to so many people – that he kept trying, even if he kept failing, to be good. That he did suffer. That his black shirt symbolized a man who walks alone – one who understood loneliness.

And loneliness is not just not having anyone; it is having someone – as Johnny Cash had a wife in the movie – who doesn't understand you. The anthem to this sense of existential loneliness was written by country music veteran Cindy Walker, who died a few weeks ago: "You give your hand to me, and then you say hello. And I can hardly speak, my heart is beating so. And anyone can tell, you think you know me well, but you don't know me."

I often wondered why Irish people like country music so much, and I suppose that easiness with songs that are as simple and stripped-down as hymns is part of it – Johnny Cash and June Carter came, of course, from a gospel tradition. But it isn't just the form of those ballads that descends from religion. What struck me as I followed the story of Cash's addiction and self-destruction was the way it relied on the audience believing certain things about the operations of love and the miraculous responsiveness of people to believing they love and are loved. There was a parable in there, too.

The Sunday Tribune, April 16, 2006

One Little Dog

I'm glad to have this space in which to praise one little dog – an ordinary, black-and-white, mongrel sheepdog – my dog, Molly, who died last week. As long as I'm writing about her I can pretend she isn't completely gone. Though she is – she is gone forever, and I have to rearrange my life without its warm center, where she was my loved and loving companion, my friend of 11 years, the only being who ever needed food and water and shelter from me, which it was the deepest pleasure to give.

I was looking forward to her becoming old and needing me more and beginning to come inside from the lane where she used to lie in wait for tractors and bound up to bark at distant dogs. Her muzzle was silvery already, but I had a clear picture of her in my mind when she would be really old, her coat mottled with gray, curled on a mat beside the fire. I thought there'd be years more of our sharing our nights. When we lived together, bedtime was always early. I'd hear her flop onto the floor and sigh heavily and swallow a few times, then slip into sleep. I'd hear her soft yapping when she dreamed in the night. Then sometimes, in the morning, she'd jump up on the bed and press in against my back and doze there while I dozed myself.

There was supposed to be more of that closeness and more winter mornings when we had the fire going long before light and the tea made, and she'd come bustling in self-importantly from a preliminary tour of her territory, frosty-cold to the touch or with raindrops glistening on her fur.

And I've lost, as well as her dear company, her good influence. She was so transparent that I knew her very well. I knew when she was anxious and uncertain and jealous and I knew when she was delighted with herself and with me. I knew who she loved and who she was afraid of. She was so open that love could flow toward her like water over a weir, and I loved her without reservation, and so did my friends who minded her when I was away. I couldn't be unkind to her or even impatient with her and that made me better than I am. It was my dream to repay her for her goodness to me by helping her when she slowed down.

You may say that she was only a dog. But I once saw it said that dogs don't have souls because they don't need them. Her innocence was so perfect that a human being could only aspire to it. And the way she ran into each day full of joy – no carrying on of grudges, no regrets – was something to imitate consciously. The way she watched over me when I hit a tree and the car turned over and the windows burst, crouching beside me where I lay on the road. The way she allowed quiet to cure her when she got a thump from a van herself, sitting open-eyed in the darkest corner of the bedroom for two days until she could get going again. The way she signaled to me to give some food to her friend the dog from down the lane. She'd wait till I did it, then watch her friend eating with an unmistakable air of satisfaction.

I know that someone will say that most dogs have Molly's qualities and that I can get another dog. But it was this dog, so gentle and hopeful, that I shared a history with. It was this dog who, from the very first day, when I saw her at the back of a cage in the pound in Finglas, used to scrutinize me with a yearning look, as if there was something she could nearly understand. This one, an expert at slinking discreetly into hotels, who came on holiday with me. This dog who was with me on the night of the turn of the millennium, when we hurried home because the fireworks frightened her and went to our usual early bed, perfectly contented with each other. For a while we walked every Saturday in the hills above Dublin with men she greeted with adoration. She'd patrol us conscientiously, up and down, but then she'd take off ecstatically on the scent of deer. I don't want another dog. I want my Molly back.

In recent years I spent months at a time in New York, and Molly lived with friends on a farm, half-an-hour farther north in Clare. I'd come home on the plane that gets into Shannon around six in the morning and I'd be at their house while it was still very early and everyone was fast asleep. I'd let myself in and give one, soft whistle and immediately I'd hear her scrambling down the stairs. She didn't even pause. She walked past me to the car and jumped into the passenger seat. Only the way she panted betrayed her excitement.

Those were homecomings it was worth going away for. I always knew exactly how many days it would be till the next one. This time it would have been a morning in late May – light, with the birds singing – when the little dog with her alert head and her white paws took up her place on the seat beside me and, both of us staring straight ahead, we started for home. But never again. Not that, or ham sandwiches in the heather, or hotels, or having our breakfast in winter mornings in the room that glowed like gold. And nothing for it but to go on without her.

The Sunday Tribune, May 7, 2006

Airport Chapels

There was a wait of five hours in Kennedy Airport not long ago, when the plane to Shannon was delayed. Some people have inner resources sufficient for a long wait; some people haven't. I haven't, which is a fact I've had to face far too many times in airports. I've therefore become quite a connoisseur of airport chapels, or rather, of the rooms usually called something like an Inter-Faith Facility for Quiet Meditation – rooms decorated in a way that vaguely invokes the chapel, though they're at the very end of the traditions of decoration that were once reserved to the sacred.

There's always pale wood, these days, and a little bit of colored, if not stained, glass, and in Kennedy the seats of the chairs are woven of a kind of straw in a gesture, I suppose, towards the antique, and the virtue of simplicity. I remember ticking off – I think it was in Ronald Reagan Airport in Washington, D.C. – the list of symbols which airport chapel designers have decided are pious without being ideological. A fish, a bird, a lamb. Images can't be more specific – crosses, for example, are in very short supply – since various denominations and sects must share the space.

But even in the chapels that most closely resemble the foyers of bleak motels, the air has, to my mind, a quality of stillness. Even if the reason you're in the chapel is that you're trying to get away from other people – even if you're doing nothing more spiritual than sitting there thinking bad thoughts about Aer Lingus – you can feel that particular stillness. And what has the air been made still by, if not by prayer? The least rooms, as much as the greatest buildings, in which many people have sincerely addressed themselves in silence to a silent deity, retain something of the extraordinariness of that act. They are more dense than ordinary places.

I begin to think upward, in chapels, as if I'm addressing a higher place or being. And I notice that I am conditioned, when I'm thinking upward, to implore. Once I tilt toward that trajectory, a crowd begins to jostle into my mind. This person has been drinking harder than ever now he's been fired; that one's teenager's wildness is wrecking the family; this old friend never returns phone calls anymore; that one is devastated by a partner's infidelity. Not to even begin on the starving children with flies in their eyes, or the women raped over and over in the course of aggression and war, or the men lost to the protections of society in secret jails, or the poor of the earth – men working in terrible mines, in quarries, children scavenging garbage heaps, cleaning women plodding through cold streets at dawn. But a strangled, hopeless wish that things might be other than they are – is that prayer?

If I say a proper prayer, in the words I remember from childhood (earnestly trying to direct them away from myself), it will be for someone who's sick. When there's nothing else to do and something must be done, it seems natural to pray for the sick. I never gave doing it a second thought, even though I don't know who or what I'm praying to, until I read about the $2.4 million experiment, sponsored by the highly respected Templeton Foundation, which recently compared how well cardiac patients who were prayed for recovered, compared to cardiac patients who were not prayed for.

The prayed-for, it turned out, did, if anything, worse than the unprayed-for. This result brought out an amusing variety of clerical defenses. It was because the praying people didn't know the people they were praying for, one chaplain said: personal prayers might be stronger. It would be bad for us, another priest said, if our prayers worked – prayers would be "a kind of commercial enterprise." Now he tells us.

But what surprised me was that modern people – reputable scientists – had ever believed that the effect of prayer could be measured. I think prayer is what you do when concern impels you to act on another person's situation, even though you know you have crossed the threshold into a situation where you have no personal agency. Prayer is how you signal that you know you have entered the dimension where fate hovers over a person, maybe to go this way, maybe that – a dimension where there are no measures, no causes, no effects and which is no more susceptible to scientific inquiry than prayer is to linguistic analysis.

That's how it seems to me. Prayer for the sick, I think, is all the more a loving act within the human community because it is an acknowledgment of powerlessness, not because it is powerful. The scientists were looking the wrong way. If prayer never does the sick or dying good, surely it always does the people who pray good? Doesn't it release them from the prison of the ego by making them move out of themselves toward imagining what it is like to be another person? Doesn't it acknowledge mystery?

But this doesn't apply to all prayer. Praying that a delay to a flight will end doesn't count – that's just superstition, not that I have anything against superstition. But to send out frail words in the hope of affecting the great, malign forces of suffering and death – no wonder special spaces are put aside to do that in.

The Sunday Tribune, June 4, 2006

Charlie Haughey

When I heard that Charlie Haughey was dead I went out of the house. I knew him slightly and it wasn't unlikely that the telephone would ring and somebody on the other end would be looking for an "assessment" of him. And I didn't have one. I've had different ones from time to time, but now I have nothing.

Tens of people have had their say about him this week, not all of them aware that estimates of a chameleon say a lot about the estimator. I know that my own circumstances – my age, my gender, what I think is my place in Irish society – condition my view of him. I've never been able to get away from seeing him within my own history – from remembering, for example, my first consciousness of him, when I used to watch his sharp face from the corner of my eye across a room packed with after-hours drinkers in Groome's Hotel. He was a very, very attractive man then, vibrant, not constricted by self-importance and wariness as he later became. It was understood that he was already on the way to being a minister, though he'd only been in the Dáil four or five years. But he was old, of course, compared to the boyfriends of girls like myself and my sister. And married. And anyway she preferred the looks of Brian Lenihan, who was usually with Charlie. She liked crinkly hair.

We would have been there with our father, who was a so-cial columnist, if that's the right term, with the *Evening Press*. He got up and went out to work in the afternoon, so the only time he might be met was late at night, when he was finished with his round of parties and receptions and went down to Groome's for a few drinks before going back to the newspaper to write "Dubliner's Diary." That's how we mixed with the actors and actresses who'd just performed at the Abbey or the Gate and who, like my father, had been on display all evening and needed to come down. The hours in Groome's modulated between the public world of work and the private world of home.

Not that the home mattered in Groome's. Very few wives had a presence in that exciting, insiders' place – the only place I ever knew Irish bohemia to be on terms of *bonhomie* with power. Because of the protection Mr. and Mrs. Groome had as Fianna Fáil publicans, for a few years artists and politicians and legal people and journalists belonged to the same loose coterie. That, by the way, is one of the ways in which the scene was pre-modern: nowadays, no politician with dealings to hide would dream of socializing with a journalist, even a journalist in as harmless a line of work as my father. But it was pre-modern, too, in the relative sophistication of it all. Married men and – mostly unmarried – women drank and flirted late into the night while, outside, O'Connell Street was silent and monochrome once the cinemagoers had caught their buses home, and beyond O'Connell Street a simple and austere country slept.

Ireland then was just discovering a new way of being a man's world. Now there were men like Charlie and my father who had cars and drivers and business that took them all over the country and no one to answer to. Men who knew every hotel and hotel manager in the 26 counties, men who knew hundreds and hundreds of people to drink whiskey and swap stories with. Men who could walk into any bar or club and be greeted with delight. Both of them were in their different ways pioneers, mapping an Ireland that was halfway between the plowshare and PR, and they thrived in that classless space. There were few celebrities in those days. They were kings of a rainy country. How much is my own view of them inflamed by envy? There'll never be such fun again, and it was never available to women. If their opportunities had been open to me, I don't suppose my personal morality would have stood up to the temptation. And if, later on, I'd acquired huge power, how real would public morality have been to me, since I'd have abandoned a personal standard? And was it almost necessary that there be a generation or two of amoral public men? Was amorality needed to unlock originality? Did men like Charlie and my father have to free themselves from the ethical norms of the quiet, decent lower middle class from which they both came, so as to do new things? They would both have claimed to be patriots, but something, after all, caused them to abandon the personal idealism once synonymous with patriotism.

What happened to the Catholic upbringing – and both Charlie and my father had devout parents and went to Joey's in Marino, a Christian Brothers' school – that confidently distinguished right from wrong? The historical questions surrounding Charlie are almost impossible to answer. And the biographical ones are just as difficult. Turn him this way and that and he looks different to different kinds of people. For example, to the child of a betrayed wife he seems both more glamorous and more destructive than he would to someone else – he looks as if he was always ripe for further transgression. And that's just one example of a circumstance that might underlie an assessment of the man. Good for those who can manage a clear line, and there has been some wonderful writing about Charlie this week. But I don't know where to start. How people choose their path – whether they do – is a mystery still to me.

The Sunday Tribune, June 18, 2006

An Unacknowledged Debt

On the mantelpiece beside me is a metal spoon with a hole in its handle, where it was attached by a cord to a soldier's belt – the spoon from my grandfather Phelan's kit, which he brought home from the First World War. It's great to see the Irishmen who fought in that war being now properly honored. Though the best way to honor them might be to go and aim a venomous spit at every monarch and general and arms-dealer in the world, and at the fat-cat ministers in their limos everywhere who are the successors of the ministers who sent uninformed and unprivileged men off to risk themselves in stupid battles. Trench warfare hardly bears thinking about, so contemptuous was it of the lives of what were frankly called at the time the lower classes. My only reservation about the belated Irish commemoration of Northerner and Southerner, Protestant and Catholic together in the trenches, is that it obscures that fact. As always, Ireland is dulled by British and Irish nationalisms to the rank realities of the class system.

But as regards our general attitude to Britain, I think that this weekend's inclusiveness is less of a breakthrough than it appears. I also think that we owe much, much more to Great Britain than we are quite ready to acknowledge. Moreover the two are related. It seems to me that though the Irish state refused to honor the Irish who fought for England, going over to England and joining up was never a thing that bothered ordinary people – at least, not until the Troubles broke out in

1969. I think that if *Irish Independent* columnist Kevin Myers had ever been able to get out and about in normal Irish life, he would have discovered that far from objecting to fellow citizens fighting in the armies of our legendary oppressor, most people were all for it. This was for straightforward economic reasons. Some of the Irish who signed up in 1914 and 1939 signed up, I suppose, for adventure or even for idealistic reasons – idealism being a shorthand word for being taken in by the propaganda of the warmongers. But mostly they did it for the money. The wife and kids got money while the man was out there. The man got fed and clothed. There was a pension afterwards. And in my grandfather's time, you had a chance of a job in one of Dublin's Protestant enterprises as a reward for your loyalty. It was well worth taking a chance on not getting killed.

The lives of most Irish people for most of the twentieth century were dominated by poverty. Wartime was only one of the times that access to Britain alleviated that poverty. In these days of abstract gestures between one nation and another – when they're apologizing as if they were people for wrongs done to each other – we should be saying thank you to our neighbor. It should be a very big "thank you."

I am certain that Irish people would have died in the streets from hunger, 30 and 40 years after getting our much-vaunted independence, if it had not been for the emigrant boat. As it was, minds died, and hearts died. There was work across the Irish Sea when there was no work here – unless you count the work of the clerks in the employment agencies that arranged our one-way tickets to menial jobs over there and took the few quid back out of our wages. The wealthy could afford the fare to the States. The rest of us could barely get ourselves to Holyhead.

It is perfectly understandable that we do not think of being grateful for work: Britain was buying our labor – there was no philanthropy on their side. But other opportunities opened to us over there that then, and even now, are not open here – ways of being trained and educated, ways of putting together qualifications, ways into professional jobs in, say, the probation service or hospital or university administration, ways of making paralegal and paramedical and business careers. Women, especially, had much wider and better chances across the water than they had here, for almost the whole of the twentieth century.

To a great extent this was due to the glorious tradition of adult education in Britain, which has managed for several centuries now to offer first and second chances at higher education to people excluded from it on grounds of gender, age, or circumstance. The Open University is the latest and the most substantial institution created to serve that constituency. It so happens that last week, at a conferring ceremony in the beautiful Symphony Hall in Birmingham, the OU gave me an honorary doctorate.

"I am a proud Irish patriot," I began my reply to the encomium that was read out, and I went on to express my gratitude to Great Britain for the employment and the other opportunities I got there, over the years, that people of my generation couldn't get at home. I feel that it in no way betrays our own history – or, indeed, takes anything away from the desirability of an all-island Irish Ireland achieved by consent – to acknowledge an individual debt of that kind. Still, it was difficult to do it. By coincidence, what I at last found myself able to say was a tiny effort of the same kind as yesterday's Somme ceremony – the effort to move away from the constricting myth in which the Irish are always victims, and nothing else, of the Anglo-Irish situation. The effort to tell a more complex truth.

The Sunday Tribune, July 2, 2006

Patronizing Women

Hollow laughter. That's the best I can do in response to the plea last week, from the Roman Catholic Archbishop of Dublin, Dr. Diarmuid Martin, that there should be a national debate on the subject of embryos. You'll have noticed, unless you've been living on the beach, that a former couple have turned to the courts to decide the fate of the embryos they had frozen when, as loving partners, they underwent fertility treatment. They've already had a child from that treatment and now the former wife wants the embryos implanted in herself in the hope of having another. To that end her lawyers argue that the embryos may not be destroyed because they are the unborn who our constitution is supposed to protect. The husband's lawyers argue that an embryo is not an unborn until it could be born; that is, until it is implanted in the womb; that outside the womb it can't turn into a baby; and that therefore the embryos can be destroyed.

Notice the position of the husband, by the way. For reasons that seem to him compelling he does not want a child of his to be borne by this woman. He wants to prevent the development of the viable, independent life of such a child. That's exactly the position of women who seek abortions: they have reasons which seem to them good not to proceed with a pregnancy. Who would have foreseen that the questions raised by abortion would become unisex – that the subject might be somewhat freed of the element of fundamental contempt for women and disgust at their bodies?

Archbishop Martin didn't live here during the so-called debates about the unborn of the early 1980s and 1990s. He was in Rome. It is usually represented as a good thing that he came back to the local ecclesiastical scene with clean hands, though of course it doesn't say much for the local ecclesiastical scene. But by publicly calling for a debate on human life – that is, a debate on abortion – he reveals himself as something of a stranger.

There are hugely important questions to be debated. Professor Ronald Dworkin, for instance, long ago published thoughts on the law and its possible responses to the different trimesters of pregnancy which have never been discussed in Ireland because the antiabortion people insist that thinking about abortion is a step towards abortion. We're not to think. Just last week, an Italian expert in the present case told the court that in her country there are no frozen embryos any more because the approach to fertilization differs from the practice here. We're not to hear about comparative technologies either, it seems, because comparison might weaken an absolutist position.

But nobody could possibly want to debate again with representatives of the Irish Roman Catholic church – by definition, a debater is on the other side. No veteran of the other side could hope for respect for women's experience and women's moral capacities. Even though there might not again be a grotesquerie like the *Late Late Show* where (to the eternal disgrace of RTÉ) "Father" Michael Cleary was allowed to present a collection of gravely disabled people to illustrate his point that if the unborn were not protected by the constitution, women would choose not to have disabled babies and the wheelchair-users surrounding him in the television studio would have been murdered in the womb. It is not beside the point that Michael Cleary was a hysteric and a hypocrite who did his best to destroy the woman he installed, when she was very young, as his concubine – as was well known to many of his priest colleagues. What matters more is the profound disrespect of the complex and morally exacting experience of bearing and rearing a disabled child, and the denial of the selfless love and care offered to such children all over the world and throughout history by people in general, but above all by mothers.

I still flinch when I think of the variation offered on Cleary's characterization of "women" by a perfectly sane cleric, Bishop Joseph Cassidy. I heard him say solemnly, on an authoritative radio program shortly before the voting, that the most dangerous place for a child to be in the world today is in its mother's womb. I know, and everyone knows, that their mothers have been the protectors of children, always and everywhere, against war and famine and indifference and neglect. Fathers are very often protectors, too, of course, but the central, overwhelming fact is that the children of the planet are brought through childhood by the women of the planet. To ignore this fact for the sake of a debating point was, and is, astonishingly hurtful. What does such a skewing of the record of women bespeak but enmity – an enmity all the more lively for being unconscious?

I'd be very interested in knowing what has changed. What part of the abortion question does Archbishop Martin think is now open to debate? That is, if he meant debate. But I think he meant what he also plainly said – that he wants influence. He wants his Church's views in there influencing whatever policy emerges from the court's deliberations in the embryo case. Well, he's entitled to that and there's not the slightest doubt he'll get it. But is there any hope he can get it just in simple acknowledgment of his position as a leader of the majority Church? Could we skip the debate bit? Insulting women and patronizing women and restating a belief about what God wants women to do is not debate. As many of us have already been unforgettably taught.

The Sunday Tribune, July 30, 2006

Islam and the West

There was an article in one of the Sundays recently so blind to its own prejudices that I haven't been able to forget it. Even though I try to make a point of forgetting anything that uses a phrase such as "Feminists believe …" It's just ridiculous to pretend that there's a whole body of women out there – of all ages, from all cultures, having had all kinds of life experiences – who all believe the same thing. There is no feminist party line on a conflict like the one recently expressed in south Lebanon. Yet this article attempted to argue, on the basis of three, or perhaps four, individuals, that "feminists" support Hezbollah.

This surprised me, to put it mildly. I know women who are pro-Palestinian alright, but I know many conscious, active feminists who are pro-Israeli. The majority of women, I assume, like the majority of everybody, see right and wrong on both sides. But the article, assuming that "feminists" are pro-Islam, asked how Western women can support cultures in which women are stoned to death for adultery, can be divorced on a man's word, cover their faces or get acid thrown on them, are denied education and health care and much more. All of which is well worth asking. I certainly wouldn't want to live in a culture where women walk behind men, to start with. Even newspaper photos of gatherings in places such as Saudi Arabia or Pakistan or Afghanistan infuriate me when the captions talk of the "people" in the photo – they're not the people, they're the men and boys.

For myself, the values of Christianity, as expanded by ideals like those of the French Revolution or the early trade-union movement or socialism, would be just fine if they were put into practice. In other words, I'm Western. But I do not, like the writer of the article, take it for granted that I understand Islamic cultures. Or that the values of Western cultures are terrifically superior.

For one thing, I visited Iran after the Islamic revolution, and brief as my time there was, I met women who had chosen to come back from modern, assimilated lives in places like Los Angeles and Oxford and Paris because that was their choice. They chose to live in a theocratic society. In general, hard as it was for me to believe it, I met many women who felt themselves protected and empowered by what I saw as the oppressive dominance of men. I met them in relaxed and unwatched circumstances – at a children's gymnastics competition, for example, and at a wedding – and they made it clear that it seemed to them their ways are better than our ways.

An example was covering up with the chador. Western commentators are appalled by women having to hide themselves. But women I met pitied Western women for having to be on display all the time and were equally appalled by the use of women's bodies in Western advertising. "Why should the seminude bodies of women be displayed on huge billboards on highways?" was the kind of point they made. And for just a few hours, when I came back to our world, it seemed to me, too, that how the female body is used in the West is, indeed, a weird thing.

If we saw ourselves from outside, we would not be as sure of our superiority as the author of the article. What is so great about a world where starving children pick over the tarmac of roads in the hope a few grains of wheat might have fallen from a lorry? Where whole communities of adults out of their minds on drink, or drugs like methamphetamine, use their children sexually and in other ways torture them? What's so great about pornography being the most popular industry on the Internet? About walking through cities at night and seeing fellow human beings asleep in doorways? About watching the toil and privation men and women endure in order just to subsist – in mines in South America, in brothels, on their knees on peasant farms – while the likes of Paris Hilton and Stephanie of Monaco and Mike Tyson are worshipped?

Just as the writer of the article picked out vivid examples of women's oppression in Islamic countries, I could talk about my culture, where women slide down poles in high heels in front of masturbating men for small sums of money, or women clean offices in the middle of the night while men sleep, or women hide with their children below window height in refuges for fear of the violence of the fathers of the children, or women are denied treatment for foetus-threatening cancers because men called priests forbid it. I would be doing what she was doing – exaggerating, for the sake of argument.

Criticism of Islamic cultures should flourish. And let it be strong and sustained: it was Al Qaeda, after all, who murdered the innocents of the Twin Towers, not the other way round. Let us be rightly glad that a Taliban could not rise to power in the Western world, however powerful the so-called Christian right may become. Let attacks on the misogyny of Islam continue. But let there be self-criticism, too. The fact has to be acknowledged that human beings have failed in the project of living together, and they've failed everywhere. There are degrees of failure, of course, and our failure is different from theirs. But we too have failed.

The Sunday Tribune, September 10, 2006

Gross Bigotry

I once had dinner in a hotel with Katherine Zappone and Ann Louise Gilligan, the two women who are at present challenging in the High Court the decision of the Revenue Commissioners not to recognize the same-sex marriage they contracted in Canada three years ago – a marriage which is valid for all purposes in Canada. They claim that the Revenue Commissioners' decision not to treat them the same as a heterosexual married couple is in breach of their constitutional rights and in breach of the European Convention on Human Rights.

They want their marriage recognized and if they don't get that, they want a declaration that they are entitled to marry each other in Ireland. It's a law case, so reports of it can't but use formal and legalistic language, and perhaps the whole thing comes across as somewhat heavy duty. But what I remember about that dinner is what fun the two of them were, and that, although we had to go to a serious debate afterwards, we never stopped laughing.

The decision in this case isn't the only important thing about it. The talk that surrounds it matters. Attitudes to it matter. It is one of a series of speakings-out which over the last 20 years or so have challenged the silences that held the old Ireland together. We've heard for the first time from rape victims; from the children of incestuous homes; from many, many people who were dreadfully abused, both inside and outside institutions, by figures of so-called authority.

Many of these revelations have been about cruelty and suffering, and many of the people concerned can't be called anything but victims. But Katherine Zappone and Ann Louise Gilligan are not only, as far as I know, not suffering – their lives have been blessed with the very best thing two people can have: a long relationship based on wholehearted love and trust. I envy them that. I saw in action, the evening we spent a few hours together – and of course I've often seen it in other couples – the truth that two people who empower each other, and who haven't ceased to relish each other, are even more of a pleasure to be with than one happy person. It's not surprising that human beings want to form couples, and want their coupleness to be recognized by others as the central thing it is in their lives.

A more cheerful pair than these two I can't imagine. Yet they are victims, too. And their account of themselves, given in court, does belong with the outpouring of witness from other individuals whose experiences have been excluded from Ireland's account of itself. They all found themselves assumed to be – by other people, or by institutions, or by the state itself – powerless.

But this couple have used their personal strength, their trained intelligences, and their contacts to mount a challenge to the way things are. When they demonstrate to Ireland that homosexual people are as proud and loving, as self-respecting and respectable, as heterosexual people, they allow the question to be formulated – why, then, are homosexual people discriminated against? (It's a pity that ordinary, inadequate people with things to hide and dodgy pasts can't be used to mount revolutionary challenges, but they can't, and we have to thank heaven that such paragons of worthiness as Mary

Robinson, or Katherine and Ann Louise do exist.) The court action also leads to the truly subversive question – what did heterosexual people ever do to deserve favorable treatment from this state? What makes their marriages superior?

The argument that marriage is about having children doesn't hold: lots of straight marriages are not and cannot be about having children and lots of gay marriages are. The argument that marriage is a sacrament doesn't hold: ours is a democracy, not a theocracy. The argument that same-sex marriage will destabilize society doesn't hold: does Canada seem destabilized to you? And as for what human beings do in bed; it may have been in the interests of the old patriarchy to con people into thinking that what the majority of men do or would like to do to women is normal and everything else is not, but the truth is that in the privacy of the bed, there's no such thing as a rule about which ridiculous act is acceptable to society and which is not. The two lovers are society.

I can't help but wonder, when I remember how light-hearted we all were the time we had dinner together, why more value isn't placed on lives that are enjoyed. Why do so many societies go out of their way to be punitive? Life is so short that you'd think humanity would make every effort to design its laws so as to contribute to the greatest happiness of the greatest number. Why shouldn't these two decent women be given the opportunity to institutionalize their happiness? I can't see that anyone or anything would be harmed by their doing so. It's true, I think, that marrying someone is perhaps the most gloriously irrational and optimistic thing most people do in all their lives, but that seems to me a reason to include everyone in the idealism: not to keep categories of people out.

Should the High Court rule in a way that doesn't support

this view, I still won't be able to see that to deny human beings, on the basis of the nature of their sexuality, the opportunity of vowing to love, is anything other than gross bigotry. And should the High Court rule in a way that does support me – well, I just hope I'm asked to the party.

The Sunday Tribune, October 15, 2006

Sex Matters

Having sex really matters. Everyone knows that. So does not having sex. What arrangements an individual makes with their own sexuality and how the individual thinks other people perceive their sexuality is a profoundly important theme during the whole lifespan from puberty to old age. Of course, this doesn't mean that people think about sex all the time; even young men bursting with testosterone only manage three times a minute. But there can have been few people so detached from the subject that when they read the reports of the survey of the Irish and sex which was presented last week, they did not pause to compare themselves to everybody else.

Good old Ireland – bringing up the rear, as always, when it comes to investigating the body, or pleasure, or any experience which has not been presorted according to hierarchies of class and gender importance. This was the first comprehensive study since the foundation of the Irish state, whereas when did Kinsey start establishing some private truths about America – half a century ago? More? No wonder some truly astonishing changes have been revealed.

What do the priests make, for example, of the slide from 71 percent of the population, 30 years ago, believing that sex before marriage is always a sin, to 6 percent now? That's not a decline: that's abandonment. It bears out what I've always thought – that the teachings of the Catholic Church, while the Church itself is much-loved and needed and an intrinsic part of our tribal identity, aren't even considered when they clash with self-interest. On a spectrum from making false insurance claims to providing hiding places for IRA killers, the adults do what they do; and now, it seems, the 17-year-olds do what they do, too.

My generation had to handle sexuality as best it could in the face of savagely punitive authorities. In that we belonged to a continuum of repression that stretched so far back that it seemed to define Ireland. For as long as anyone could remember, girls who got pregnant before marriage were hunted out of the community, without pity. To this day I can't bear to think about some of the suffering I witnessed then. So my first reaction to reading this survey was to go into a church and thank whoever or whatever brings about societal change that those days are over.

Not, by the way, that I approve of 17-year-olds having sex. I think it's far too intimate a thing to share with some hottie picked up at a disco. And I think there should be a new sin called risking having a baby just because the two of you are too excited and shy to check that one of you is using contraception. Leaving the baby aside – babies manage to thrive, it seems, no matter what – a young person's life is inclined to stop dead when they take on the responsibility of parenting. They drop out, for example, from education.

And one of the most unexpected things this study does is provide a motivation for staying in education. I was attracted to the section on frequency of sex because I've always been struck by how regret for moderation surfaces on the deathbed. The poet Keats, who had much else undone to mourn for, said about the girl he loved, "I should have had her while I was well." John Betjeman said his main wish, looking back at his life, was that he'd had more sex. W. B. Yeats, as he aged, did everything he could to stay in touch with all forms of creativity (that's putting it very genteelly). And if having lots of sex is an aim in life, then it's a good idea to stay in school. "There is evidence," this study says, "of a greater frequency of sex among people with higher educational qualifications."

You still won't be at it as often as some of the young, who manage to have sex daily. But then, they probably have a much larger pool of partners to choose from than you do. "The availability of partners is the crucial factor in how often you have sex," so any amount of PhDs or even professorships won't help if you live in semiretirement under the eye of one, watchful, spouse.

Yet the real surprise of this study, for me, was the figure for satisfaction. I've always associated sex with difficulty – that it is difficult to find the right partner, and then difficult to reach a happy intimacy with them, and then difficult to keep the intimacy going through all the many events of a busy life. And literature could hardly exist without accounts of unwise passion and passion frustrated and intense sexual loneliness and tragic misalliance. But then along comes this survey to tell us that no less than 70 percent of Irish women and 57 percent of Irish men are satisfied with their sex lives. That's very hard to believe. I mean, that's probably more than are satisfied with the performance of the Ireland soccer team or Bertie Ahern as Taoiseach.

The suspicion can't but arise that they're satisfied with the first of these – as they are perhaps with the second and the third – because they have low expectations. But to join in the general cheer – what's wrong with that? To be reasonably pleased with whatever hand life has dealt you, sex-wise, is a fine, sensible thing to be. And it's very good for your health. Think of all the great romantic heroes and heroines who risked their all for a perfection of bliss. Where did they end up? Right. Dead. They ended up (a) brokenhearted and (b) dead.

The Sunday Tribune, October 22, 2006

Tribal Icons

I feel vaguely but pervasively guilty when I forget about Northern Ireland. Not that bearing it in mind ever did me or it any good, but I've taken on board decades of scathing reproach about us pleasure-loving, bourgeois-collaborationist Free Staters, who sold our Northern brothers and sisters out so as to cling to our own comforts, and to the unearned pseudo-freedoms which we have done nothing to extend to them. And that's our friends. I take it for granted that the other side doesn't daily heap brimstone on my head only because its tactic is to pretend that the Republic isn't there at all, and that if it is, it has no right to comment on matters Northern.

Insofar as I understand what's not going on up there, the sticking points seem extremely serious. It will be a huge change in their culture when Loyalists share some kind of genuine executive with Republicans. And it will be the end not just of an era, but of eras stretching back to the early seventeenth century, when Republicans accept an order and laws for which Westminster is ultimately responsible. But that doesn't mean it is at all interesting for the outsider to sit around waiting for these concessions to be made. It certainly seems to me that, not only will they be made sooner or later, but that if it is later, it doesn't greatly matter – that life has settled down in Northern Ireland in an irrevocable way (bar the crazies) and will go on being settled, no matter which bits of what agreement are supposedly in force.

In other words, there's no hurry, lads. No one's holding their breath.

But I was made sincerely ashamed of my own flippancy by the near-unbelievable suggestion, made, it seems, by "British government representatives in Rome," that the Queen of England and the Pope be invited to visit Northern Ireland more or less simultaneously to celebrate the bringing about of so-called peace by the latest ingenious attempt to establish power-sharing that doesn't look like power-sharing – the one that would be referred to as the St. Andrew's Agreement, if in fact it was ever mentioned in normal conversation.

For one awful moment, I felt what it must be like actually to be from Northern Ireland, or to live there, and to have to put up with being patronized from a height by every idiot in the English establishment, who, if this suggestion is anything to go by, privately think of the North as if it is inhabited by cartoon characters – mad papists on one side, mad royalists on the other. People who think that a response to a very difficult political settlement can be manipulated by rushing symbolic figures onto Northern territory for a few hours. It would be a few hours, I need hardly say – the diaries of the demigods are booked up years ahead. But whoever made the suggestion must believe that even a short visit, from behind 20 layers of bodyguards, would be enough to dazzle the people of the North.

What kind of people do these distant governors think Northern people are? Something on the lines of natives of New Guinea, who worship bits of airplanes? Britain's colony in Ireland has had hundreds of years to perfect internal structures of exploitation, oppression, and bitter subversion now being painstakingly dismantled. There is a well of malice there that is practically bottomless. Very recently, each side watched without pity their neighbors being gravely wounded. The worst is certainly over, but the bar has been set almost impossibly high for cooperation. And with all this, some civil servant or diplomat thinks that parading the very tribal icons that started the Troubles off in 1611 or whenever is a lovely little idea.

My outrage has nothing to do with practicalities, though I assume that someone sane pointed out that the logistics of a simultaneous visit would be impossible. For one thing, you couldn't just bring in Her Majesty for the Prods, and not let Catholics with a lively interest in the monarchy get a look at her. The Pontiff, on the other hand, couldn't be paraded around Loyalist areas at all, due to sincere fundamentalist objections to his very existence. Is Pope Benedict the Whore of Babylon or is he not? That's what the people Ian Paisley has fed on bigotry would want to know, and it would put the Queen in an impossible position – she owning the place, and Pope Benedict being her guest. That's just for starters.

But the point is that a visit from anyone at all would be nothing but a sideshow. Patsy McGarry of *The Irish Times* – who got this story from "sources" – should go back to the sources and break the news to them that the people in Northern Ireland are both as simple and as complex as any other people. That most of them want what people the world over want – to live with normal access to education and employment and advantage, with a normal amount of self-approval, under fairly competent managers who are backed by a reasonably even-handed judicial system. That waving relics at them – and both the Queen and the Pope are, politically speaking, relics of ancient regimes – does not send them home to bed starry-eyed. And that if it did, the place would be in even more trouble than it is in today.

The Sunday Tribune, November 5, 2006

Marriage and the Constitution

What is the magic ingredient in marriage, I ask you? Is there a magic ingredient in marriage? I have no firsthand experience of the state, but I firmly believe that it does change each person's view of who they are and what relation they are in to each other. I base this on the curious fact that not one, not two, but three different women, at different times, have told me that they knew on their wedding day, without doubt, that they shouldn't have married their husbands. These were women who'd been more or less living with their men perfectly happily. That's what makes me think that the vows themselves are potent, though whether for good or ill I don't know.

Our constitution also thinks that marriage is in itself a transforming act. The natural parents in the Baby Ann case got their child back because they married. The Irish Constitution pledges itself "to guard with special care the institution of Marriage, on which the Family is founded, and to protect it against attack." So the poor adoptive parents hadn't a chance. Ann's natural parents married and therefore, with their child, they form a family exactly within the meaning of the constitution.

But it's not that the constitution believes that married people make a more stable family unit than unmarried people who choose to live together. It's not, in the case of adoption, that anyone argues that it is easier for a child to fit in with the norm than with the exception to the norm, though I think that's very likely true. The adoptive parents in this sad case are married, too, don't forget. Defining the family as the natural children of parents who are in the contractual relationship called marriage must be about conception and about ownership as well. It is the definition that places as many restrictions as possible on the variousness of humanity. It makes it more likely than any other arrangement that a man can look around his table at the children gathered there and say complacently, "these are mine."

I remember hearing that when Éamon de Valera was working on the constitution, he used to go around to Blackrock College on his bicycle and talk it over with his pal, the priest who was president there. I don't know whether their conversations were minuted, but if they were, I'd like to know whether they understood the implications of shoring up the privileged position of marriage. The natural parents of Ann marrying meant, Mrs. Justice McGuinness said this week, that the question was no longer the best interests of the child but the lawfulness or otherwise of the adoptive parents' custody of her. "This meant," she said, "that it was no longer possible for the court to look at the matter from the point of view of the child."

Many people believe that tremendously difficult questions such as the Ann question shouldn't be asked in the courts at all. They shouldn't be fitted to the template of legal argument in front of a judge or judges. There might be instead some sort of tribunal which reached some kind of legally binding outcome, but by a reflective rather than an argumentative process. I see no reason to believe that psychologists, social workers, or teachers are necessarily better than lawyers at judging the outcome of adoption decisions. But they live and work with children, so they build up expertise in this area, which lawyers do not. And they're less arrogant and self-seeking, and they don't try to separate themselves from ordinary experience by tons of money and fake British accents.

Above all, a tribunal might be able to work quickly. One of the outrageous aspects of this case is that Ann's natural mother first tried to get her child back 10 months ago. You don't have to believe everything psychiatrists and other commentators say about a child's formative years to see that the delay in deciding who may act as parents to Ann is the most harmful thing that has happened to the child so far. Not to mention that the natural parents had a particular right to expedition, in a case where delay may have enormous adverse consequences for them as a family unit.

We'll never know what will become of the five people concerned. I hope not, anyway. I hope Ann will now disappear into the anonymous, win-some, lose-some, generally warm experience of growing up that most people know. I hope the adoptive parents, whose loss must be in some ways worse even than death, will find a child they can keep to give new love to. I hope the cowardly politicians, our so-called legislators, who have never had the vision or heart to reform the adoption laws, will prepare themselves to do so soon.

And I hope we'll find some way to institutionalize the fact that in the latter part of the twentieth century, there was another blossoming of the meaning of the injunction laid down by Christ and other great teachers that we should love one another, and that those latest insights inspire us to extend full human and civic rights to social units other than husband, wife, and child of husband/wife. That, in other words, the referendum on the rights of the child promised for next year will rethink what marriage in itself is, and whose rights –

272

if anyone's – it favors, and that it will release us from constitutional concepts created in the 1930s by a devout Roman Catholic man born, and forever a child of, 1882.

The Sunday Tribune, November 19, 2006

Humanizing Economics

I'm never invited to talk in clubs in Ireland. In fact, I don't know that there are many clubs in Ireland that organize evenings of serious talking. But I'm in America at the moment and professional clubs matter here, perhaps because, in such a huge country, networking is something people in the same line of business have to do because they can't rely on bumping into each other. The rather grand Overseas Press Club in midtown Manhattan is basically for and about foreign correspondents. Thanks to Ireland's present status in the world, it held a panel discussion recently that examined the question – how has Ireland managed to surge forward economically? I was one of the speakers – something of a wild card. The other speakers actually knew something about the subject.

But economics doesn't exist independently of the general culture. Being a poor country or a prosperous country is a matter of the detail of lived experience for the people in that country. The speakers the other night kept referring to the Irish labor force. But what is a labor force, or rather, who is it? How is it linked with the past and future? I brooded about that on the long subway ride home.

It was agreed by all concerned the other night that a major reason for our sudden economic well-being was that in the 1990s, when profitable American companies were looking for an EU country to open up in, they chose Ireland because of its labor force. And what was so great about the labor force? Well, they said, it was and is large, well-educated, and English-speaking. I amused myself by looking at each of those words.

Take "English-speaking." If we were not English-speaking, which we are thanks to our specific responses to colonial oppression by Britain – Wales, you notice, was also oppressed, but the Welsh did not lose their language – we would not be enjoying our present prosperity. Property is much cheaper in Italy or France or Germany and the roads and railways are indescribably better and the food is in a different and higher league, but if you were an American or Asian CEO setting up a business in an EU country all that wouldn't count against the problems presented by any other language than English. So – thank you, England.

Then take "well-educated." What does it mean to say that the Irish labor force is well-educated? Against whom is it being compared? And what is the educational goal the workers have well achieved? Have they learnt to be independent thinkers? Have they found their way to identifying their own gifts and to releasing their own creativity? Perhaps well-educated means nothing more than that for the last 35 years or so most Irish students haven't left school till they're well into their teens and nowadays a high proportion have gone on to third-level study. But the same could be said for the young people of many other countries. What is it about Irish education that makes the Irish so suitable for employment? It doesn't just mean, does it, that they're good at obeying American bosses?

Now take the seemingly innocuous word, "large." Behind this word, I decided – as I raced across the platform to change trains – a massive cultural shift is hiding. How did the Irish labor force become so large? Well, I'll tell you. It got large by Irish mothers having big families – very, very big families, followed over time by big families, followed by families declining in size towards the EU average. And why did Irish women have so many children?

They had them because they had few options but to have them, until, in 1979, Charles Haughey defied the majority Church and those who follow papal teaching in this matter and brought in limited access to contraception for married couples as an Irish solution to an Irish problem. As soon as there was widespread access to contraception, family size fell dramatically. So the economic miracle owes its existence to *Mná na hÉireann*! Had you realized that? How often do specialist commentators make that point? We'd be nowhere today without all the workers our mothers and grandmothers provided us with.

What's more, as soon as the adult lives of the women of Ireland were not wholly spent in childrearing, the women sought paid work. They came from a standing start to constitute the biggest addition to the Irish labor force in recent decades – in fact, for a time more or less all its growth was due to the entry of women. And there are more women to come. Even now, there aren't as many women working outside as well as inside the home as there are in most other EU countries. The jobs women get at the moment are clustered at the bottom end of the pay scale, where they may be the foundation of personal power, but they don't add up to social power.

But just you wait. Even as things are, women's entry into the labor force means changed childrearing, changed parent-to-parent and parent-to-child relationships, and in the end it will mean changed women. Which is not unexpected, they just having given birth to the Celtic Tiger. And with this little exercise in humanizing the "dismal science" of economics completed to my satisfaction, the train rattled into my station.

The Sunday Tribune, December 17, 2006

Nouveau Materialism

I had a bet on with myself, whether Diarmuid Martin, the Catholic Archbishop of Dublin, would go on about greed in his Christmas homily, and I'm sorry to say he did. All the spiritual leaders seem to be worried about our values now that we have money, as if our values were just fine when we were half-desperate from the lack of it. Our values, note. Our greed. Not Charles J. Haughey's greed or Ray Burke's greed or George Redmond's greed or the greed sloshing around the Fianna Fáil tent at the Galway Races. Not a word about that. Just the greed of people who until recently were in no position to be greedy.

I personally hope that you have lots of money in 2007. Money is the great facilitator. It opens the door to new experience. It buys services. It can't protect you against illness or death, but it can make all the difference to how you endure the one and stay comfortable when the other begins to loom. Friends can't be bought, but the opportunities for making them can. Attention can be bought. Education can be bought. You name some good that can't be approached by being bought and I'll be very much surprised.

Including being good. Money can help us to be good – or at least, the absence of money made us bad. We know for sure, as a matter of bitter experience, that when Ireland was poor it was a horrible, unjust, miserable, tight, and mean place, exceptionally cruel to women, children, and the poor. The only excuse for the condition this country was in by the 1950s was poverty. Only seeing children as rats who would eat the last of the grain can begin to explain why they were treated as they were. Not that poverty of itself makes children seem a burden. All over Africa, for example, in situations of deprivation and even hunger, children are loved and enjoyed. It took the churchmen we had then, as well as mass poverty, to create the Ireland where children were treated like animals who invited punishment, and men and women were afraid of each other, afraid of their own sexuality, afraid of their minds, and in despair at the destiny that shoveled them onto the emigrant boats. The "orphanages" and industrial schools and mother-and-baby homes of that era were excrescences of a society rotten in multiple ways. Still, the best defense against it was money.

A few months ago there was a horrendous car-crash in rural Ireland in which several young people died, and the priest at one of the funerals preached a sermon on the theme of how the past 20 years or so have ruined the values by which Irish people once lived. What this had to do with the tragic loss of those young people, I do not know. As far as I understand it, their last hours were spent having a few drinks in the local pub, where they thoroughly enjoyed themselves. I don't see how the rest of us are implicated at all. Still – the sermon was highly praised. There must be quite a hankering for the generalized guilt which was such an effective instrument of ideological control in the past. There must be a kind of hankering for the bad old days.

Archbishop Brady took up the theme recently. In his view, "more and more people are fearful of the future, isolated, and make no life commitments" – though if he'd ever drunk in Kilburn or Coventry or Springfield, Massachusetts, with some of the elderly Irish people who were human exports from the old Ireland, he'd really know what fear, isolation, and the incapacity to make life commitments are like. At least if you're in this state, when you have money in your pocket, you have some agency in it. Up to now, it was a state imposed by poverty.

The primate went on to link morality with manners. The nuns used to do the same, especially the more snobbish orders. To be genteel was to be holy. What is our senior churchman, in the face of the human condition, doing, linking the bad language used by Podge and Rodge in a puppet show with "where we are going morally and spiritually?" Ah, I see. He says he wants back "decency and respect." Well, decency is perfectly compatible with potty language. And respect? Respect for his or any authority is not at all the same when you've money in your pocket and you don't need a priest's reference to get a job. Deference, in modern Ireland, has to be earned.

This isn't to say that our nouveau materialism isn't going through a phase of gross ostentation, waking up gross envy in the people who aren't being ostentatious. Sure we've had no practice – most of us don't know how to have money and be nice or have money and be good. But at least now we are in a position to find out. At least now, if we don't cherish our infants, educate our children, give to the needy, and pay our taxes, it will be evident that those are our choices. But it is perfectly possible that, in time, we'll settle down into quite a decent little society.

The churchmen who berate us for our vulgar enjoyment of wealth have never themselves wanted for a meal, never tried to get a child a job, never watched a clever man or woman drink away their cleverness in the absence of an educational or any other opportunity. If they had – if they were inured to the lowest of expectations, the way we used to be – they'd pause now to thank God for the change that has come over Ireland, and to face the consequences for themselves of us not being sheep and this place no longer being a vale of tears.

The Sunday Tribune, December 31, 2006

A Generous Life

My friend Seán Mac Réamoinn died on Wednesday. He was my friend since I was 17 years old, and I last saw him a week ago, and a whole sphere of reference dies for me with him. And I can never thank him again, now, for all that he showed me.

He did important public things in his life, and one of them, which no obituary will omit, was that with his friends, a marvelous band of bilingual and Ireland-loving men and women, he founded Cumann Merriman. The Merriman people relished the language and what's more they relished life – they liked other people and drinking and singing and listening to singing and arguing and being attracted and set-dancing and gossip and the acquisition of detailed, intimate, loving knowledge of every corner of this island. Their summer school aimed to rescue Irish for pleasure and emotion.

It was Seán's personal inclusiveness lightly institutionalized. It was his mentoring energy finding a form. And that's what the obituaries may not capture – that what he was in the Dublin where I was lucky enough to settle into being his combination pupil and gofer was a mentor. Since most of the social, not to mention the intellectual, life of the time took place in pubs, young gofers were almost a recognized caste. It was they who had to go off to try to collect a check or to leave in a book review just scribbled on a bit of paper borrowed from the barman or to buy the pound of sausages intended in the long run to be brought home to the wife or to place a bet or, above all, to make a phone call. And the telephone boxes of the time – remember the steel boxes with button A and button B? – were not for the fainthearted.

The important person in the group, you see – the one who was on form, pouring out anecdotes and jokes and information and working by instinct to stimulate everyone there and unobtrusively coax them into the company – that person, who was often Seán, couldn't move. Once that person put on his coat – I never knew a woman to be that person – the whole thing was over. So that person had to send out the student – apprentices like myself were known as students even when we weren't actually studying anything anywhere – to establish where everyone else was. Because there was a population then, mainly of men, who migrated between the newspaper offices and Radio Éireann, then in the GPO, and various departments of the civil service, and UCD, then in Earlsfort Terrace, and a large and varied selection of pubs; and they were always looking for each other. (Women journalists had not yet been invented, except for those writing on the women's pages, but there were Radio Éireann women and a few girlfriends and mistresses and the occasional wife.)

The most characteristic action of this population was putting the head around the door – of the pub, or the snug, or the back lounge – to see who was there. The incomer had to gauge whether they were entitled to join such-and-such a company. They had to estimate how long everyone there had already been drinking and how likely it was that they were heading for trouble. The incomer had to weigh the duties of the job and home against the attraction of the present company – and I never saw anyone turn away at the door for fear of being bored by Seán Mac Réamoinn. And for peripheral figures who had done nothing to distinguish themselves – for example, myself – there was the question of whether they were wanted.

Even wit and erudition and personal distinction wouldn't necessarily make a person wanted; the only thing that was certain to, just like in *Ulysses*, was the money to buy a round, since everyone concerned was either poor or grindingly poor. I had no money and if it wasn't that Seán was my patron, I would have had no entrée to hours, days, years of sitting in pubs listening to the best of talk. Golden times.

Seán could do his jobs on the hoof, well able to scrawl a thousand-word article or script on more or less anything while constantly on the move; I remember him in joyous talk all over Rome and London as well as the most remote corners of Ireland – though he couldn't type and couldn't drive. But he settled down, of course, into the substantial work and service to the country that the obituarists will document. Yet to me that era in his life when I first knew him was the truest to his nature. He was profligate with his personality. He never said a sentence that he didn't make interesting or have an encounter that he didn't put energy into. He was a feeling man with a rich store of mind anyway, but what made him hum and buzz and sparkle was society. He wanted to love his fellow man – he believed in Christ and Christ's injunction that we should love one another. But it surely never crossed his mind that his way of living his life exemplified that love – that when he bustled around Dublin, creating little outposts of the life-force wherever he held court for a while, he was celebrating other people as well as himself. But it crossed my mind, without my knowing the words for it. I saw him make a gift of himself to other people, conferring value on them through nothing more magic than talk. I saw him and thank him for demonstrating, without for a minute meaning to, that there's such a thing as living generously.

The Sunday Tribune, January 21, 2007

Irish-American Culture

March is always a great month for Oirishry in Manhattan, and there's more than ever of it this year, because of the success of Garry Hynes's production of Brian Friel's *Translations*, which has generated a series of discussions, and because there'll be an event in honor of the late Ben Kiely, organized by the writer Colum McCann, who also sets up a day of readings by Irish and Irish-American writers in a bar called Puck Fair every St. Patrick's Day. And because of a terrific program of music and lectures at Glucksman Ireland House, including a big commemoration of the late, great John McGahern and a couple of lectures by women academics – one on the truths behind the stereotype of the Irish servant girl, one on the key role played by Irish nuns in the development of care for the sick in New York – exactly the kind of fields of inquiry, by the way, which are thriving in the U.S. for reasons which the managers of National University of Ireland, Galway, who are in the process of downgrading their respected Women's Studies program, would do well to ponder.

And there's much more Irish-flavored stuff around. There's an Irish-American television series called *The Black Donnellys* – "We can't compete with *The Sopranos*," Frank McCourt said. "We haven't the cuisine" – and then there's Scorsese's *The Departed*.

Last week, the wonderful Lower East Side Tenement Museum organized a panel discussion with Frank McCourt, Terry Golway, Pete Hamill, and other famous Manhattan Irish-

Americans about where the Irish presence is in New York now, and whether it is mostly a legacy. A large audience shoehorned itself into a trendy corner bar – which would once have been a saloon – to listen to these stars on this subject. There probably hadn't been as many Irish people in the area, Peter Quinn remarked, since the Draft Riots (riots by poor Irish immigrants in 1863 against being drafted by Lincoln to fight in the Civil War on behalf of blacks, with whom they habitually vied for jobs).

I made the rather obvious point that where Irishness resides in Manhattan now is in high culture. And that, in some ways, equals a retreat from importance. The only visceral, deeply felt bond between Irish-America and Ireland was green nationalism, and now it is a spent force. Since the Anglo-Irish and St. Andrew's agreements, the urgency has gone out of the identity politics of the island, and therefore out of any Irish-American political issue, except immigration policy. The old bulls – Teddy Kennedy, John Hume, and Martin Galvin, for example – have not been replaced by young bulls.

What there is is status on the performance side of the entertainment business, in most of the arts and, up to a point, in the print media. But there's not, to my mind, a Manhattan-Irish intelligentsia, or an Irish philanthropic/social establishment or, indeed, any Irish establishment. The Minister for Arts, Sports and Tourism, John O'Donoghue, said – when he recently launched a plan for an Irish cultural center in Manhattan, to which Gabriel Byrne is generously giving his time and energy – that "the Irish in America have made a significant contribution to American culture in business and politics. It is only right and fitting that we celebrate this proud tradition … by developing an Irish cultural center." But why culture to celebrate business and politics? Why celebrate one thing with another thing?

Why not, to celebrate business success, develop mutually beneficial business strategies? The Chinese and Egyptians and many another immigrant group are powerful commercial forces for each other. Why not, to celebrate the importance we once had in politics, work to establish a post-Northern Ireland Irish-American political presence? It is very noticeable here, when full-page petitions to do with foreign or domestic issues are printed in the newspapers, that few if any names beginning with Mac or O have signed. And why is there no Irish-American journal of current affairs? The Jews of New York are a vibrant presence in talk, action and publication in the politics of the city and the country, but the Irish are not.

Any truthful description of Irish-American culture – of the entire ethos and way of life – would place it firmly in blue-collar America, away from high culture or from any of the arts, even the domestic ones. The macho American-Irish image even takes on a slightly antisocial coloring on St. Patrick's Day, at least in the area where I stay when I'm in New York – a middle-class, family-oriented, very Jewish area. The local parade is by no means something I hear praised. The big, tired men in Windcheaters, jeans, and white sneakers and the women who look as if they've been around the block come out of the bars and take over the occasion. And drinking can't be shared, as distinctive foods can, or dancing can, or decorative styles, such as you see in parades in Chinatown, can, and it has no iconography. There's nothing in the Irish drinking culture for children, and modern America worships children.

If the government of the Republic of Ireland wants to do something vibrant for itself and its Irish-American element, why doesn't it recognize this disconnect? Why not think along the lines of education and media and job and professional opportunities we might assist in providing to the diaspora? "Culture" sounds great, but it is the easy option, not to mention that it is dependent on gifted individuals and not on the state. Where are John O'Donoghue's fellow ministers? What are they doing for the Irish presence in New York?

The Sunday Tribune, March 11, 2007

A Social Contract

If they had to forgive each other, I don't think it could be done. I have an exceptionally lurid picture of Northern-Irish community relations in my head, of course, since most of the time I knew the place mainly as a journalist, and journalists weren't sent up there to cover the ordinary and the uneventful. My feelings were never of consequence and I could always leave the next day, yet the extremities of emotion to which I was forced almost every time I went north of the border are traced on me like high-tide marks. And I think with awe – what are the inner marks gouged on people who lived there?

I stood once on the wet grass verge of a mean housing estate, looking at a burnt-out house. The grass was wet from the firemen's hoses. Three little boys had burnt to death in the house in front of me not many hours before, for the crime of being Catholic in a Protestant enclave. Up and down the street, people who knew who'd torched the house – people who'd heard the children screaming – peered from their doors. The neighbors, I thought. Just think what that word means when it goes bad. And if I haven't a balancing example of the depths of sectarian hatred as inflicted on the other side, it is because of the difficulties in the way of reporting from that side. But I know what was done. I know that when it comes to the unforgivable, everybody has a share.

If the new Northern deal depended on owning up to bigotry, I don't suppose it would hold. The old hands sneered at me for not knowing about bigotry before I started going north. But we'd lived sheltered lives in the Republic. I had to learn – incredulous – that I had only to open my mouth, or people had only to note the registration number of my car, to be disliked and mistrusted and excluded. The contempt was sometimes naked. I was going around an exhibition about the Famine era in his town in County Armagh with the local mayor once, and he said, looking at an old photo of dreadful slums: "Of course, there's nothing like that now. They have the best of housing and health care." By "they" he meant Catholics – then and now the poor people in his town are Catholic people. And he turned to me and said with shocking venom: 'And still they're not satisfied!'

If that man had to own up to his hatred for his own neighbors, I don't suppose he could do it. If they in turn had to utterly abandon for ever the consolation of lethal fantasies, not to mention of a united Ireland in which his power would be wiped out, I don't suppose they could do it, either.

But bigotry is going to be different, uncoupled from threat and fear. Societies don't have to forgive. People do – I suppose that personal maturity isn't achieved until hurt and insult are detached from obsession and put in some kind of perspective. But societies have less integrity than people. The distances between people are wider and better ventilated than the distances within a person. A society with reasonably fair structures and rules and watchdogs and monitors, and more or less impartial avenues of appeal, can be viable even though everyone in it is still angry. A benign political system works at making spaces and devising stratagems by which people can live side by side whether or not they despise each other, whether or not they say they can never forgive.

The world is full of such places. Not just the United States, where Orthodox Jew lives beside fundamentalist Christian, Armenian beside Turk, Shiite beside Sunni – though the U.S. is surely humanity's most impressive achievement in the line of functioning tolerance. Europe, too, has celebrated this week the structures, marked in their youth by the Treaty of Rome, into which, in the last half-century, ancient enmities have been dispersed. And these were enmities that in our lifetime seemed ungovernable. There's a great monument to the Canadian dead of the First World War at Vimy Ridge in France which was still not quite finished when the Second World War broke out – as it were, around it. There were barely 20 years between the two huge bloodlettings. People forget that. And it's an excellent thing that they forget it.

The control of hatred is a separate thing from social justice; the same United States that allows multiple coexistences is as unequal as you can get. Disadvantage will be a long time shifting its many shapes in Northern Ireland. But the basic social contract has to be secured before anything else. The fact is that there are quite a few people on this island who burned or bombed or shot at or tortured other people, and who don't regret that they did it and, if circumstances reverted to what they were, would do it again. There are very many more people whose lives have been completely deformed by that violence and hatred. Northern Ireland, and to an extent the rest of Ireland, is full of people who don't forgive. It is full of people who can't be forgiven. It is a lesson in social maturity to accept that; and to accept that the politicians move in now to construct a political entity that works, not to build a society in which people are good.

The Sunday Tribune, April 1, 2007

On Citizenship

There's many a footnote to be added to the recent-election, mild and consensual as it was. One might note how extraordinarily old-fashioned the campaign was. They ought to fly tourists in and take them around to watch, in one of the world's wealthiest countries, old-style political parties running perfectly preserved old-time elections. Fáilte Ireland could offer general elections as events mixing folklore, faith, and entertainment, something between climbing Croagh Patrick and the All-Ireland Finals.

Most of what was said in the campaign was so much hot air. What the politicians want, as a good in itself, is to be elected. And what the Average Irish Voter wants is, in truth, to get into the Dáil or keep in the Dáil one of their own, by which they mean a person known, seed, breed, and generation, to themselves. Or, at least, a local person. Having got him in (women are an anomaly), they want that man to ascend through Minister of State status to Minister status and come home in a big car like some great African chieftain waving a magic stick. And why? Local pride? No. Keen awareness of the person's abilities and his suitability as a legislator for the nation? No. Proud contribution to the political well-being of the state as a whole? Are you kidding?

They want it because – and I quote – "otherwise we'll get nothing." No bypasses. No ever-open hospitals. No four-and-a-half civil servants decentralized at huge cost. No prisons, under-used arts centers, trips to Strasbourg to observe the European Parliament. Nothing.

Yet again, this time, we failed to use an election for wide and important purposes, though that is what our neighbors to the east and west are doing. For example – I was walking down a boreen from the hill behind Roundstone last Sunday when a lumbering SUV passed, pausing only for the canvassers to offer a piece of what is called election "literature" starring the FF candidates for Galway West. Energy awareness, when there's an Irish election on? Are you joking? Back in the city, the shoal of "literature" – fiction – behind the door didn't have a single piece printed on recycled paper, not even the Green Party flyer.

Small things, you may say. Yet the biggest nonideological issue of today is that our planet is in trouble, and it is going to be in ever greater trouble as the Far East emulates the environmental excesses of the countries of the Northern hemisphere. It is in trouble from population growth; I read last week that just one state in India – a state which is four times the size of Leinster – will soon have a population of 242 million. How are our planet's people to find food and work and education and shelter? And, accepting that we cannot reverse the climate change our demands on the environment have already brought about, how are we to prevent further damage? The effects of global warming are now as much a part of everyday consciousness of the world – outside Ireland – as night and day. A man from Vermont remarks that the maple sugar industry is being destroyed by erratic weather. A woman says without thinking it anything out of the ordinary that her family are not going to buy a cottage in the Lake District because the coast there is very vulnerable to rising sea levels. The sales figures for Toyota's mass-produced hybrid car rise all the time. Outside Ireland, that is. Here, only about 1,000 Prius have been sold in two or three years.

Next door to us in the UK, Gordon Brown is pressing ahead with five new towns which will be environmentally friendly because, politically, he is trying to trump David Cameron on green issues. Tony Blair, too, has announced large policy initiatives in the area of energy and conservation as the crowning glory of his time in office. He's going to set out plans for nuclear power stations. He's going to set up a national "pay-as-you-drive" scheme. Here, such issues didn't detain the candidates in the recent election for one second.

Rather, the universe appears to bore them. And us. As does, apparently, the big issue closer to home – the war between human beings which began with 9/11. It and what it led to have transformed electoral politics in our neighbor to the west so completely that the Democratic Party will very likely choose between a person of color and a woman as their presidential candidate next year, thus shattering two of the taboos that have shaped politics throughout recorded history. We ourselves are involved in the Iraq and Afghanistan wars, through Shannon airport, through the EU, through our self-identification as ardent Christians and through the vulnerability we share with all other travelers. This mattered to some of the stalwart moralists – Michael D., for example. But it didn't matter to the likes of Bertie.

"We'll get nothing," people say. "I'm voting for X or Y because, otherwise, we'll get nothing." Whence this sullen, dependent, greedy, self-pitying attitude to the business of being citizens? Is it part of post-colonial damage, that we're so good at entitlement and so bad at responsibility? If it is, is the post-colonial phase going to go on for ever? Elections are opportunities for a society to express its preoccupations and articulate its desires. But all we've learnt from this one is that though we now seem to be a wealthy, modern, well-educated country, underneath we're still too frightened and parochial even to think about giving. All we want is to get.

The Sunday Tribune, May 27, 2007

Afterword

If there is a single phrase that sums up the second wave of feminism that emerged in the 1960s, it is "the personal is political." It turns up in these pages. It means, not that lovers or family members need to form parties and have elections, but that private relationships, especially those between men and women, involve the use of power and are shaped by public, social forces.

Nuala O'Faolain certainly believed that. In her columns, she is always acutely sensitive to the inner workings of both power and powerlessness, the way they shape, not just the big external world but our most intimate sense of who we are. She got that knowledge in part from growing up in an Irish Catholic society where: "The individual was a nobody, in a world of more powerful beings. Power was always out there, in the hands of the wielder of punishment. The notion of personal authority, of rightly having your own place in power relations, simply couldn't develop in the climate of fear."

She got the knowledge, too, from being a woman. Hovering around much of her journalism, sometimes in the background, occasionally front and center, is a haunted awareness of the sense of threat that is always there for women: "The potential violence of men toward women – the readiness with which they will rape and batter and murder – is part of the context within which the equable and affectionate relationships between the mass of men and women take place." Feminism is always a moral and intellectual touchstone for her reactions to the world around her.

And she got the sense of how political the personal really is, oddly enough, from reading. Encountering her marvellous columns again, it is hard not to be struck by how deeply and passionately well-read she is. But the result of that reading is not a display of erudition. It is something much more all-encompassing and humane. It is the sense that what she has read – all those books that put structure and form on external experience – have been entirely personalized. It is as much a part of her experience as the people she encounters and the places she inhabits. When she writes about James Joyce's Dublin or "the country lanes" of John McGahern's novels, it is not as an academic or literary historian, but as a witness. She has seen and lived in them. And conversely when she writes of the process of learning to read ("I remember the exact moment myself and it was the only transcendent thing that ever happened to me"), it is with the feeling that to be deprived of that moment is to be denied human dignity. In her way of looking at things, reading is the crossroads where the personal and the political, our social and collective lives on the one hand and our most intimate selves on the other, meet and converse.

But what made Nuala O'Faolain such a powerful and distinctive writer was ultimately not this engagement with the notion that the personal is political. It was that she also understood the phrase in reverse – the political is personal.

Her journalism eschewed the gnostic pretense at Olympian insight into events that was the mainstay of "serious" columnists before her. She once wrote hilariously, indeed, of her gift for false prophecy. In her early days in England, a pollster showed her the first issue of *Cosmopolitan*. She said it would never catch on. She confidently predicted on RTÉ's *Questions and Answers* that Ben Dunne's huge donations to Charles

Haughey would never be linked to a particular politician. She told Mary Robinson, whom she admired hugely, that she had no chance of being elected to the presidency.

Her insight was of a very different order, and her gift was to find a language that was equally distinctive. She found a way of writing, a literary style, in which the personality could be politicized and politics personalized.

Take two more or less random examples.

Politicizing the personal, she wrote brilliantly of the way ordinary Irish behavior could be shaped by the vagueness of our sense of citizenship: "People have to be prodded and beaten into taking any kind of care of the landscape. Individuals insist on trashing their own part of it for their own reasons: The overall picture has nothing to do with them. People roll down the windows of their cars and throw their litter out. That's somebody else's territory they're moving through."

Personalizing the political, she could write of Northern Ireland in the early stages of the peace process as if it were an awkward, unloved child trying to squirm out from under a burden of self-hatred: "It is a society that does not yet like itself enough to relax its sectarianism. And my impression is that it does not feel liked." Or she could even use a gesture of her own, leaning forward to hear a priest discourse on sectarianism, to develop a subtle and brilliant insight into the link between violence and male domination in Northern Ireland: "I understood from that movement of my body – leaning forward to be told what to do – one of the reasons why Northern Ireland is such a patriarchy."

These apparently easy shifts from concepts of citizenship to litter, from political violence to personal psychology, from bodily gesture to large-scale social analysis, demanded a style whose simplicity came from an enormous sophistication. That style was, for anyone who had to write a column in the same paper, terrifyingly assured.

For all her self-doubt and hesitation in person (the uncertainty that made her smuggle the extraordinary memoir *Are You Somebody?* into print as a mere introduction to a collection of her *Irish Times* columns), she achieved, when she wrote, a seamlessly comprehensive tone.

That tone is what made her unique – her ability to write about, say, mobile phones and abortion, St. Patrick's Day parades and sectarian violence, in exactly the same voice. She had perfect pitch for a note that was precisely halfway between the intimacy of confession and the objectivity of reportage. She personalized public issues without trivializing them, and gave a public dimension to personal experience without falling into solipsism.

This was, in itself, a considerable literary achievement. She solved one of the most difficult problems a writer can face – the use of the word "I." In journalism, it can be used to create a comic, self-deprecating persona, or to bear raw witness to an extraordinary event. It can be deployed as mere egoistic display, filling what ought to be a public space with inflated foibles.

Only very rarely can it be used with sincerity and integrity on the one hand and a cool objectivity on the other.

And yet this was precisely the combination Nuala sought. And she sought it for a profound moral reason. She understood her job in writing for newspapers to be the making of some tiny contribution toward the diminution of indifference. She needed some answer to the human inability, as she puts it in a column from 2002, to "feel for the whole world." She needed some way not to be overwhelmed by the sheer scale of the planet's horror and injustice and unhappiness. And she found those things – tentatively and contingently – in her fashioning of a public "I," a kind of intimacy with her readers through which those large questions and emotions could be filtered and humanized. She forged that miraculous literary self that was at once immediately personal and yet sufficiently capacious to register the movements of the great outside world.

In this regard, Nuala's devotion to Marcel Proust was not accidental. She learned from him how to construct a coherent sense of self in writing, one that could be intimate and immediate but also infinitely expansive. Often her columns started, and remained, with herself, but brought political and moral issues within the frame of her own vibrant emotion and luminous intelligence.

They could begin like strange, strung-out short stories: "Imagine wanting to die"; "Someone I know bought a derelict cottage recently"; "Laois had always seemed to me to be one of the flatter counties"; even "Well … I don't know … "

Or, as with the 1997 column "Questions of Relative Rights": "For Christmas week I was stuck in a small, litter-strewn Bulgarian ski resort, where there was no snow, and therefore no skiing and therefore nothing much to do." This situation leads, via reports of a dancing bear in a nearby town, to a Proustian memory of seeing such a bear and his master in Istanbul: "He was inflicting whatever it was on the animal because he himself was trapped and had no other way to survive."

And just as the reader is wondering what this has to do with anything, the symbiosis of the bear and the bear-master is turned into a brilliant, brave metaphor for her own complex feelings on the thorny public question of abortion. No one else could have done this without being gauche, crass, or merely scatty, and she could do so only because she found a tone and a language with that distinctive fusion of intimacy and analysis.

It was a tribute to her brilliance as a stylist that no one quite noticed how raw and angry, how fragile and exposed, the "I" of her columns really was, until she herself traced its lineaments in *Are You Somebody?*

Her deep reluctance to write that book suggested that, at some level, she understood the way it took apart the self that made her one of the greatest columnists ever to inhabit the English language.

Fintan O'Toole
January 2010